Carnival and the Formation of a Caribbean Transnation

New World Diasporas

Florida A&M University, Tallahassee
Florida Atlantic University, Boca Raton
Florida Gulf Coast University, Ft. Myers
Florida International University, Miami
Florida State University, Tallahassee
University of Central Florida, Orlando
University of Florida, Gainesville
University of North Florida, Jacksonville
University of South Florida, Tampa
University of West Florida, Pensacola

New World Diasporas

Edited by Kevin A. Yelvington

This series seeks to stimulate critical perspectives on diaspora processes in the New World. Representations of "race" and ethnicity, the origins and consequences of nationalism, migratory streams and the advent of transnationalism, the dialectics of "homelands" and diasporas, trade networks, gender relations in immigrant communities, the politics of displacement and exile, and the utilization of the past to serve the present are among the phenomena addressed by original, provocative research in disciplines such as anthropology, history, political science, and sociology.

International Editorial Board

More Than Black: Afro-Cubans in Tampa, by Susan D. Greenbaum (2002)
Carnival and the Formation of a Caribbean Transnation, by Philip W. Scher (2003)

Carnival

and the Formation of a Caribbean Transnation

Philip W. Scher

University Press of Florida

Gainesville | Tallahassee | Tampa | Boca Raton

Pensacola | Orlando | Miami | Jacksonville | Ft. Myers

First cloth printing, 2003
First paperback printing, 2004

Library of Congress Cataloging-in-Publication Data
Scher, Philip W., 1965–
Carnival and the formation of a Caribbean transnation / Philip W. Scher
p. cm. — (New World diasporas series)
Includes bibliographical references and index.
ISBN 0-8130-2612-1 (cloth: alk. paper); ISBN 0-8130-2799-3 (pbk.)
1. Carnival—Trinidad and Tobago. 2. Carnival—New York (State)—New York.
3. West Indians—New York (State)—New York—Ethnic identity. 4. Brooklyn
(New York, N.Y.)—Social life and customs. I. Title. II. Series.
GT4229.T7 .S24 2003
394.25'0972983—dc21 2002075081

The University Press of Florida is the scholarly publishing agency for the State
University System of Florida, comprising Florida A&M University, Florida Atlantic
University, Florida Gulf Coast University, Florida International University, Florida
State University, University of Central Florida, University of Florida, University
of North Florida, University of South Florida, and University of West Florida.

University Press of Florida
15 Northwest 15th Street
Gainesville, FL 32611–2079
http://www.upf.com

For Audrey

"And for many nights she lost her rest
Step by step you gradually grow
You never miss the water till the well run dry
Like a mother when she closes her eyes."

King Radio, New York, 1936

Contents

Figures

Foreword

Extremely indifferent to the Barnum and Bailey Circus's self-depiction as "The Greatest Show on Earth," Trinidadians use exactly the same exaltation for their Carnival. In this book, Philip W. Scher argues that what the "show" that is Carnival displays is multiplex and manifold. It entails but cannot be reduced to the individual motivations of participants, the artistic expression of the producers, gender relations and public sexuality, a national narrative in the service of state aggrandizement, a burlesque of colonial (and postcolonial) dominant norms of respectability, a reified and commodified vision of "culture," high stakes identity politics, calculated economic investment, and a typically Western preoccupation with leisure time. And while Carnival might be tied to a particular fixed (national and personal) place and time in the minds and representations of Trinidadians at "home" and "abroad," one of the compelling aspects of contemporary Carnival that becomes the central theme of Scher's book is that the meanings, practices, and symbolization of Carnival are anything but fixed. They are transformed as Carnival itself travels, simultaneously blurring and reestablishing the permeable boundaries between "home" and "abroad." As such—and this is one of the remarkable accomplishments of this book—Scher addresses himself to perhaps the main puzzle and theoretical stumbling block in the burgeoning and overdetermined (popular and academic) discourse on "globalization": Why and how is the production of "culture" implicated in seemingly contradictory processes that establish more and more connections across political borders, creating so-called decentered identities? That is, how particularism and differentiation on the one hand, and hybridity, creolization, and even sameness on the other, imply each other. And unlike much globalization theory Scher is anything but silent on the nature, role, and efficacy of the state and political institutions.

Substantively, Scher focuses both on the rise of Trinidadian-style Carnival in Brooklyn, New York, and on Carnival in Trinidad. He builds a theoretical framework to explain how Carnival functions in the formation of what he calls the Trinidadian "transnation." This he sees as a feature of some groups within diaspora. The transnation employs what Scher terms the "reproductive imagination" to present itself as a collectivity with a set of identifiable cultural traits that are associated with what is taken to be the "national culture" of the homeland, currently understood by those involved to be exemplified in and by the form of the nation-state. But for the transnation to exist requires not only an act of imagination but actual and active on-going interaction, reciprocity, and negotiation, of social relations embedded in ties of kinship and friendship, between those at any particular time residing in distinct national territories. As such, "transnation" does not so much describe a kind of community as a kind of identity. This identity, in turn, depends on the idea of culture—but an older idea of culture as whole, homogeneous, and bounded, internally coherent, authentic, deeply historical and associated with "tradition"—that owes its origins perhaps to anthropology's past but which is being slowly abandoned by anthropologists (like Scher) themselves. Here, Scher is sympathetic to the advantages of maintaining this conception of culture for the groups who put it to use in their various projects, but firm in his decision to forge ahead and construct the theoretical tools adequate to his task.

Carnival-as-objectified-culture becomes part of a "politics of recognition" as indeed these politics depend on *a something* to be recognized. At the same time, the production of Carnival as a commodity form gives affirmation that members of the transnation produce something of value that can stand for their value as a group and even, in the logic of postmodern capitalism, that they can produce something that can be exported. But this is not a commodity that becomes unknown, anonymous. Quite the opposite. It always bears their signature. In Trinidad, Carnival in the post–World War II era was defined as an authentic working-class Afro-Trinidadian cultural form by the middle-class creole nationalists who would supplant the British upon Independence in 1962. Post-Independence politics have involved a contest between Afro- and Indo-Trinidadians to secure the state and part of the strategies employed revolve around propagating and instituting a "national culture." Carnival is made to stand as a metonym for "Trinidad." In promoting Carnival, the state's representatives ensure national sovereignty and their own efficacy—again, vis-à-vis "culture"—and the state becomes identified with the politically ascendant Afro-Trinidadian population. The nation-state conjuncture is both projected into diaspora and challenged at the same time. Here, both centrifugal and centripetal forces are evident.

New York City since 1965 has received more than half a million West Indian migrants—about twice the population of Barbados. In Brooklyn, Carnival is used in "culturalist" movements—involving the conscious mobilization of cultural differences—as part of an on-going tournament of distinction between New York's ethnic groups, competing for recognition under a regime of what Scher calls "bureaucratic multiculturalism," a kind of politics of recognition with the added element of social control. Here, a dialectic is at work where the city has an ability to bestow recognition in a resource competition model but only to groups who have the requisite corporate signs of distinction. This is where Carnival comes in. It helps to establish the Caribbean community as a political player by making the community visible via its display of culture. Trinidadians in Trinidad and in Brooklyn worry about the other's Carnival. In Trinidad, the state cultural apparatus worries about Carnival being appropriated. It seeks control over the proliferation of Carnival culture, hoping in the era of structural adjustment policies directed by the International Monetary Fund and the World Bank—with their demand of compliance to U.S.-oriented capitalism—to make Carnival into a copyrighted, marketable, exportable, standardized commodity. When autonomy is attenuated in the economic sphere it appears that "culture" becomes emphasized and asserted.

In Brooklyn, where many musicians and Carnival artists from Trinidad come every year to perform and produce Carnival bands, changes in Trinidad's Carnival are often the subject of consternation, especially for earlier migrants. The nostalgia for "home" gets disrupted. But when Trinidadians based in Brooklyn actually encounter the Carnival of home, and they often do, organizing their yearly vacations around the pre-Lenten event, they sometimes decry what they see as the lack of attention to artistic detail, a forgetting of the traditional Carnival themes and Carnival characters of their youth, as well as an overemphasis on scantily clad bodies winin' (dancing in a sexually provocative manner, hips gyrating) in the street. These narratives of degeneration, of decrying the present degraded, inauthentic state of today's Carnival, are indicative of Trinidadian (and Trinidadians') modernity. It was the Trinidadian theorist C.L.R. James who showed how the Caribbean was historically involved in the framing of "the West" and of modernity. Narratives of degeneration are the mere flip side of narratives of progress and indeed are essential to visions of a linear march toward a better future. Carnival is also about the embodiment of modernity.

This book is on a hot topic. The proliferation of Caribbean Carnivals—London's Notting Hill Carnival, Toronto's Caribana, Brooklyn's Labor Day Carnival are certainly the best known, but there are now literally hundreds of Carnivals abroad and even within the Caribbean itself there is the export of Carnival from Trinidad to other islands—means that "playing mas'" (i.e., masquerade) has become yet another "deterritorialized" cultural artefact of our globalized age. The place of Carnival in the lives of migrant populations overtly maintaining their transnational ties calls out for the kind of understanding and analysis provided so clearly by Scher in this book.

Mas'! Mas'! Caribbean Carnival might just be coming to a street near you soon.

Kevin A. Yelvington,
Series Editor

Acknowledgments

This book really began a long time ago, when I was a university undergraduate. The development of my interest in Trinidad Carnival came together in a quite unlikely way. I was involved in an intensive independent study with several friends called "Couch, Carnival and the Criminal Kind." In that seminar I was introduced to the works of M. M. Bakhtin, and my curiosity about rituals of inversion and laughter grew. At the same time one of my close friends, a Trinidadian named Avery Ince, had introduced me to the Trinidad Carnival. I suppose that I grew tired of reading about archaic carnivals and what it was they were supposed to be accomplishing and decided that a more anthropological approach might be rewarding. As the study grew my interests changed. First, through performance-centered approaches encouraged by Roger Abrahams at the University of Pennsylvania's Department of Folklore and Folklife. Later, with a focus on transnationalism and globalization, inspired by Arjun Appadurai in the Department of Anthropology, I began to look at the Trinidad Carnival and its offspring, the Brooklyn Carnival, as important parts of a process of identity formation. Balancing a respect for the history of the festival, its main contributors, and brilliant artists with a theoretical emphasis on the politics of culture has been the greatest challenge. I would like to thank Webb Keane and Sandra Barnes for making me pay attention to the ethnographic materials while I was busy theorizing. If there is any success in that regard in this book it is as a result of their encouragement, while any shortcomings are my own. In the process of writing this book, I considered a wide range of materials as "ethnographic," not merely my interviews and participation in Carnival events. I approached the materials produced in the service of the production of Carnival as much a part of the "evidence" as anything else, especially since so much of my emphasis here is on the intersection between individual and group identity formation and official national and administrative rhetoric. In this book the words and images that accompany the Carnival become part of the greater dialogue about the event.

Michel de Certeau once wrote beautifully about standing high above New York City, looking down and realizing the almost erotic thrill of gaining "perspective" on a usually confused and disorienting mass of streets and people. For de Certeau, though, the idea of mastering the city through the all-powerful eye was illusory. On the streets, we who walk them know that they are never stable. And the shifting cadence of peoples' routes, the undulation of the crowd, is what there is. The authority of the avenues may be, in some utopian sense, undercut by the passing of walkers: out for a stroll, changing the world. Looking at Carnival was very much like that for me. There was a craving to have someplace to stand, not only metaphorically but also, sometimes, actually. On many Carnival Tuesdays in Port-of-Spain I found myself being invited up to one or another friend's apartment overlooking the action, taking a drink, wolfing down food. But the views only ever extended so far. What was happening to those masqueraders when they turned the corner? So Carnival is not to be mastered, and I make no claims to have mastered it here. What I am writing about is how the Carnival seems to be playing out in a specific historical context. Toward that end I quickly realized that a multitude of people make the festival. Not only is Carnival the masqueraders, calypsonians, steelbands, and all who stand behind them and facilitate their performances; it is also the police, the politicians, the tourist boards, the airlines, the restaurants, the vendors. And so every year something like a whole event is made, but only as a collective enterprise.

I like to think of this book that way too. And so here are some of the revelers who made my Carnival. At the University of Pennsylvania, in addition to the people I have mentioned, I want to thank Linda Lee of the Department of Anthropology and Marco Manzo of the Center for Folklore and Ethnography. During and after my fieldwork I have had enormous help from students who have come before or were there afterward. Kevin Yelvington, Stephen Stuempfle, Diana Wells, Lisa Meyers, and David Scott have all been a source of great encouragement. But I reserve my greatest thanks for Garth Green. While in the field we had many occasions to discuss our research, play mas' and ponder some of the mysteries of ethnographic fieldwork. In the end I gained a close friend. A whole host of Trinidadian scholars and friends helped make this process a joy: Laurel Ince, Grace and Winston Carr, Roma Quan Soon and Romeo

Cunin, Robert K. Lee, Betty and Sankar Baldeosingh and their entire family, Garry Chin, Christopher Cozier, Irenee Shaw, Gregory and Tessa Sloan-Sealey, Che Lovelace, Charlotte Elias, Annie Paul, Skye Hernandez, and Georgia Popplewell. Many thanks go to all the masmen and bandleaders who gave me their time and enthusiasm. These include Ray Morris, Kevin Davis, Pepta Pierre and her family, Carlos Lezama, Arden Knox, Richard Afong, Elsie and Stephen Lee Heung, Raoul Garib, Cito Velasquez, Geraldo Vieira and his son Geraldo Vieira Junior, Neville Hinds, Stephen Derek, Todd Gulick, Peter Minshall, Katheryn Chan, and the inimitable Jason Griffith. At the University of the West Indies I want to thank Keith Nurse, Funso Aiyejina, Marsha Brooks, and Gordon Rohlehr. At the *Trinidad Express*, Kay Baldeosingh, Melissa Richards, Kathleen Maharaj, and Terry Joseph. Wayne Headley and Marlon Rouse at the *Trinidad Guardian* helped me find wonderful photographs, as did Timmy Mora at Visual Art and Production. I also want to thank my family, my brothers, David Scher and Tony Chase, my sister, Susan Chase Breyer, and my stepmother, Janie Woo. My father, Dr. Stephen K. Scher, started me on this road a long time ago, and I thank him for it.

Finally, to my wife and best friend, Constance (who could not have been more aptly named), I say this: like the heroic travelers who people this book, we have made a family and a home on the road. There is no place I would rather be than where you are.

Introduction

In my view, the problematic intellectual heritage of Euro-American modernity still determines the manner in which nationality is understood within black political discourse. In particular, it conditions the continuing aspiration to acquire a supposedly authentic, natural and stable identity.

Paul Gilroy, *Small Acts* (1993)

Mas', Mas', I know you by your nose hole.

Trinidadian expression used upon recognizing a masquerader

This book addresses the issue of identity formation in the transnational experience. My goal is to use an ethnographic approach to offer insights into the ways in which a people's sense of ethnic and national identity is developed in a situation that transcends many of the categories for self-definition that are available. The rise of the Trinidad-style Carnival in Brooklyn, New York, provides an excellent opportunity for observing how cultural forms and the meanings that surround them may change in a diasporic situation. As Trinidadians have had to make lives for themselves in New York City, Carnival has played a variety of roles. From liming (hanging out) site (see glossary on page 184) to ethnic identity marker to political forum, Carnival itself has been made to play mas' (masquerade), to change its faces, and to yield new meanings in shifting contexts. The result has been that Carnival has become a central symbol in the formation of a Trinidadian *transnation*. At some level this entire volume is dedicated to understanding the very idea of a transnation and will therefore require frequent returns to this notion. Briefly, however, we might see a transnation as a group in diaspora that imagines itself as a collectivity with a specific history and a body of quantifiable traits and characteristics in relation to a nation or nation-state that exists in the present in a putative homeland. What must be present is an active and ongoing interaction with the home nation in several spheres. Economic ties, ideological ties, and cultural ties must all be active. Such involvements set this kind of community apart from other kinds of immigrant communities that may continue to utilize an understanding of their cultural heritage but do not have an active, multidimensional involvement with the home nation. I make a distinction here because newer waves of immigrants and other mobile populations have the ability to preserve—and even the necessity of preserving—active ties back "home." This ability is not only potential, it is actively used; therefore, the term transnation describes a process or an ongoing relationship that must be maintained. Embedded in the process is a constant negotiation surrounding the construction of national and/or ethnic identity that figures prominently into the creation of a public life and a public image for the group. This book explores that very delicate and complex process.

In the course of learning about the lives of Trinidadian transnationals, I had occasion to live in Trinidad and in Brooklyn and to play mas' in multiple Carnivals. My experiences were comparatively short-lived. Trinidadians who divide their lives between North America and the Caribbean have made a life out of movement. They have created a system of familial networks and international travel, a matrix of telephones and emails in the service of maintaining their personal ties with those who have stayed behind. In the process, they also have created a new kind of "imagined community" (Anderson 1983).

After spending my first ten months in Trinidad for my dissertation fieldwork, I returned to experience once again the mas' on Labor Day. I met a colleague and his wife at the Brooklyn version of the Trinidadian Panorama steelband competition one evening before Carnival. As we sat in the bleachers eating roti, a curried stew wrapped in Indian bread, I watched the crowd mingle. The evening din was punctuated by shouts of recognition, cries of joy at meeting up with friends or relatives "from home" who may not have been encountered in quite some time. I began to feel for the first time some glimmer of understanding as to why Trinidadians and other West Indians went through so much trouble and expense to play their mas.' In New York the event served as a kind of winnowing tray, separating the West Indians from the mélange of New Yorkers into which they were integrated on a daily basis. It was not that outsiders were not welcome—never have I felt so uniformly welcomed into a cultural event as I have in my experiences with Carnival both in New York and in Trinidad—it was more that a kind of self-selection was in place. This self-selection seemed to operate on the personal level as well as on a more general or "social identity" level. During Carnival, West Indians find each other in the crowd while simultaneously presenting themselves to the crowd.

When Ray Morris, Kevin "Fuzzy" Davis, and other masmen spoke of Carnival as being "we ting," or "our thing," I began to realize that there were many valences to this idea, that I was experiencing a genuinely transnational event and an event that literally "took place" on the Parkway every year. By this I mean that Carnival not only took over a space but took a place and created another place out of it. The parade carried a kind of memory of place with it as it approximated Trinidad Carnival in Brooklyn; as the urban air was overpowered by the humid smoke of Caribbean cooking; as reggae, soca, zouk, merengue, and other music transformed the aural spectrum of New York City. And for a few days every year Brooklyn could not help but notice this presence.

As I began to explore the nature of this transnational event, however, I saw it shot through with contradictions and shifting elements. Most importantly, I wanted to explore the outward spiral of connections that held Carnival in the center of a transnational vortex. This required looking at political economy, nation-state cultural policy, migration, city politics, and ethnic identity while still considering the activities and practices of groups of people negotiating life between two countries, two regions.

General Theoretical Background

In *Anthropology as Cultural Critique*, Marcus and Fischer write:

> An interpretive anthropology fully accountable to its historical and po-
> litical-economy implications thus remains to be written. How to write
> about multiple cultural differences that matter in a world system that
> seems to be developing either toward homogenization or a simple polar-
> ization between rich and poor? How to take account of a reciprocity of
> perspectives, which requires the ethnographer to consider seriously the
> de facto counterethnography of subjects who . . . are often equally, if not
> more, aware of [the world system's] operation than the anthropologist
> himself? Most importantly, the assumption of a sociological unit, spa-
> tially and temporally isolated, is deeply embedded in the conventional
> framing of subjects for ethnographic analysis and must be modified
> (1986: 86).

More than fifteen years later, however, the interpretive anthropology that Marcus and Fischer spoke of is still in its infancy. There have been very few studies that have attempted to scrutinize the "conventional framing of subjects for ethnographic analysis" by examining the various ways subjects participate in their own framing, both consciously and unconsciously, by engaging with the institutional rhetoric that purports to describe them. At issue here is the notion of self-consciously employed cultural forms and identities, with special attention paid to expressive culture, measured alongside the actions and attitudes of people as they go about the business of living.

The activities of Trinidadians in New York and Trinidad only occasionally relate to "culture" as it is understood by official bodies such as the state, local government agencies, and tourist organizations. I want to examine culture as it is used in this way, however it is not my intention to privilege this notion of culture over others as a definition. I am more concerned about the ways such ideas of culture become integrated into lived practice. We may say, as anthropologists, that this particular concept of culture is too narrow, essentialist, and ethno-nationalist, and serves the blatant political agendas of mono- or multiculturalists alike. The manifestations of this idea of culture appear on the right as well as on the left, yet retain a common feature of being functionalist; a means to an end. I am interested in the ways people discuss and self-consciously act upon the understanding that culture is a collection of reified expressive forms, while their unconscious activities, those that analysts might also call properly "cultural," contradict these consciously held notions.

In what follows, I provide a discussion of culture not as I believe it is understood by anthropologists but as I believe it has come to be regarded by official, politically oriented organizations and by the "average" person in the street. Culture in its academic sense (or senses) is rarely available to people outside anthropological debates. Yet it is this notion of culture that I am tracing in its external manifestations among Trinidadians who discussed their "culture" with me. I believe that culture in this sense is an important feature in the lives of transnational migrants who find themselves in situations where cultural display becomes an important element in their integration into a new society. For most of the people I spoke with, their understanding of culture is shaped through whatever interactions they have with a public discourse of culture. In this case I examine how state rhetoric from Trinidad, generated in the context of national culture-building, is repeated by masqueraders in Brooklyn in a discussion about ethnic identity in New York City.

In exploring this type of "metacultural" discourse, I am not claiming that understandings of culture end there. I do feel, however, that future anthropological investigations of culture must take into account the increasing importance of identity politics or the politics of recognition to the people in question. Increasingly, the subjects of anthropological study are profoundly aware of and concerned about their "conventional framing." Not only is this true in cultural anthropology but in archaeology and physical anthropology as well, such that dig sites have become potential platforms for separatist and/or nationalist movements, and the search for the land where mankind "began" fuels debates about race, entitlement, and human civilization.

In cultural anthropology the disciplinary concern for "culture" and the fundamentally comparative nature of anthropological theory have entered into a much wider discourse. In the past, descriptive ethnography played a major role in forming a popular public conception of culture as the sum total of a "location's" expressive forms, cuisine, language, and, slightly more abstractly, attitudes. These notions have entered into common currency in distorted form, yet they remain important to anthropology, even as anthropologists work beyond them. Thus, recent anthropological theories that challenge older notions of culture have come face to face with their own past.

In a recent issue of *Cultural Anthropology* edited by Daniel Segal (1996), scholars dealt with how anthropologists who, in the name of cultural constructivist theory, have exposed certain cultural forms as examples of "invented tradition" and their performers as essentialists, now have to face down the angry responses of "native" culture bearers and others who resent the insinuation that what they have been doing is "false" or, worse, politically suspect. Yet it seems possible to negotiate an anthropology that is both anti-essentialist and sensitive to the role that "essentialisms" play, without condemnation.

In this work my aim is to explore some aspects of the transnational experience from the perspective of those who live it. It is an inquiry that focuses on a particular cultural form and those people who work in and around its promotion and performance: the Carnival of Trinidad and Tobago. By studying its exportation and development in Brooklyn, New York, I aim to provide an ethnography of transnationalism with special attention given to the ways in which Carnival is discussed and to the ways in which Carnival is actually performed and produced. I look closely at various kinds of objectification, with special attention to what happens with the commodification of the festival. By exploring what I see as different types of exchange, I want to suggest that objectified cultural forms are essential to metacultural discourse and therefore to identity formation. Official bodies such as the state in Trinidad or the city of New York have a powerful role in providing dominant narratives of culture and cultural forms, which serve to objectify those forms but do not determine the ways those forms will be encountered by participants. Carnival in Trinidad and Tobago provides a wonderful forum for this project as it so deeply involves notions of personal and national identity. I also believe that this investigation can make a helpful contribution to festival studies in general by eliminating the need to distinguish between authentic and inauthentic forms.

The phenomena described in this ethnography will go some way toward illuminating the relationships between home-nation nationalist politics, the rhetoric of international recognition, and the construction of a local politics of ethnic identity. By looking at Carnival—an event of national symbolic importance in Trinidad—and the rise of its centrality in the construction of a national culture, we can begin to see how its development in New York has fed off of its development in Trinidad. Similarly, the rise of Carnival's importance in New York (and in Toronto, London, Miami) requires a continuing relationship with Trinidad on many levels, not the least being a source for Trinidadian-ness.

The organizing principle of this introduction revolves around certain key words and concepts that recur throughout the text, including a thumbnail description of Carnival itself in order to ground later references to specific events within the festival. Beginning with recent work on transnationalism, I will tease out the relationship between what Arjun Appadurai has called "the work of the imagination" (1996: 5–11) with the "politics of recognition" (Taylor and Gutmann 1994; Fraser 1996) in a global setting. The relationship between an emigrant "community" of Trinidadians in New York and their home nation is one of continual action and reaction. The two places and their constituents do not live cut off from each other, but in constant contact. Their mutual dependence encompasses cultural exchanges, economic and political exchanges, and the actual physical movement of people and goods. The transnational traffic between Trinidad and New York has created a transnation that I will briefly define below and more fully develop in chapter 2.[1]

Transnation and Transnational Literature

Throughout the text I will be drawing upon the notion of the transnation, a term that I have proposed to describe any collectivity that exists outside of yet in some relationship to a home nation-state from which it draws concepts of itself, its history, and its culture. The transnation does not describe a kind of collectivity (diasporic community, refugee, exile); it describes a kind of identity that emerges from the experiences of people within such communities. The rise in the importance of such a notion can be linked, at least in part, to the flourishing of the ideological principles that celebrate multiculturalism, diversity, and ethnic difference and reward those distinctions in various ways. Even as older notions of ethnicity are modified in anthropology (i.e., ethnicity as primordial or as functions of resource competition), ethnicity seen in precisely this way becomes a powerful concept in contemporary politics (Eriksen 1993). As the transnation develops a sense of itself, it is partly supported by the independent development of political systems that, on the one hand, seem bound to uphold the morality of acknowledging difference but, on the other, are threatened by the erosion of any sense of a larger collective identity that can contain the fragmentation that multiculturalism encourages.

Transnationalism and Identity

A cursory glance at developments in anthropology over the past several years reveals an increasing focus on globalization, transnationalism, migration, deterritorialization, tourism, and other related subjects (Kearney 1995). The scope of anthropological investigation has widened to take into account the operations of the "world system" (Wallerstein 1974), dependency and development theory (Escobar 1995), and other global developments. One important result of these endeavors has been the fundamental transformation in the way traditional anthropological subjects have been framed for analysis. The advent of studies of time-space compression, for instance (Harvey 1989; Massey 1995), have inclined anthropologists toward seeing the larger political-economic and cultural environments in which "locals" live.

Anthropology, in return, has contributed to our understanding of the impact global developments have on the lives of the people we study (Glick Schiller et al. 1992). Ethnographic studies of "local" responses to "global" phenomena have greatly modified the "cultural imperialism" thesis and have shown that mass mediation does not necessarily lead to cultural homogenization throughout the world (see Tomlinson 1991). Yet in the rush to advance cultural theory in anthropology the role of the idea of culture in the popular imagination was all but left behind (but see Gupta 1992; Gupta and Ferguson 1992). As social scientists focus more and more on the breakdown of traditional nation forms, on the phenomenon of global capitalism, and on movements of people for purposes of labor or as the result of war, the idea that "identities" will likewise fragment and, if not disappear, then become fluid, increases in currency (King 1991).[2] In a recent overview of transnationalism and anthropology Michael Kearney, citing Nancie Gonzalez (1992), writes that "diasporas include a full cross-section of community members who are dispersed to many diverse regions of the world and yet who retain a *myth* of their uniqueness and an interest in their homeland" (1995: 559, emphasis mine). My experiences with Trinidadians who live and work in New York but who have intimate connections—through both frequent travel and constant communication—with Trinidad have led me to the view that such "myths" are powerful parts of the imagination of the transnation and are actively used in the construction of identity. As such they are not "false" or unreal, as the above usage of myth implies, but are concrete representations of the collective that have an objective and material existence. In that sense perhaps, Trinidadian understandings of their culture as "we *ting*" (our thing) communicate this phenomenon in the best manner.

Theories of cultural constructivism, therefore, must be careful to distinguish between (a) an understanding of culture as constructed through social processes that include the mobilization of primordial notions of identity and (b) those primordial notions themselves as evidence of a kind of false consciousness of essentialism against which cultural constructivism labors. If this distinction is not heeded, anthropologists run the risk of focusing on specific kinds of cultural forms as evidence of essentialism instead of contextualizing those forms in the larger cultural and political environment in which they exist. Furthermore, one runs the risk of seeing such forms as merely "touristic" or "official." The impulse to denigrate supposedly "invalid" cultural forms such as art for tourists, government-sponsored festivals, and the like reveals more about the anthropologist and his or her craving for authenticity than it does about the cultural forms themselves.

One strategy, for instance, toward furthering anti-essentialism has been the "invention of tradition" approach in which cultural forms are exposed as examples of fraudulent tradition (Hobsbawm and Ranger 1983; for a fuller discussion see Segal 1996). The purpose of such approaches was to lay bare the manufacture of cultural forms by groups in power and to show such forms as tools in the manipulation of public sentiment. That is, they assumed a kind of "false consciousness" on the part of the audiences in question. "Invention of tradition" projects implied that there were real traditions somewhere to be found. Yet the strategy has also been adopted by cultural constructivists to show, not that there are "real" traditions, but that *all tradition* is a social construction. However, in adopting a purely cultural constructivist, anti-essentialist standpoint on ethnicity one may run the risk of devaluing the identities of ethnic groups and, contrary to the stated goals of anti-essentialism, "extend[ing] and legitim[izing] scholarly control over the discourses of Others" (Briggs 1996: 463), which is what the "invention of tradition" literature has recently been accused of doing. Yet there are three problems that emerge from focusing on cultural forms in this way. First, one cannot assume that specific forms produce only certain meanings; second, one cannot assume that the meanings associated with cultural forms that can be "shown" to be invented or "inauthentic" are themselves inauthentic by association; and third, that elites are the only ones actually producing such forms. One of the chief drawbacks of seeing "official forms" as the result of elite strategies is that such a view is not equipped to address the phenomenon of subaltern and marginalized peoples adopting the same strategies for their own political purposes.

I would suggest, then, that a more fruitful approach to the study of ethnicity and identity is one that emphasizes the processes by which collectivities stress their differences from each other through cultural means on the conscious level but takes into account the practices and behaviors that are not fully conscious. In that case, we have to make a clear distinction between "ethnicity" and "ethnic identity" on the one hand and culture on the other. But we must be aware that the limited sense of culture used in the politico-institutional rhetoric of multiculturalism and what has become known as the politics of recognition itself *becomes* part of lived practices and experiences. Anthropologists can look at the cultural forms that exist as "emblematic" on many different but conjoined levels, placing the emphasis back on cultural constructivism and the work of the imagination yet incorporating many different sources for these imaginings.

This work seeks to situate Carnival, which has a relationship to the government and is touristic yet which is not wholly defined by those relationships, within both the larger context of the "politics of recognition" and the realm of personal practice and private activity. In doing this I want to show that collective "identity" exists somewhere in-between these worlds, in processes of "imagination" (but not myth) that constitute an idea of a collectivity called the transnation. In doing so I engage with current literature that approaches the issue of constructed identities from several angles and multiple disciplines. Specifically, I turn to the sociological and philosophical literature on the politics of recognition for insights into the socio-political climate that creates a context in which public cultural forms become of paramount importance.

Nancy Fraser has termed this radical rendering of cultural constructivism "the deconstructive version of antiessentialism" and indicates that its most salient feature is the belief that the proper task of projects of identity is not to construct workable forms of subjectivity or collective identity but to deconstruct all other attempts at such constructions. Although there are positive elements to deconstructive anti-essentialist politics, the major drawback is its indifference to "social structures of domination and to social relations of inequality" (1997: 183). That is, anti-essentialisms relinquish a major factor in the importance of ethnicity, which is their "emancipatory" quality, their role in struggles against oppression, cultural domination, and the like. Stressing "invention" in cultural production disengages the cultural form from its bearing on reality, on what may be "anticipated" and acted upon. This is where a view of ethnicity that stresses *reproductive imagination* becomes viable. Ethnicity conceived of along these lines takes into consideration the social structures and political-economic constraints experienced by groups of people and sees ethnicity in its relation to them. Such a view sees ethnicity in the political environment of multiculturalism, which helps determine its shape. Therefore the question of construction, which does violence to and undermines the emancipatory power of ethnic identity, must be dealt with alongside the kinds of state and administrative policies that shape the *public form* of ethnic identity such as multiculturalism (Eriksen 1993). That way, as researchers we are able to contextualize the shape of ethnicity and identity without necessarily making potentially pejorative statements about their objective reality.

Reexamining the Festival

While I am interested in trying to forge a path between essentialism and anti-essentialism, I am doing so with an expressive form of culture, Carnival, and especially with the ways in which this form relates to issues of national, personal, and ethnic identity. In that regard, then, this work is indebted to a long history of festival scholarship in both anthropology and folklore studies. Festival studies have often been closely intertwined with studies of ritual inspired by the work of Arnold van Gennep (1960) and the works of Victor Turner (e.g., 1969) in which the social role of the festival is explored from the perspective of individual status transformation or rites of passage. Turner expanded upon this focus to include a many-layered consideration of the individual's connection to the social order, and further saw the festival as a symbolic embodiment of underlying social structures (1983). Yet Turner, as well as others, saw the festival as a locus of play, of reflexivity, and of social commentary (1982; Babcock 1978; Abrahams 1982; MacAloon 1984; Manning 1983). This conception of the festival continues to yield important insights, especially insofar as it is concerned with representations of the social body to and by the individual. Such studies drew heavily on play theory (Bateson 1958; Huizinga 1955; Caillois 1979) and, in the main, saw festival as an area for play within social structure, yet developed such theories beyond a strictly functionalist approach. Turner, Babcock, and Abrahams all began to stress the importance of seeing the dialectical nature of festival "which moves from structure to antistructure and back again to transformed structure" (Turner 1983: 110), thereby highlighting the idea that agency is structured but also structures.

Abrahams, however, rejected the utter divorce of festival behavior from the rest of the year. By showing that festival behaviors have precedent outside the festival moment and by drawing a stronger relationship between festival and "daily life," Abrahams pushed us away from studies that emphasize the rejection or reversal of acceptable social norms and values. There is a sobering effect to these insights. For analysts of a form like the festival, during which there are clear and visible yet often highly fanciful and stylized transformations taking place, it is easy to lose sight of the self-consciously political and socially normalizing affects of an event like Carnival.

I do not wish to suggest in this study that it is better to ignore festivals and carnivals as rites of reversal or to reject a more psychological approach to the study of masquerading and celebrating. I would rather see a level of integration, in which the festival may be about the exercise of personal fantasy but also about the display of commodified culture. Carnival may be a way for individuals to improve their social standing while, conversely, participation in Carnival may be seen as socially ruinous. Events like Carnival in Trinidad are full of contradictions, yet it is in the workings of these contradictions that we as anthropologists and folklorists see the subtler sides of representation, recognition, and ritual. Carnival in Trinidad exists in a political world. It has, for a long time, been seen as an object of culture and therefore the object of much discourse on "culture." One important ideological frame that helps contextualize Carnival as "Culture" is its place in the politics of recognition.

Recognition and Politics

In a recent work Webb Keane (1997) has noted that the concept of recognition involves a close relationship with objectification and the idea of repeatability as well as the larger context of power and social structure. Objectification and recognition are bound together through a process wherein objectification takes place through the act of recognition. It is a recognized and repeatable form that becomes the object, clearly bound (Keane 1997: 14). There is in this formulation, and in the problem of recognition itself, the problem of circularity. That is, objectification takes place through an act of recognition, which itself requires an object to recognize ("an instance of something that is already known" [1997: 14]). Some of this problem is resolved by taking larger issues of power and knowledge into account that figure into the framing of experiences (Foucault 1980). Such a view would suggest that what individuals recognize as objects have been shaped always already outside of the subject.

What seems certain is that recognition and objectification take place in a process of interaction. The social nature of recognition and objectification means that all such acts are open to negotiation and are rife with ambiguity. It also means that different types of recognition and objectification, such as self-objectification, are inherently acts of exchange in which understandings of identity are traded and at the same time constructed. Objectification and recognition not only occur in mutual cooperation, they are always "working." That is, objects are never stable and depend continually on acts of recognition, which in turn impart a kind of materiality to the object. Thus it is through exchanges of recognition that objectivity is established and it is upon these objects that recognition may proceed in dialectical fashion. When issues of collective identity arise the problem is compounded enormously. Suddenly there are a multitude of variables in the equation.

In the Trinidadian example I have come across a collectivity that is defining itself across multiple worlds. Caught between Trinidad and Trinidadian nationalism and New York City's ethnic politics, the transnation emerges as Trinidadians mobilize the rhetoric of the former in the service of negotiating the latter. For many Trinidadians in New York it is Carnival that exemplifies their relationship to the home country and helps them negotiate the host country most effectively. That being said, however, the way in which people actually play mas' often bears no relationship to official discourse or even to their own sense of culture and identity as it is consciously expressed. The process of self-conscious cultural display requires the presence of tangible cultural forms. As we shall see, these get created and "objectified" in many ways. Creating an understanding of "Carnival" that may be shared among Trinidadians and also cross-culturally requires many kinds of objectification.

In discussions among Trinidadians in the mas' camp, one variety of objectification is achieved. Yet the display of "culture" to non-Trinidadians and even to non-West Indians, requires a different sort of objectification and needs to enter into a different sort of discourse of culture. Culture for display requires the presence of *culturalisms* that are commodified. The commodified cultural form achieves a level of materiality that is different from the form objectified in other ways and lends itself more fully to situations of exchange. The buying and selling of cultural objects is one sort of exchange, but it exists in the shadow of more abstract forms of exchange: recognition. Recognition—or what I, following more general usage, will be calling the politics of recognition—is a kind of exchange relationship in which cultural display serves to legitimize multiculturalist policy (while facilitating social administration in general) in return for which the displayer receives access to goods and services. I must stress that this form of exchange is only one part of the context in which Carnival exists. It is not its defining context, nor does it determine the way in which Trinidadians gain an ethnic identity.

Objectification versus Commodification

The standard, economic definition of a commodity is something that exists in a system of exchange wherein the item in question has both a use value and an exchange value (known simply as value in Marxist terminology). The object's use value is determined by its power to satisfy some human want, while its exchange value is determined by its power to command other commodities in the system of exchange. The commodity form, in the traditional Marxist understanding of it, extends to other areas of social life such that human relations and object relations become confused in what is known as commodity fetishism. I do not wish to enter into a discussion of commodity fetishism here except to point out that Marx used the concept of the commodity to "analyse forms which . . . are not themselves in the primitive sense, commodities" (Bottomore 1996: 102). That is, commodification, in the Marxist tradition, becomes something that grows out of a particular mode of production to inform relationships that people have with other people or other forms in social life.[3]

Recent treatments of commodities in the anthropological literature emphasize the transient quality of the commodity form. That is, the commodity moment in the "social life" of a thing is only one of many identities that thing may have (Appadurai 1986a; Kopytoff 1986). In his discussion of object "biographies" Igor Kopytoff notes, for instance, that only certain things may be regarded as properly commodifiable; that the commodity life of the thing may be limited and, perhaps most importantly, that "the same thing may, at the same time, be seen as a commodity by one person and as something else by another" (1986: 64). A cultural form may be commodified therefore, without fixing the form's meaning everywhere and for all time. Yet when the object's chief property is its exchangeability, it can be said to be in its commodity form (Appadurai 1986a: 8–10). The question is, however, what kinds of systems of exchange are being assumed here? If the notion of exchange includes more than a traditionally economic definition, the commodity form might be extended to include economies in which other kinds of capital are being sought.

Furthermore, as Appadurai has noted, the commodity context must be taken into consideration. That is, in what situations is an object (or in our case an objectified cultural form) likely to be seen as a commodity? Appadurai gives the example of marriage transactions in certain societies wherein a woman's exchange value is foregrounded (1986a: 15). In the case of Carnival, in certain situations of cultural identity negotiation the festival's commodity form exists alongside its other social identities. The larger contexts that situate the commodity moment are also contexts in which Carnival bears many different kinds of meanings. Thus, even within the commodity form the properties of the object in question are not wholly determined. Ambiguity or uncertainty may arise in at least two different situations, one involving things and the other involving people.

In the first case the object in question is a thing and is only considered a commodity by one party. This, it seems to me, is quite often the case in acts of exchange between a merchant and a consumer in contemporary Western society. For instance, if I go to buy a gift for a friend, the item I purchase is not defined by its property of exchangeability, although it may be so considered by the merchant. The second situation speaks to Appadurai's example of the woman involved in a marriage transaction. In such a case the woman, herself the "item" in question, may not think of herself primarily in terms of exchangeability. No doubt one can find more examples and subtypes to these exceptions. To me, then, commodification is an example of the sort of recognition and objectification noted above. For if the commodity is one kind of object, its recognition as such is social and therefore open to negotiation. Things may have "biographies," but they may also have split personalities depending upon the different frames brought to the interaction by different people. Finally, commodification involves exchange.

I therefore propose that if a commodity is, broadly conceived, that moment in the life of a thing in which its exchangeability is foregrounded, we must focus on the systems of exchange that might arise from such a definition. In addition to considering money exchange systems and barter as legitimate forms of commodity exchange, we might include the exchange of recognition and of what Bourdieu calls both "symbolic" and "cultural" capital (1993: 75).[4] What would emerge from this would be both a narrowing of the distinction between object and commodity and a way of theorizing the role of culture in presentations of identity without assuming that any relationship culture has to commodity exchange delegitimizes the cultural form or determines the meaning of the form for participants. Finally, I would suggest that it is through the act of commodification (in this new sense) that the transnation has access to sources on which to found acts of reproductive imagination. Simply put, the transnation is not merely a collectivity imagining itself in various ways. We must see the transnation as existing in an "economy of identity," which requires that it imagine itself in *specific ways,* as a coherent cultural group. In order to achieve this the transnation must produce quantifiable products of itself to consume and to exchange in acts of legitimation. In what follows I will show how the transnation is restricted in imagining itself by looking at the ways in which received notions of culture impose limits on the cultural imagination through what I call "bureaucratic multiculturalism."

The Politics of Recognition

The politics of recognition is a concept made popular in the work of Charles Taylor (Taylor and Gutmann 1992). Simply put, it is the political position, adopted most visibly by "multiculturalists," that one's identity is predicated upon recognition by others. The failure to recognize another's identity is the failure to grant them full human status *as themselves.* It also means that continual failure to recognize some person or group will result in their misrecognition of *themselves,* leading to alienation, low self-esteem, self-hatred. Identity, in this case, is played with very loosely. It can mean gender, ethnicity, age, "race," or many other things. Recognition in this sense depends upon the notion that an authentic and immutable identity preexists the recognition of it by others; therefore, the politics of recognition has been called essentialist. Multiculturalist politics have been decried by, among others, those interested in the "politics of redistribution" (Fraser 1997), which is characterized by a focus not on identity per se but on economic injustice, and is therefore associated with socialist politics. Recognition politics has also been targeted by anti-essentialists or deconstructionists who claim that all identities are socially constructed and, therefore, that any claims to a primordial identity are spurious (Fraser 1997: 173–88). My aim here is not to formulate another criticism of multiculturalism or even of antiessentialism. I am interested in seeing the manifestations of cultural politics in the lives of transnationals and in seeing the ideological implications of recognition politics in the formation of the transnation's collective sense of itself.

Reproductive Imagination, Fantasy, and the Transnation

I would like to begin here the discussion of imagination that will underlie the following sections. Over the course of this text I will take different perspectives on the acts of imagination and the practices that ensue from them. In the interactions between the state, the transnationals, and the city of New York, different imaginations are at work. What I will be calling the imagination is defined specifically by the *Oxford English Dictionary* as "reproductive imagination," where it is differentiated from a more general notion of the imagination. As the *OED* has it, reproductive imagination is "that faculty of the mind by which are formed images or concepts of external objects not present to the senses and of their relations (to each other or to the subject): hence frequently including memory" (1989: 1377). What is chiefly useful about this distinction is that there is not the same emphasis on some relation to reality. The traditional definition of the imagination stresses that what is imagined has no basis in reality, and the imaginant understands this.

In reproductive imagination, however, the imaginant is drawing inferences from memory and forming an impression of what is likely or what may be anticipated and therefore what may be acted upon. Yet the memories upon which people draw are not merely the recollections of their own personal experiences. In the work of Adorno (1981) and Horkheimer (1972), in the "nostalgia for the present" of Fredric Jameson (1984), and in the hyperrealities of Umberto Eco (1986) and Jean Baudrillard (1983), critical theorists have emphasized the power of mass mediation and other forms of public or official representation in the acts of remembering that a collectivity performs. The collective process of reproductive imagination is rooted not only in the amalgamation of memories of individuals but in the interested mobilization of narratives of lost pasts engaged in by the state, by the tourist industry, by culture brokers, by local government, and by other groups who may control the public representation of cultural histories. It is this understanding of imagination that I want to use here.[5]

The imagination, as I conceive of it then, requires not only historical narratives but publicly available images and cultural forms that support and reinforce those narratives. Public monuments, festivals, and historical sites are all material markers that give evidence to the enduring and powerful reality of events narrated. Discussions in the literature of parade often point to the carefully choreographed nature of the processional route as it makes its way past important landmarks, imbues certain spaces with ritual import, or creates a moment of sacrality in an otherwise profane locale (Davis 1986; Marin 1987). In all of these cases a degree of visibility or material presence helps create impressions of power and legitimacy. Susan Davis points out that even in parades meant to burlesque the "establishment" act of marching, masquerading carries powerful legitimating properties (1986: 158–59).

The public arena, then, clearly has great significance for the reproductive imagination and remains a highly contested forum. Later in this chapter I will discuss the importance of the festival from this particular perspective. However, first I will introduce some basic concepts, which will inform my later discussion of public cultural forms and their relationship to the act of cultural legitimation engaged in primarily by the state and by its allies in civil society. In a later chapter I show that part of the state's bid for legitimacy, in Trinidad, requires the impression that it has full control over the flow of goods and services across its borders. This flow includes the production and distribution of cultural forms as well. State control over cultural forms is facilitated by the general understanding that such cultural forms are themselves also commodities in the more traditional sense of objects intended for economic exchange.

The commodification of cultural forms on this level achieves two things at once. First, it transforms the cultural form into a particular kind of object that has roughly the same status as other kinds of commodities, such as petroleum and agricultural products. In its commodified incarnation the cultural form can be bought and sold, given value, copyrighted, cataloged, and inventoried. Reification has an additional consequence. Commodification is a form (one of many) of objectification. The state's policy to promote the commodification of cultural forms also allows it to define the public shape of such forms, to determine the "look" of the cultural form as material object. Yet the state's interests are not always internally harmonious, nor, as I have said, do the results of state actions with regard to cultural forms wholly determine their reception in society as a whole. In Trinidad, representatives of state agencies, masqueraders, Carnival promoters, musicians, and costume makers may all conceive of Carnival differently; they might see the future of the event or its importance to Trinidad very differently, yet they are operating with objectified notions of Carnival. And in some cases, at least, there is commerce between understandings of Carnival, especially as it relates to national culture or national identity.

In my many discussions with Trinidadians concerning Carnival, it was immediately clear that the type of discussion one was having shifted the way in which the festival was discussed. Thus a conversation on the personal meaning of Carnival to an individual could produce one kind of response—typified, for instance, by a focus on liming—while, even within the same conversation, an inquiry into the meaning of Carnival as Trinidadian culture produced a whole different set of issues. These issues would also be linked in specific ways. By way of example, a particular interview I conducted in Port-of-Spain with celebrated carnival artist or masman Neville Hinds is worthy of note. Mr. Hinds is one of a growing number of carnival artists making his living not only in Trinidad but in Brooklyn as well. In addition to bringing out his own bands, Mr. Hinds also designs bands for others who then hire people to build the costumes. These Carnival bandleaders are not, in Mr. Hinds estimation, "real" masmen (Neville Hinds interview, Jan. 23, 1994). To Hinds the distinction can be likened to the difference between someone who writes music and someone who performs other people's songs. For Hinds producing Carnival costumes and designs is something one does through trial and error and through the careful mastery of the art. One cannot achieve the status of designer through certificates or "papers." Hinds is here referring to the influx of Carnival entrepreneurs who began bringing out bands as commercial ventures and who claimed the title of bandleader without artistic qualification or who sought such qualifications through the National Carnival Commission and their sponsored programs. Hinds's definition of masman must take into consideration developments within the state and their incursions into Carnival. Their very presence affects his definition and what can be considered properly "professional."

This is to be expected, of course, and shifts in context reveal that Carnival is objectified in several different ways by the same people. Much of this work focuses on the narratives and acts of objectification surrounding Carnival specifically as national culture. These narratives are most salient in exploring the formation of the transnation. I found that there was a great deal of homogeneity from one actor to the next and that similar notions of Carnival could be found in official documents, in tourist literature, and in private statements both in Trinidad and in Brooklyn. Yet despite their similarities, these notions of Carnival could be used quite differently given the context.

In Trinidad state policies indicate that Carnival is seen as a growing industry. In New York Carnival is seen less as an industry and more as an example of an authentic ethnic identity. In both of these cases, however, Carnival is objectified in relation to an act of exchange. The assumption underlying both of these phenomena is that culture (as a collection of cultural forms) can be used in what we might call "the economy of identity." By this I mean a system of exchange that emerges from a larger ideological framework in which identity is seen as an objective or material reality that can be possessed and exists as a fully conscious property. The ideological foundations of this system, I grant, have a very specific genealogy. The economy of identity, furthermore, is part of a political framework exemplified by "multiculturalism" that I do not believe is shared everywhere in the world. It is, however, a reality in the lives of Trinidadians both at home in Trinidad and "abroad" in New York City. Within the economy of identity a very specific notion of culture is used. I have described that conception of culture very briefly here and will elaborate it more theoretically and ethnographically later on. Within the economy of identity, commodified cultural forms are presented as "evidence" of authentic culture. Although these forms themselves have elements that exist in the traditional money economy (i.e., one can hire dancers, charge admission to festival activities, sell souvenirs, food, tapes of music, etc.), they also exist as markers for the exchange of symbolic and cultural capital. Cultural forms also exist in systems of exchange wherein these other kinds of capital are at stake. When these moments are foregrounded or present, such forms may be called "culturalisms."

Culture versus Culturalism

In *Modernity at Large,* Arjun Appadurai makes a useful distinction between culture and culturalism. In tracing the concept of culture Appadurai marks a four-step approach that carries the notion of culture away from a purely substantive set of attributes, to those features of a group that foreground dimensions of difference, to "culture as group identity based on difference," and finally to "culture as the process of naturalizing a subset of differences that have been mobilized to articulate group identity" (1996: 15). Appadurai moves us toward a more instrumental understanding of ethnicity and away, as he says, from a "primordial" one. Introducing the concept of *culturalism*, Appadurai wants to highlight the self-conscious, political mobilization of difference for a wide range of purposes. The climate for such projects is hospitable, especially using the tools of market capitalism. What Appadurai also points out is that the interaction between culturalist enterprises and individual subjects is not always going to produce an interpellated subject in the Althusserian sense (1971), nor does it guarantee hegemony or alienated subjectivity (a position taken by some Frankfurt School scholars and, in a different sense, Foucault [1980]).

However, what is of greatest interest to this work is the problem of exploring the relationship between the culturalist movement and the subject. In other words, how do we account for "the process by which certain criteria of difference, mobilized for group identity" become "(re)inscribed into bodily subjects, thus to be experienced as both natural and profoundly incendiary" (Appadurai 1996: 14). Furthermore, in what manner can a treatment of such processes illuminate the ways in which the very movement of people from a home country sparks the state to engage in culturalist enterprises that reverberate through the transnation and return once again to the homeland? It is my contention that dual-sited ethnography provides the intellectual space for such an exploration. In the following chapters various factors in the exchange between the agents of culturalism and the subjects they address will be discussed. Yet as long as culturalisms exist in relation to people who must incorporate them into their lives, the chance of multiple and conflicting meanings exists.

The State

Throughout this text I make frequent mention of the state. I would like to clarify here who exactly is meant by this sometimes ambiguous collective noun. The ideas of the state, of sovereignty, of democracy derive from debates concerning the emergence of the "modern state" from older centralized state systems. The transformation of the state from an absolutist political entity governed by a supreme executive power, such as a monarch, and dependent on that ruler for its existence *(l'état, c'est moi)* to an independent system of rule governed but not determined by the person of the ruler was accompanied by controversies regarding the source of political authority: sovereignty (Held 1995: 32–47). From Hobbes and Locke to Rousseau differing notions of the state's mandate were offered. From state sovereignty to popular sovereignty such debates shaped the discourse of modern statehood. Rousseau's theory that citizens "should be involved directly in the creation of the laws by which their lives are regulated" (Held 1995: 45) was based upon the larger concept of the "general will," the collective contemplation of the common good. As the state became, more and more, the model for legitimate political authority it became the locus of struggles for access to resources and power and grew more and more into the site from which rule was administered to a bounded territory (Held 1995: 47).

The feature of the modern nation-state, then, that figures heavily into my usage is the understanding that the state "works for a living." Legitimation is an ongoing affair both at home and abroad, and, although no one is specifically challenging the contemporary state in Trinidad and Tobago in violent or demonstrative political activity, the state is under continual pressure from sources external and internal to itself (Structural Adjustment agreements, for instance, which Trinidad entered into in the late 1980s, put restrictions on the state's economic and social policies).

I agree with Dietrich Rueschemeyer et al. (1992: 262–63) in their emphasis on the state not as "a mere reflection of power relations in civil society" but, as an entity that can "act autonomously of civil society," one that can "profoundly shape it." As they point out, this has been true throughout the history of the British Caribbean (1992: 264–66). However, whereas Rueschemeyer et al. are particularly interested in the political and economic end of these relationships, I am more concerned with showing the cultural end.

Throughout what follows, when I refer to the state I am referring less to the autonomous structures of the government, which remain in place despite the transitory nature of the political parties that inhabit them, and more to specific policies issued from the Trinidadian state. That is, I am concerned with the state's public position on a given matter. Thus, in that spirit, I make less of a distinction between the officials of the state—its ministers, its civil servants—and the class from which such employees are drawn. Part of the state's ability to govern is lodged in its ability to demonstrate its legitimate concern for and stewardship of the sentiments of the nation or of the people who live in the bounded territory the state controls. The appearance of consent derives, in some measure, from the fact that opinions of the state are reproduced in the private sector. These ideas, independently given but subsequently reflected in state policy, can give the appearance of consensus. However, as I will show later, there is a confluence of state interests and class interests, especially with regard to issues of culture. Also there is a great deal of movement between the private sector and the state within, particularly, the middle class. The same people are in positions to pronounce the nation's views from outside state organizations (through the press, for instance) as are in the government (which I will take as roughly synonymous with the state). For example, during the course of my interviews I had occasion to meet with a number of individuals who at one time or another had served both in state cultural ministries or organizations and in the newspapers, television, or radio. There are many examples, for instance, of artists or musicians taking posts in the government in areas of their expertise. Where there are differences in view among members of the same class or within the government, I note them. For example, the opinions that many artists have concerning Carnival differ slightly from the opinions of people in the state who are not themselves artists but who have experience in the business world or the world of tourism promotion. In sum, my use of the term "state," although necessarily loose in some cases, reflects the porous nature of government and the exchanges between public and private sectors within Trinidad.

Outline of Chapters

Each chapter highlights some part of the theoretical issues brought up in the introduction. In chapter 1 I provide a history of Carnival in Trinidad from the perspective of the middle classes and show that this group gradually appropriated the festival for nationalist purposes and forged a sense that Carnival should be the national festival. In the contemporary instance Carnival figures prominently into the state's bid for sovereignty in the global "family" of nations.

Chapter 2 details the history of Carnival in Brooklyn and demonstrates its importance to the growing community of Trinidadians who migrated there in the 1960s. I also make a case for utilizing a dual-sited ethnographic methodology in order to explore the complex relations between home and host country.

Chapter 3 is an exploration of the mas' camp in Brooklyn and shows the role that Carnival plays in the lives of certain Trinidadian New Yorkers. The mas' camp is an area in which people discuss and participate in the production of Carnival. It is an area that exists outside of the "official" festival itself as seen by the city and Trinidadian culture brokers. The mas' camp provides insight into one of the ways in which the transnation imagines itself that is not immediately related to "official discourse" about culture.

In chapter 4 I return to the world of "official" discourse and New York politics to show the environment in which Carnival exists. Drawing upon an incident that threatened Carnival and the West Indian community in general I show how Carnival lends itself to multiculturalist politics and inter-ethnic negotiation.

Chapters 5 and 6 take us back to Trinidad to witness two Carnival-related competitions. One of these was highly unsuccessful, while the other was enormously popular. I explore some reasons why events transpired the way they did, focusing on the role that transmigrants had in determining the outcomes of each competition and suggesting that success is at least in part attributable to an appeal to the transnation.

Carnival Schematic

Although the various parts of Carnival will be described in greater detail as the work progresses, the following is a brief sketch of the events of Carnival as they appear in order. These events apply to both Trinidad and New York, unless otherwise specified. The main difference involves the Parade of the Bands; in New York there is only one day of bands marching, while in Trinidad there are two. The main events are as follows.

• *Saturday before Carnival: Panorama Steelband Competition*
Steelband finalists play one selection (approximately ten minutes) before a panel of judges. All participants are ranked with prize money and awards allocated accordingly. The winning band plays for the public the following Saturday night at a celebratory event, "Champs in Concert."
• *Sunday before Carnival: Dimanche Gras*
The Calypso Monarch competition, like Panorama, pits Calypso finalists against each other. Competitors sing two new and original compositions. The winner, crowned Calypso Monarch, is typically awarded a motorcar and performs at "Champs in Concert" the following weekend. There is also an extemporaneous Calypso competition.

The King and Queen competition features the largest and most spectacular costumes produced by individual bands. Costumes, which generally represent the theme of their sponsoring band, must be carried across the stage by an individual masquerader. A king and a queen are chosen from the competitors.

• *Carnival Monday morning: J'ouvert celebrations*
J'ouvert begins at 2:00 A.M. after Dimanche Gras. Wearing Ole Mas' costumes (many of which are visual puns meant to lampoon current political events) or covering themselves in mud, oil, and paint, people begin the revelry. Marking the official opening of Carnival, the keys to the city are given to King Carnival, the spirit of Carnival. J'ouvert ends at 8:00 A.M.

• *Carnival Monday day: Informal Parade of the Bands (Trinidad only)*
Dressed in only part of their costumes, masqueraders join their bands and march through the streets.

• *Carnival Monday evening and night: Monday Mas'*
Monday night mas' features a city-wide procession of steelbands accompanied by followers.

• *Carnival Tuesday day: Parade of the Bands*
Masqueraders emerge onto the streets in their full regalia at 8:00 A.M. Masquerade bands congregate and proceed to judging venues, accompanied by roving sound systems.

• *Carnival Tuesday evening and night: Las Lap*
After the bands have crossed the final judging station, Las Lap begins. The bands roam until midnight.

1

Carnival in Trinidad

A Selected History

This chapter provides a historical perspective on Carnival in Trinidad. In dealing with this subject my aim is not to present a detailed and total view of the festival, which has been carried out elsewhere (see Hill 1972; Crowley 1956b; van Koningsbruggen 1997; Liverpool 1993; Anthony 1989), but to focus specifically on the transformations within the event that have been sparked by middle- and upper-class involvement. I do this primarily because it is here that the roots of Carnival as a national festival can be found, and it is the nationalization of Carnival that has become so important to Trinidadian cultural identity both at home and abroad.

"Race," Color, and Class in Trinidad

In approaching this complex historical material it is necessary to say a few words about terminology. Trinidadian historical sources are not consistent in their use of terms especially with regard to race and class. Race sometimes means color and sometimes means "ethnicity" or place of origin, such as the African race or the Indian race, now quite archaic. Class generally means one's position in the economic hierarchy, yet because there are color associations with class there are overlaps with ethnicity (M. G. Smith 1965, 1991; Braithwaite 1975 (1953); Ryan 1991; Segal 1993). Trinidad has a colonial history, one that has engendered a population that is diverse and intricately interwoven. Thus, the relationship of color to class is never entirely a case of black and white, upper and lower, even though these are the basic parameters. Also, within color and class categories there are long histories of divisions and animosities, some of which persist.

The white population, especially in the nineteenth century, was deeply divided between French Creoles, or descendants of French planters—invited to populate the island by the Spanish in a series of Cédulas de Población culminating in the heaviest immigration in 1783–and the English, who came after the British captured the colony in 1797. Furthermore, there were so-called free colored in various socio-economic positions—some wealthy landowners—who were themselves divided between French free colored and English free colored. There were, in addition, prior to emancipation, the slaves of the French, the slaves of the British, the slaves of the free French colored, and the slaves of the free English colored. There were, finally, free blacks, whose ancestry was "unmixed" and predominantly African, many of whom were from other West Indian islands, both Anglophone and Francophone. After emancipation in 1838, waves of indentured laborers came to the island, including Chinese and Indians. In the early twentieth century very few immigrants arrived, with the exception of a small population of Syrian and Lebanese, who nevertheless have had an important influence on Trinidadian society. Liberated West Africans, over 8,000 of them (many of them Yoruba), came to Trinidad between 1841 and 1861. Surnames such as Africa, Yarriba, and Congo attest to their presence after the 1840s (Brereton 1979: 136). Other free Africans came from the disbanded West India Regiments that were demobilized after 1815, and were joined by Americans of African descent who arrived after having fought for the British during the War of 1812.

As for Europeans—German, Irish, Corsican, Italian, Portuguese, Venezuelan, and Scottish immigrants found their way to Trinidad's shores as well. It was also in the post-emancipation years that many more "small islander" immigrants came, primarily from the British West Indies. Interaction between these groups was frequent, especially in the urban center of Port-of-Spain, and political loyalties were never guaranteed purely by race, class, culture, language, or religion but by some mixture of all of them.

In this work I will refer to Trinidadians of primarily African descent either as black, as African, or as Afro-Trinidadian, which is common practice in Trinidad currently.[1] Similarly, people of Indian descent are generally referred to as Indians or Indo-Trinidadians.[2] Distinctions among kinds of white people have lessened over the years, most likely due to their dwindling numbers and their withdrawal from public political life. Even so, a distinction should still be made between French Creoles and English Creoles. The term "Creole" here refers both to people of European and African descent born in Trinidad. It is common to refer to white Creoles as "French Creoles" despite their actual nationality of origin, especially if they are Catholic.

The colored population presents the social scientist with perhaps the greatest difficulty. This is at least in part because determining who fits into what category is so heavily determined by who the classifier is. Yet in general the common term is still "colored" for this group. Within this broad category, however, there exist subtypes, each with its own particularities such as "red," "Spanish," and "high-brown." Who fits each of these subtypes is problematic and depends upon the speaker, the encounter, and the relative social positions of each. In all cases, it has been noted, the effort, especially in colonial Trinidad, was to appear lighter, closer to the European end of the spectrum (Segal 1993: 87; Braithwaite 1975: 91–92). In Trinidad people from all classes tended to use intricate systems of classification that "divided [people] . . . into the white, fusty, musty, dusty, tea, coffee, cocoa, light black, dark black. He [the West Indian] never doubted the validity of the prejudices of the culture to which he aspired" (Naipaul 1962: 73).

Beginning from immutable categories of "race" such as African, European, and Indian, colors signified the degree from which one was removed either from the top (white) or the bottom (black) of the social hierarchy. The foundational categories of the spectrum itself remained, for the most part uninterrogated. That is, European, African and East Indian were generally understood as the unmixed sources from which other combinations derived (Segal 1993). Yet it is the "very fact of combination and ambiguity [that] foregrounds the fluidity of ethnic identity" (Khan 1993: 180).

For instance, in speaking of the type known as "Spanish," Aisha Khan (1993) emphasizes that in Trinidad and in other "mixed" societies, the act of classification and the content of the category are mutually dependent. That is, using the example of a "Spanish" or someone with the general features of dark, straight, or softly curly hair and light-brown complexion, Khan points out that ancestry ceases to be of sole importance and is tempered with phenotype, class, and geography to produce a category that has variable application. This variability signals the fluid and often historically mutable categories of ethnicity and race. In contemporary Trinidad, although the term "Spanish" does tend to be used as a description of phenotype and even of personal comportment (cultured, polite, upper class, and even "respectable"), its use highlights the qualities and associations reserved for the "pure" categories. Thus a Spanish is less threatening to an Indo-Trinidadian than an Afro-Trinidadian who is seen

to possess certain undesirable traits, but does little to interfere with the association of those traits with Africans and may even reinforce them. A "Spanish" may elicit envy, contempt, or admiration depending on the speaker and
the situation. In my own experience a woman who identified herself as a
"black, Caribbean woman" showed disgust for a woman whom she felt was
using her "Spanish" appearance to gain easy entrance to a Port-of-Spain night-
club known to be tacitly discriminatory against black Trinidadians. "Anywhere
else she goes outside of this country? I tell you she's black!" Conversely, in a
discussion about advertising in Trinidad a friend told me that looking Spanish
was the ideal for many women, and that is the image they are given on television. Spanish, however, is not itself an ethnicity in Trinidad in the broadly
political sense. When discussing ethnicity in institutionalized political arenas,
most people refer to the "pure" types of race or nationality, and these are
mainly the Indians, the Africans, the Chinese, the Portuguese, the Syrians, etc.

Ethnicity, however, is only one factor. Since independence ethnic politics in
Trinidad have mainly been about African versus Indian, these being the two
largest ethnic groups. The recent victory of the traditionally Indian United
National Congress party has markedly invigorated this division. Yet the focus
on race and ethnicity, by stressing primordial group identities, has largely
thrown discussions of class aside.

Although current discussions of national identity involve ways to appease
the largest two ethnic groups (Indian and African), the initial impetus for
having a national culture historically derives from the "mixed" group: the
colored middle class. The colored population of Trinidad agitated for independence from England and spawned the first cohesive nationalist movement in the country. Their disenfranchisement under Crown Colony rule
coupled with their marginalized economic and social position led them to
this. The colored population has been described as a group marked by ambivalence and uncertainty, a feeling of insecurity derived from the fact that
they shared the opinions and prejudices of the white elite but were inextrica-
bly linked to their black, and therefore inferior, ancestry (Powrie 1956). An
ambivalence about their position within Trinidadian society was perceived
in the late nineteenth century by Charles Kingsley, the English writer, who
noted that "they [the colored population] claim and justly, to be considered
as our kinfolk and equals. . . . What faults some of them have, proceed mainly
from a not dishonourable ambition, mixed with uncertainty of their own
position" (Kingsley 1871: 151). This "class insecurity," as Brereton calls it,

derived not only from social barriers, erected by the white establishment, but by economic ones as well.

The colored population could be divided into two basic groups. The smaller group comprised wealthy planters living mainly in the southern part of the island. The larger group were the civil servants, printers and publishers, teachers, lawyers, doctors, and clerks. Very few of this latter group had sufficient capital to invest in business ventures either commercial or agricultural (excluding, of course, the group of colored planters mentioned above) and were discouraged from doing so when they did have such funds. Included within this latter group were the free blacks who had achieved middle-class status and who frequently aligned themselves with the colored population (Brereton 1979: 89–90).

The relationship between being colored and occupying a distinct class position, although difficult to support in any pure sense, was based on the general principle of limited social mobility through color and phenotype (Khan 1993). This situation evolved over time in Trinidad and was shaped by the transfer of power to the British after the Spanish capitulation in 1797.

The free colored planter class had come primarily from the French West Indian colonies. Accorded a lower status economically but not necessarily socially under the Spanish, they suffered even more greatly when the British arrived. While Chacon, the last Spanish governor, permitted the free colored to mingle socially with their white planter counterparts, the British subjected this group to humiliating conditions and discriminated against them socially as well as economically (Brereton 1981: 24–25, 36–37). The social and economic mobility of even the highest free-colored citizen was restricted by issues of "color" and racial ideology, such that there was a ceiling of sorts under which there was limited room for advancement. In that sense at least, class and color have been intimately connected in Trinidad since both before and after colonialism (Braithwaite 1975).

For my purposes here, then, I use colored to mean those people of "mixed" African and European ancestry, including the group of southern landowners and "middle class," to mean civil servants and midlevel managerial staff members, including bank clerks, accountants, secretaries and administrators as well as teachers, editors, and other like professionals.

In the Trinidad of today the middle classes are no longer exclusively colored, but the general profile of the middle class remains intact. That is, the class tends toward the same particular viewpoints, opinions, and values of its predecessor even though the ethnic makeup has changed and diversified. I concur with Kevin Yelvington's approach (1995), which follows Bourdieu in seeing class as an amalgamation of economic, social, and cultural "capitals" ensconced in a habitus (1984). I see Bourdieu's conception of the habitus as useful also in relation to the embodied quality of class and class-related consumption practices. Bourdieu maintains that the consumption practices of given classes help to "shape the class body" (1984: 190). Segal, using a semiotic and social constructivist approach, has noted that color and phenotype in Trinidad are often "read" by Trinidadians and that whole narratives, including conceptions of class, are produced from such readings. They constitute "bodies of knowledge" that draw upon "facts of racial ancestry," each with a corresponding history and habitus (1993: 86–87).

Daniel Miller sees class in Trinidad not as an irreducible fact, nor as a "prime mover," but as an aspect of his dualistic model of transcendence versus transience.[3] He is right, I believe, to remind us that class is not often used by Trinidadians as a self-descriptive. He suggests that this rejection of class is due to a refusal to accept the rigidity of hierarchical social structures that recourse to class distinctions would imply. Miller states, "The argument against using class as central to self-reference is made by Trinidadians themselves in discussing their ability to undermine the pretensions to class through their self-confidence and wit" (1994: 270). Miller thus finds the use of class "of variable utility" and seems to subsume emic uses of the term ("class as subjectivity") to his dualistic model and therefore to specific subject positions within his larger scheme. At the same time he is willing to accept a traditional Marxist (etic) view to provide explanations for economic inequalities (Miller 1994: 271–72).

The middle class in Trinidad comprises a constellation of specific histories, values, and consumption practices. In turn, over the years, the values of the middle class—and for that matter a great portion of the upper class—have been relatively consistent and have been given a voice in the public sector through media held by the middle class. The newspapers, television stations, radio stations, and other organs of public opinion have generally been in middle-class hands largely because of the historical circumstances noted above.

Recently, class loyalties and interests have been frequently undermined by loyalties to race or ethnicity, especially in the much more economically and hierarchically fluid Trinidad of the past thirty years or so, which has seen a more diverse population in positions previously held by the "nearly white."

Despite the divisions that have fragmented class solidarity, a general moral tenor prevails across ethnic divisions that can be said to be middle class. This attitude has been treated in the anthropological literature of the Caribbean a great deal. My aim here in describing what has come to be called "respectability" is not to offer suggestions about its origins in the region but to see its application and rejection throughout Carnival. Respectability and Carnival have been linked since the middle class began to take an active interest in the reformation of the festival, and the legacy of competitions, control, and "improvement" have found their way into Trinidadian life with a variety of consequences.

Respectability

Respectability is a key concept in the anthropology of the Caribbean, usually coupled with the binary opposite concept of "reputation" (Wilson 1973; Abrahams 1983; Miller 1994). It is of interest to me here more as an aspect of the discourse of middle class-ness than as an objective sociological fact pertaining to the structure of West Indian society as a whole.[4] In that regard, then, I see respectability as a feature of being middle class inasmuch as it figures prominently into discussions of what it means to be middle class and colored in Trinidad.

Respectability in the anthropological literature of the Caribbean, however, first emerged as part of a basic dichotomy of respectability and reputation delineated by Peter J. Wilson in his seminal work *Crab Antics* (1973). In Wilson's scheme respectability and reputation were aspects of West Indian life that were divided along gender lines and provided society's fundamental structural framework. In Wilson's analysis women are associated with respectability, which comprises domestic values, morality, and propriety. Women traditionally take up a strong position vis-à-vis the maintenance of kinship links, domestic order, proper conduct, and the education of children. These features of feminine-based respectability are further linked with the colonial order, place a great deal of weight on the hierarchical structure of colonial society, and manifest themselves as an embodiment of Euro-colonial values.

Men, on the other hand, are associated with reputation, which is public, "immoral" or potentially so, and decidedly improper. Behaviors in the realm of reputation are characterized by loud, demonstrative talk; going to the rum-shop; extramarital sexual activity; and valuation placed on success in contests and activities that are fundamentally egalitarian in nature and outside of the legal, colonial order. Reputation, as Wilson saw it, was a feature of Creole-African society and ran counter to European values.

Anthropologists have added terms to this dichotomy even as they have criticized its finer points (Abrahams 1983; Miller 1994; van Koningsbruggen 1997), yet the powerful model of a dualistic structure to the Caribbean socio-cultural complex has endured. As mentioned, in the original Wilson model the dichotomized variables of respectability and reputation were associated, respectively, with acquiescence and resistance to the colonial order. Daniel Miller rejects both the strict gender segregation of the model as well as its easy relationship to issues of colonial complicity/antagonism.

With the issue of gender Miller shows how this dichotomy could very easily be stood on its head to produce an equally viable, alternative conclusion. That is, respectability can be seen as resistant to colonialism inasmuch as it helped to foster strong moral codes, kinship ties, and the disciplined pursuit of property as the antidote to the harsh and unstable conditions of slavery (1994: 262–63). Miller's solution is to substitute the respectability/reputation model with a dichotomy based upon transience versus transcendence.

I agree with Miller that respectability does not necessarily indicate the presence of successful colonial hegemony, nor does reputation equal an authentic, Creole-based counter-hegemony. Yet Miller leaves the association of respectability with the female world intact and merely offers an alternative explanation for that association. I would caution against the strict association of respectability with gender in general as it does not seem to account for roles women have played in the public sphere of "reputation," which adherents to Wilson's model traditionally associate with men.

Within the history of Carnival itself, and even to this day, there have been women actively involved in the culture of reputation building. Although generally in the service of building a particular man's reputation, women certainly have been known for creating and defending their own formidable reputations as fighters, singers, and lovers. In the underworld Carnival of the late nineteenth century, women often sang the praises of their favorite calinda or stick-fighting men. These women, called matadors, were skilled speakers, strong fighters, and often able singers of praise in their role as "chanterelles" for the various "societies" in the 1840s. Such societies have been considered precursors to the contemporary masquerade bands (Hill 1972: 56).

Matadors and chanterelles, members of the jamette class, were fully within the tradition of what Abrahams calls "talking broad" and were not above public disturbances. In 1868 a Port-of-Spain newspaper reported on seven bands of women dressed in "fantastic dresses." Many of these women were notorious "nymphs of the pavement" or prostitutes and convicted criminals who carried concealed batons. They formed societies whose membership may have centered around religion, territory, and language and were self-proclaimed "societies for dancing and fighting" (Cowley 1996: 60–61) and existed alongside similar male activities. In one instance two well-known jamettes, Bodicea and Alice Sugar, fought. The fracas "lasted a full hour and they ended up completely battered. They fought like animals over a celebrated stickman, Cutaway Rimbeau" (Sampson 1988 [1956]: 161). Later, when Rimbeau took a fancy to Alice Sugar's younger sister, another notorious jamette named Piti Belle Lily, Bodicea "mauled him into cringing submission with his own poui (hardwood stave)" (161).

Today such women are rarer, but the passing of older, well-known "flagwomen" or standard bearers for the steelbands still occasions mourning both in the Carnival world and even in the press. Their continued presence at steelband competitions bears witness to the fact that women still occupy positions of "reputation" within Trinidadian society.[5] Furthermore, the competence many women display in verbal duels, in calypso singing, and in other forms of oral performance that are not generally considered respectable is a highly visible part of Trinidadian life.[6] Later in this work I show how certain expressive forms previously associated with unrespectable behavior have been "reformed" into respectability through competitions and careful monitoring. Women have entered into these reformed versions in much greater numbers, for instance in the steelbands. In these cases I do see the entrance of women into spheres of "reputation" as an aspect of the influence of middle-class involvement in Carnival and a sort of expansion of the field of respectability. But that is slightly separate from the issue of gender, and I see that as part of the same trend that has witnessed young men from "respectable" backgrounds joining steelbands as well. In other words, respectability exists apart from gender in my view, although there are gender divisions *within* reputation and respectability.

This represents only a cursory history into an underinvestigated aspect of West Indian and Trinidadian society. But the notion that "women are constantly involved with norms and expectations which arise from their activities within a network of kin, a factor which is connected with the close bond between mothers and children . . . [and] in the institutions of the family and the home [which] correspond[s] to the values of legitimate society and thus with respectability" (van Koningsbruggen 1997: 178) does not seem viable as a total explanation. I would tend to see respectability (and reputation) as a larger body of values related to ethnicity and class with gender being a factor in the roles taken within those spheres.

Respectability in Trinidad, however, is a reality derived from the colonial experience, but no doubt also comes from other sources as well. It has had the greatest impact on the colored middle class, who have historically been in the position to champion its values publicly, but it is by no means restricted to that class alone. For my purposes here, however, I want to focus on the what exactly these values are and how they have played a significant role in the middle-class domination of Carnival after the latter part of the nineteenth century.

Perhaps the best description of the colored middle-class exemplar can be found in Edgar Mittelholzer's brilliant novel *A Morning at the Office*, which takes a typical pre-independence Port-of-Spain office as its setting. The novel explores in microcosm the complex relations between color, ethnicity, and class that existed then and persist even now, nearly fifty years later, in Trinidad. In the novel, the character of the accounts typist, Miss Henery, is debating whether or not to accept a proposal of marriage from a colored man, Herbert McGlenny. In weighing the advantages of this union Miss Henery provides us with a wonderful archetype of the colored middle-class gentleman: "He came of good class, had a light olive complexion and hair with large waves ('good' hair, Miss Henery thought of it as; as a member of the West Indian Coloured middle-class, she conceived of human hair in terms of 'good' and 'bad'. . . . 'Good' hair is hair that is European in appearance)" (1950: 58).

Herbert McGlenny is employed with his father's commission agency, which is doing very well. He can be seen at the DeLuxe movie house that, even in today's Port-of-Spain, tends to show the films that appeal to middle-class audiences. He has good parentage, and his uncle has been the mayor of Port-of-Spain.

As Barbara Powrie has explained, "Respectability is the keynote of colored middle-class existence." For Powrie, however, "The ideal person and form of behavior is still white, and life is patterned to conform as closely as possible to all that is felt to be contained within this ideal" (1956: 94). Whiteness and therefore the colonizers stand as the measure of positive value. It is from them that standards of respectability come and to them that one must look for validation. Toward that end certain professions are more generally sought after than others, including the civil service as mentioned above. Such a view persisted in Trinidad for as long as the white presence was a visible and prominent part of Trinidadians' life. For instance, C. L. R. James wrote that the "nearly white" hang "tooth and nail to the fringes of white society" while the darker groups do everything they can to minimize contact with those darker than themselves (1933: 8). This view of Trinidadians society also marks Lloyd Braithwaite's study of stratification in Trinidad conducted in the 1950s (1975 [1953]).

Yet after independence the white presence on the island diminished. As whites ceased to be involved with public life, the dominant aesthetic that had privileged whiteness began to fade. In its place grew up an aesthetic of light-brownness. The specter of the old colonial hierarchy of values continued to linger, but the ascendancy of the colored class provided an opportunity to occupy the new, top position on the pyramid. Anthropologist Peter van Koningsbruggen traces the rise of beautiful brownness to the post–World War II years and sees the American presence as instrumental in changing the popular image of whites (1997: 105; see also Klass 1973).

Although I agree that American whites had a definite impact on Trinidadian popular consciousness (see below), I am less certain that American sailors participated in the devaluation of white beauty. An increase of whites, no matter what their character, does not necessarily lead to an aesthetic devaluation. If anything, white soldiers provided many women with an opportunity to "lighten" their children and increase their chances for success in that color-oriented world (an indication that the hierarchy was in healthy order). Rather, I see a decrease in whiteness and the growing irrelevancy of whiteness *in public* as the major contributing factor to the shift in aesthetics. Thus, although white soldiers were prominent during and after the war, the general trend over the long term was toward white absence. The growth of a local aesthetic of brownness can also be seen in relation to middle-class nationalism and a desire to see "native" culture championed.

Again I must stress that things European and—even more so—American have not declined in significance at a deep level. American television, American music, American images of beauty are still a significant part of Trinidadian popular culture. They do still inform the system of values. However, qualities that can be said to be European are more abstracted in their local realization and direct imitations of American advertisements, for instance, are often produced locally with local actors. American culture functions to shape the surface level of aesthetic and cultural priorities in very meaningful ways, but does not determine them in their specificity. That is achieved locally and through local negotiation.[7]

The growth of a local consciousness has been a part of middle-class involvement with Carnival since the end of the nineteenth century. In order to gain a better understanding of the role the middle class has played in Carnival, it is essential to focus on their bid to make Carnival a national symbol during the drive to secure legislative autonomy from England. Carnival carried with it the potential to rally the predominantly black masses behind an essentially colored political agenda. The nationalization effort consisted of a two-fold strategy of selective censorship and reform. In the former (censorship) the middle classes were often in accord with the white elites, who generally favored complete abolition of the festival. It was in the process of reform that the middle class gained the backing of the masses, who began to see the colored group as their protectors. This strategy was the predecessor of the contemporary effort to secure national sovereignty and legitimation through the management of national culture.

The Middle Class Takes Over

As mentioned, under the French rule of their home islands and under Spanish colonial law, the colored populace were more or less favored for the white blood they had. Under the British, after the capitulation in 1797, blackness was the distinguishing feature. This shift of policy had far-reaching effects. In the eyes of the new administrators, the glass was now half empty for the colored population. Consequently, coloreds were summarily stripped of many of their former rights. Although these rights were legally restored in the 1830s, continuing acts of prejudice were reported in newspapers such as the *Trinidad Sentinel*, whose editor was a colored gentleman. These reports illustrated the degree to which the practices of colonial society lagged behind the legislation enacted many miles away in the metropole. While there are many indications that the colored population were taught to despise their African roots, there is ample evidence that at least some regarded their mixed past with pride (Brereton 1981: 130). "Passing" for white was perhaps a prudent strategy in a colony with limited opportunities for nonwhites, but it does not necessarily follow that such strategies were conceived of as anything more than pragmatic.

On the other hand, for coloreds complete identification with their African past and with the black population of Trinidad was circumscribed both by the negative social effects of such an alliance as well as by the palpable animosity often directed toward them by blacks, especially of the lower classes. Wood has described it in this way: "For them [coloreds] there existed a limbo of insecurity in which the conventions of social intercourse between the classes were shifting and uncertain, in which they were sensitive to real or imagined slights, a No-man's-land where they were exposed to crossfire from both sides" (1968: 253). Yet during the nineteenth century the colored population began to slowly work toward appropriating political control over the island.

After emancipation in 1838 more and more blacks rose to take their own places amongst the middle class. With this development came a greater degree of solidarity between black and colored Trinidadians of the same class. Various associations arose that promoted race pride, such as the Pan African Association started by H. S. Williams, a Trinidadian lawyer in London. After the dissolution of this organization, many of its members joined a newly formed organization, the Ratepayers Association.

The RPA, as it was known, provided a forum for the airing of grievances against Crown Colony rule. Toward the end of the nineteenth century and into the early twentieth century the middle classes, through the press, attempted to gain the support of the masses in favor of representative government. Culturally this took the form of the middle-class appropriation of (or attempted appropriation of) Carnival. Politically, perhaps the most celebrated event was the Water Riots of 1903. Utilizing the issue of the unfair regulation of the water supply by the government, the Ratepayers Association, through their sympathetic press, attempted to forge a link of solidarity between themselves and the black masses. The actions of the RPA in the political realm go hand in hand with their efforts in the cultural realm. These efforts against Colonial rule came from the class and "color" most injured by English colonialism. The French, Catholic, colored, and black middle classes suffered on every front. They were denied social privileges granted to others of equal or greater wealth who were white, their religion and French customs were constantly under attack in the nineteenth century by English Protestants, especially Charles Warner, the attorney general, whose main mission in life seemed to be the eradication of all French influence on the island, white, black, or colored. The variables present in the condition of the colored and eventually the black middle class made it difficult to find allies in the French Creole (white) upper classes. However, common cause could be found or manufactured on racial, religious (for many), and political grounds with lower-class blacks.

The Water Riots proved this. Water had been a frequent point of contention throughout the latter half of the nineteenth century. In 1874 the delivery of water to Port-of-Spain amounted to between sixty-five and seventy-one gallons per day per person. This was twice the amount cited for London during the same period (Williams 1962: 180). The vast majority of this water usage came from the wealthier sections of Port-of-Spain in which families had constructed huge plunge baths into which flowed steady streams of water to keep them perpetually fresh. The government resolved to curb the waste by metering the water supply and by randomly checking and shutting down the stand pipes in the barrack yards, the communal water supply of the very poor. The proposal to meter the water supply, penalize the wasteful, and increase water rates affected the upper and middle classes the most. It was a blow mostly to those who stood to lose a luxury to which they were accustomed. Middle- and upper-class colored, however, painted the government's attempts at water regulation as yet another example of authoritarian Crown Colony government and mobilized nationalist sentiments for their cause. A protest outside the main government building, the Red House, in 1903 turned into a riot with sixteen people killed and forty-three wounded and the Red House (Parliament) burned to the ground.

The riots were part of a sustained effort by the colored classes to push for legislative reform. The Borough Council of Port-of-Spain had been abolished a few years earlier under the policy of Joseph Chamberlain, the secretary of the colonies between 1895 and 1903. Chamberlain was "openly hostile to the grant of representative institutions to colonies where the majority of the people were not Europeans" (Brereton 1981: 146). The Borough council had served as the only forum for the articulation of black and colored issues during this period. The removal of the council was a terrible insult.

The 1890s was also a period of reform in the realm of Carnival. Merchants, who were themselves not often colored, had enjoyed a growing business due to the festival and enjoyed the increased profits as a result of Carnival-season spending. Even the poorest inhabitants of Port-of-Spain liked to spend something on their Carnival costumes, if possible, and often saved the whole year for such purposes. It served at least two interests for the merchants and other middle-class members to fight for the preservation of Carnival. First is the reason already mentioned. Second, Carnival represented an indigenous cultural expression that could be mobilized effectively as an area of common cultural ground against foreign incursion and alien rule. But how had this happened?

Throughout the 1860s and 1870s and for much of the 1880s Carnival had been taken over by "the lower orders." Commonly known now as the Jamette Carnival, the festival was the province of those people who dwelled below the "diamètre," the imaginary line that bisected society and divided it into the respectable and the criminal. Those who dwelled below this line were "persons without any settled occupation subsisting by theft or by the favor of prostitutes, whose wages they share. They have no charitable, political or other definite object, but are called into operation only for the purpose of fighting with other bands" (Colonial Office cited in Brereton 1979: 124). The jamettes "owned" Carnival in the latter half of the nineteenth century, and nearly all members of respectable society decried the wanton lawlessness and moral turpitude that they witnessed in the event. Generally, the higher classes blamed the small islanders and Venezuelans for the corruption of the honest laboring classes of Port-of-Spain, the irony of which is fittingly displayed by the fact that the police force at this time was made up largely of Barbadians as well (Brereton 1979: 128). Carnivals of 1881 and 1884 resulted in large-scale rioting as the police attempted to stop processions of torch-bearing masqueraders from parading in the city. The torchlight parade was a continuation of the cannes brûlées or canboulay, a ceremonial reenactment of the gangs of slaves mustered late at night to put out cane fires. Whites had also reenacted this event, but most probably for very different reasons. For the planter classes putting out a cane fire was one of the few excitements and "colorful" events that plantation life had to offer in a remote colony. For ex-slaves, whose forbears had in all probability started those fires, it was a commemoration of the success of their on-going resistance to that abominable institution.

The Canboulay had been shifted to the night before Carnival Monday, from the August 1st, Emancipation Day celebrations at some point in the nineteenth century, but it is unclear as to when. Although the precise circumstances of the shift may not be known, it seems certain that the combination of the celebration of Emancipation, as embodied in the Canboulay, with Carnival eventually contributed to Carnival's survival and its appropriation by the more radical and progressive elements within the colored and black middle classes, who defended it against its detractors in the more conservative colored and white circles. Ultimately, the middle classes "rescued" Carnival from abolition by the government through persistent agitation. Yet, as we shall see later, their rescue was steeped in the rhetoric of the dominant class.

In 1888 plans were being made to celebrate the Emancipation Jubilee. Those members of the colored intellectual and social elite who were more radical in their "race pride" organized a ball in which the true horrors of slavery and the great triumph of the African over servitude were to be justly addressed and acknowledged (Brereton 1979: 107). A more subdued version was also organized by the government and members of the white and colored upper classes (it has been suggested that the primary colored opposition to Carnival came from Protestants, the result of English and African intermixing).[8] The more radical affair was held by some of the same notable men of color who would, over a decade later, be involved with the Water Riots of 1903. These men were searching for a rallying point, if you will, and they found it in the culture of the ex-slaves they championed. In addition to Carnival, other aspects of slave culture were defended against debilitating ordinances. For instance, Philip Rostant, a colored leader of the constitutional reform movement, supported African drumming and dancing against an ordinance that would have prohibited it in 1883. The ordinance was replaced by the governor with a more moderate one that called for a drumming license. In this way "the radical elements of the reform movement seized this opportunity and used the attack on drumming as an example of the inequities of the colonial order" (Trotman 1986: 265).

African religion, which was a favorite target of the establishment, was ably defended on at least one occasion by a colored lawyer, Vincent Brown, who helped overturn a conviction against the leader of an African religious sect in the Belmont section of Port-of-Spain. Brown claimed that the defendant, Papa Antoine, was the leader of a "genuine African religion" and not a practitioner of obeah, defined in the law as "the assumption of supernatural powers for the purpose of making money" and doing mischief. Members of the colored middle and upper classes, make no mistake, were not in favor of such practices; their feet were too firmly planted in the soil of Western religion and culture. They were not champions of African culture on the grounds that it merited equal consideration and esteem alongside European culture.

Vincent Brown, in claiming that Papa Antoine was a "genuine" African priest, qualified his assessment by asking the court for clemency despite the fact that the religion, however genuine, was "false" and "misguided" (Brereton 1979: 155–56). Even J. J. Thomas, the celebrated black author, member of the

Philological Society in London, and defender of black rights and Creole culture, had no illusions about the state of culture in Africa versus the possibilities of Africans outside of Africa who had become advanced through education.[9] In other words, support of African culture by the black and colored middle classes was carried out in the attempt to justify the presence of people of African descent within the civilized world, the world of the colonists, the Western world. The goal was to favorably compare the potentialities of Africans with other human beings, not to justify the achievements of Africans per se.

Although many of these ideas would change in Trinidad, especially after the Black Power movement in the late 1960s and early 1970s, the underlying desire to be counted as legitimate contributors to a world standard of culture remained a foundational principle. This same principle exists today in the rhetorical strategies of middle-class reformers and nationalist culture brokers. It is the continuing legacy of the middle class's relationship to colonial ideology in the postcolonial world.

Ultimately the gradual formulation of a sense of race pride as well as a sense of nationalist Creole identity combined in the image of Carnival as the true expression of the nonwhite, native-born people of Trinidad. Carnival became, for the constitutional reformers of the nineteenth century, the perfect hook upon which to hang a nationalist banner, or, as Rohlehr has put it, the "Carnival issue was important not only for itself, but as a symbol of the felt need for self-determination" (1990: 91).

Before its appropriation could be fully realized, however, there was the matter of Carnival being decidedly repugnant in many ways to the elite colored population. As I have already mentioned the so-called Jamette Carnivals of the later nineteenth century were often violent, sexually explicit affairs. If there was one thing the colored classes and the white elites could agree upon, it was that something had to be done about Carnival. The difference lay in just what that was supposed to be.

The negative impression of Carnival is explicit in the colored newspapers. The general tone of these papers, however, was that Carnival, although it should be morally improved, needed to be preserved as the exemplar of Trinidadian national culture. In direct contrast the conservative, planter-oriented journal, the *Port-of-Spain Gazette,* was consistently anti-Carnival as well as anti-black in general. It is easy to see, with a growing enthusiasm in things African combined with a growing anti–Crown Colony government, why Carnival should be adopted by the radical colored contingent. Although the colored population had traditionally avoided actual participation in the streets with their black working-class countrymen, "this class was deeply resentful of any interference with Carnival by the Government and was ready to use it if necessary as a means of indirect attack on the Governor and the upper [white] class whenever tension rose" (Pearse 1988 [1956]: 23).

One might point to the Canboulay Riots of 1881 as a watershed event. Certainly colored participation in the streets and behind the scenes rose after this event. However, the takeover of Carnival was more likely a gradual occurrence. The Riots occurred when Captain Arthur Baker of the police attempted to stop and seize the torches of a group of revelers. He had been successful in this endeavor the year before and had, imprudently, pledged to "put an end to this nocturnal sortie" (qtd. in de Verteil 1984: 73) at a pre-Carnival dinner party the following year.

The "masses" were armed and ready and indignant. The melee that ensued caused many injuries and much damage before it was over. The governor of the island mollified the crowds by going before them and pleading for peace while pledging not to interfere with their amusements any further. The colored middle-class press walked a fine line, criticizing ordinances intended to prohibit the event but supporting those ordinances designed to help control the event. *New Era* editorialized against the actions of the police and Captain Baker and suggested that Baker's "discrediting of the populace" had been done in the service of "a clique" whose intention it was to turn the new governor (Sanford Freeling) against the population and against Carnival. The political maneuverings of the radical colored class were finally successful. Throughout the course of the 1890s a series of ordinances were passed that tightened the grip on Carnival and helped purge it of its underclass character. In the words of de Verteil, "Canboulay could be killed, because the middle-class blacks and coloreds were willing to have it so and in fact cooperated in its suppression as Special Constables. Carnival was kept, because it could be made to conform to their wishes and their understanding of tradition" (de Verteil 1984: 115).

A pattern would emerge from these events that would mark the attitudes of the colored middle classes toward Carnival, in some measure, even to this day: namely, that Carnival consistently contains features that attract the middle class in theory but must be reshaped in practice. This generally results in the disappearance of those elements that are meant to represent "true" Carnival, and subsequently the rhetoric of the middle classes becomes perpetually characterized by a kind of terminal nostalgia (see chapter 6). For example, the arts and crafts or local musical forms that appear at Carnival time are immensely attractive to middle-class ambitions for a "national" culture. However, such forms and musical styles often contain "obscene" elements such as references to sex, violence, or other immorality. The appropriation of Carnival by the middle classes in the nineteenth century ultimately led to the objectification of Carnival as a national festival in the twentieth.[10]

But what exactly are the features of Carnival that are attractive? What are the features that are so repugnant? Who are these reformers and how can we get a better sense of what motivations were behind their actions? According to Bridget Brereton, "Nothing alarmed respectable people so much as the extent of 'vagrancy' among the Port-of-Spain lower classes. The Victorian belief in the virtue of honest labour was outraged by the spectacle of able-bodied men and women lounging around the streets with no apparent means of supporting themselves" (Brereton 1979: 123). The newspapers of the period are full of indignant condemnations of the indolence of the lowest orders. This "vicious idleness" led to criminal activity, prostitution (not considered an occupation), and vices of all sorts such as gambling, drinking, and fighting. This class of "loose men and women" were a nuisance in very specific ways. In addition to their unemployment they monopolized public thoroughfares and banded together for the purpose of brawling with each other and harassing members of the upper classes (Brereton 1979: 124–25).

The protestations of the elite point repeatedly to two basic concerns: idleness and immorality. Yet the colored elite were reluctant to agree to the banning of Carnival. As we have seen, Carnival was something like a diamond in the rough of national culture. Their solution was to institute a reform process that began with restrictive ordinances but continued with the ubiquitous competitions that continue today.

In order to eliminate the offensive elements from Carnival, merchants and other members of the middle class instituted competitions, offering prizes for the best-costumed bands, best Wild Indian bands etc. The competition is, in effect, the productive use of the "national" talents of the poor and disadvantaged. Competitions function as a rationalization of artistic endeavor, herding it from display into enterprise. In the competition one has to work for a prize, the process of which teaches diligence, dedication, and discipline.

In the early years of the twentieth century, competitions began and commercial sponsorship of Carnival bands became prevalent. In 1907, for instance, there is a report of a donkey making its way through the streets adorned with a placard that read "I do not wear Waterman's hats because I am an ass" (Anthony 1989: 17). By 1909 commercially sponsored competitions appear to have become commonplace, and the now legendary Ignatius "Papa Bodi" Bodu, a prominent Port-of-Spain merchant, had established his competition on Chacon street in downtown Port-of-Spain.[11]

The institution of competitions, however, did not signal the end of "authentic" Carnival, and not merely because some more genuine version continued to exist on the fringes (although a different and somewhat antagonistic Carnival *did* continue to exist outside the middle-class Carnival). What it did, however was provide a set of parameters for the expressive forms being judged within the competition. These parameters were not only shifted into the hands of the competition judges and administrators,[12] they created an objective version of the expressive form itself, complete with "proper" formal and aesthetic criteria.[13] It became possible for the middle class to shape expressive forms to suit their standards and at the same time produce a catalog of tangible Carnival "items" that would later comprise the highly transportable elements of the transnational Carnival. The organization of Carnival into competitions, each with a distinctive focus (i.e., calypso, steelband, masquerade) and oriented toward a capital reward, lay the foundations for the commodified cultural products that are part of Carnival today.

Yet, by entering into the competitive system through the calypso tents or the masquerade contests, the singer or mas' maker gained a wider audience, possibly some remuneration for his efforts, and a kind of fame that derived from the "official" nature of the event. Furthermore, the competition venues were only part of the Carnival scene. There continued to exist other venues for the practice of Carnival arts, outside of the official ones. I want to make clear, however, that those "outside" venues (barrack yards, private or neighborhood-oriented masquerades, etc.) do not constitute the "genuine article," the authentic Carnival. The calypso sung in the tent, for instance, may be the same one sung in the home, or even put to record. The moment of its commodification, that stage in its "social life" (Appadurai 1986a: 12) is only one of the ways the form may be viewed. That is, too great a focus on the commodity property of the calypso when it is being sung for money, or sold for profit, can ignore the status of the calypso in other kinds of relationships that occur simultaneously with its commodity relationship. The commodity form may even be salient to only one or a few of the parties involved in the calypso performance event. Thus the fact that commodification has been present, or even dominant, in some aspects of

Carnival since the middle class became involved, does not eliminate all other possible meanings and relationships for Carnival forms. Neither is the commodity "moment" the only relationship involving exchange as its primary feature.

For example, Donald Hill recounts the story of the first island-wide calypso king competition in 1939 (Hill 1993: 76–79). The competition was organized by the Victory Tent, which was managed by a government bureaucrat named Reynold Wilkinson. The tents (which started as actual tents but later moved into more permanent venues) were showcases for singers. They were not always official competitions but were sometimes merely concerts with paying customers. The Victory Tent catered to patrons of all classes but was particularly interested in attracting middle- and upper-class patrons and tourists. The first calypso king competition was organized as a kind of gimmick to attract calypso fans to the Victory Tent. It was enormously popular and showcased the talents of some of the era's most popular singers. Yet the participants in this highly commercial venture were primarily concerned with earning the calypso crown. Their actions, undertaken for a variety of reasons including a bid for status within the calypso world, helped legitimize the contest even as it won them fame. Thus commodification of what had been informal competitions (Picong) did not necessarily destroy the form itself. Any cultural form or practice that undergoes commodification in some way requires levels of participation from all different types of actors, including performers and artists.

Although descriptions of these early Carnival competitions are few and far between, after World War I many more descriptions of Carnival and Carnival competitions become available. Once Carnival attained a modicum of respectability, the newspapers gave their wholehearted support to its success. One of the earliest newspapers to get involved was the then newly formed *Trinidad Guardian* newspaper, which helped to organize and sponsor the Carnival of 1919, known as the Victory Carnival. From the detailed accounts of the Victory Carnival plus the records of the fledgling Carnival Committee (the first of its kind), it appears as though the Carnival of 1919 signaled the ultimate triumph of the middle class over the jamettes (Anthony 1989: 20). The year 1919 marks the first time that Carnival moved to the Queen's Park Savannah, as the *Guardian* sponsored a major competition at this site. The *Guardian* offered attractive prizes and respite from the "dust and heat of the town as against the pleasant coolness of the Savannah" in order to lure people from the competitions sponsored by merchants in the city center (*Trinidad Guardian* cited in Anthony 1989: 19).[14]

The *Guardian*'s appeal was to the wealthier classes who wanted to enjoy Carnival in more familiar and congenial surroundings. The middle and upper classes, through their organ, the *Guardian*, were actually trying to change the social geography of Carnival, to redirect the flood of humanity through channels of its own devising. Decorated cars made their appearance, slowly gliding around the enclosed arena, festooned with flowers or, in one case, disguised as an enormous red shoe, or a military tank, or a basket of fruit. The presence of automobiles, having only recently made their appearance in Trinidad, signified that these were clearly the floats of the well-to-do who found Carnival once again to be sufficiently safe for their indulgence. The Victory Carnival also marked the first calypso competition as sung by masquerade bands.

Ultimately, the classes remained apart. The poorer members of the city stayed with their downtown competitions and traditions and the middle and upper classes enjoyed the comfort of the Savannah. The *Guardian* reported primarily on its own Carnival and offered greater prizes and attractions for the wealthy. The Victory Carnival represented the first of the middle-class Carnivals that would slowly but surely come to dominate more and more of the Carnival scene.

Perhaps even more telling than the *Trinidad Guardian*'s Carnival enterprise was the campaign launched by the *Argos* newspaper. Beginning in 1912 but coming to full fruition in 1919, the *Argos* had become the most outspoken proponent of Carnival reform movement. Calling for reform over abolition, this paper was, in the wake of the *New Era* paper, the mouthpiece of the colored middle classes. Merchants who sold goods relating to Carnival, such as costumes, masks, cloth, and the like, were wont to display these goods in their shop cases as they might appear on masqueraders. Thus, they portrayed jamette characters and "such like monstrosities." *Argos* suggested that businesses replace such masking figures with more appropriate models for emulation such as "continental peasants, Spanish toreadores, milkmaids, Danish women, etc. etc." and other characters whose relationship to the population would have been distant indeed. The *Argos* further encouraged that businesses "offer small prizes for the best dressed band of a certain costume exhibited in the show cases" (Rohlehr 1990: 89). The *Argos* newspaper defended Carnival, not only against its own worst instincts and the Crown Colony/elite denigrations, but also against naysayers drawn from the ranks of the "foreigners" in Trinidad.

Rohlehr discusses a petition sent to all the major newspapers and the major figures of authority on the island by a group calling themselves the Trinidad Brotherhood, a collection of fundamentalist Christians. The *Argos* repudiated the petition, not so much on moral or theological grounds, but on the grounds that the signees were off-islanders.[15]

A rivalry then sprang up between the *Guardian* Carnival, whose clientele tended to be the more elite members of society, and the *Argos*, the self-proclaimed paper of the people, who wished to lead the reformation of Carnival in its own image. The showdown occurred over the venue for Carnival competitions in Port-of-Spain, with the *Argos* arguing for the maintenance of the downtown spot. A nice bit of propaganda was printed by the *Argos* to support its position, generally calling on the black (Creole) population to support the "true" Carnival. These exhortations, it must be remembered, were coming from the very same group who wished to purge the "true" Carnival of many of its original characters to make way for milkmaids and Dutch women. Both papers vied for the leadership of Carnival, and both papers had Carnival committees which helped erect tents and visited existing tents to make suggestions as to how to improve the moral tone of the masquerades and the songs being sung. The *Argos* campaign was decidedly specific in its aims and with its instructions. Certain Creole songs, sung either in patois or English, were not only permitted but encouraged, as long as the instruments accompanying the songs were *not* African-derived, with an emphasis on tamboo bamboo and bottle and spoon, favorite instruments of the jamettes. "The proud aim of all these people was to abolish the Ole Mas' of the unwashed and put in its place the pretty Mas' of the respectable" (Rohlehr 1990: 97).

The campaign for cleanliness in Carnival, pursued by both the *Argos* and the *Guardian* newspapers was in some ways a kind of surgery performed by the middle class on the popular entertainments of the working and unemployed poor. Those elements which, according to the middle classes, served the purposes of defining a national culture, were duly kept, while the elements which reflected poorly on the society or were perceived to be dangerous and without merit, were excised. The interesting thing to note is the degree to which this campaign was successful. According to newspaper accounts from the time, many calypsonians were willing to modify and "clean" their calypsos. Masqueraders appeared willing to don the continental costumes suggested by the newspaper elites. Other evidence, however, shows that the many elements of the Jamette Carnival died hard. Tamboo Bamboo bands, for instance, lasted throughout the early years of the twentieth century and were replaced with noisier metal instruments, which evolved into the steel-band movement in the 1930s and '40s.[16] Various styles of masquerade rose up to replace those that had been discouraged by middle-class efforts. The portrayals of the Jamette Carnival that had been most offensive, such as the *pissenlit* in which a man paraded about in women's clothes soiled to represent menstruation accompanied by caricatured sexual movements, were actively cried down by "public" sentiment. Other costumed portrayals were suppressed, especially those styles of clothing most associated with the jamette world. Yet the acceptable costumes that were to replace them were worn in the continuing spirit of the Jamette Carnival. "Pretty mas'" as it is called did not stamp out the jamettes, nor were jamette portrayals never themselves "pretty." The lower-class Carnival found a way to survive in its adaptation of the pretty aesthetic.

A full accounting of the types of costumes and characters that have appeared and disappeared over the years in the Trinidad Carnival cannot be fully enumerated here (see Crowley 1956b). Many costumes arose in parody of contemporary issues or developments in Trinidadian society. Such costumes were of direct relevance to everyday life for the average Trinidadian of the period. For instance, the rise of the popularity of sailor bands in the 1940s was directly attributable to the presence of American sailors at the naval base in Chaguaramas. Trinidadians poked fun at the "bad behavior" of the sailors and imitated their drunken walks, their dirty uniforms, their occasional penchant for carrying ladies underwear, and the like. Many variations on the sailor costume emerged due to the popularity of the basic form. The expansion of the form and the focus on its development reached a high point sometime in the 1950s. With the war over and the naval base an issue of national sovereignty in the face of coming independence, sailors ceased to occupy the same position of popularity they once had. Other concerns found their way into public expression at Carnival time. There are still sailor bands today, many of them carrying on the traditions of their forbears with skill and a great deal of comic ingenuity, but they in no way can be said to be the focus of the general populace. They are not au courant but are recognized and appreciated as nostalgia (see chapter 6).

The middle-class incursion into Carnival fundamentally changed the nature of the event. The "official" administration of Carnival after 1919 created a new set of priorities that could not but affect the way in which all mas' players participated. Sanctioned competitions, of a much more lucrative order than the more modest competitions of merchants such as Ignatius Bodu, arose and flourished. Many of the fundamental justifications of the earlier competitions remained intact, however the competition itself, as a fundamental feature of Carnival, outgrew its original purpose. The Dimanche Gras and Carnival Queen competitions (see below), for instance, became wholly the province of the middle class itself. Here were competitions directed primarily at the wealthier classes with many winners chosen from those classes.

The Eurocentric aesthetic that dominated the judging of the contestants was a sore point for many Trinidadians, especially the predominantly African lower class, but also African members of the upper classes. This aesthetic was marked by a tendency to award prizes to the girls with the most European features in the Carnival Queen competition and to support and approve of elaborate masquerades based upon European themes. Furthermore, a wide gap existed between the Queen's prizes and the prizes received by other competitors such as the calypsonians, who were predominantly black. The interwar years were fraught with territorial struggles.[17] After the relative successes of the first postwar Carnivals it became clear that Carnival was no longer in danger of dissolution. No governor in his right mind wanted to face the obstreperousness of a Carnival community denied. The stakes that were now being played for were over the legacy of "bourgeois caretakership" (Rohlehr 1990: 405).

Dimanche Gras and the Colored Middle Class

The Dimanche Gras (or Fat Sunday) has its roots in Trinidad in the masquerade balls of the late eighteenth century. These fancy dress balls continued even after emancipation drove the elites off of the streets at Carnival time. Such galas continued right through the nineteenth century as the chief form of Carnival amusement for the upper classes, both white and colored. Such events were marked by rich pageantry and fantastic costumes, often portraying historical themes and styles of dress. In his *History of Trinidad* (1838), E. L. Joseph gave a description of one of the more fantastic dresses worn by the wife of a Venezuelan general: "It was of the finest gauze, puckered (I believe I use the right phrase); between these puckers small and great fire flies were introduced: the effect of this costume was splendid beyond description; the phosphoric scintillations were tri-colored—the cincindela, as it respires, emits a pale blue light, while the greater insect displayed its deep azure and dark red sparks. This dress was worn at a masquerade; but it put an end, for that night, to all masking, as on its appearance every one in the room removed his or her mask through astonishment" (1838: 72).[18]

Most of these early balls were held in private homes, but beginning with the Victory Carnival in 1919, more and more reports indicate that attendance at large-scale Carnival stage shows at the Prince's Building in Port-of-Spain became a popular Carnival pastime. The Prince's Building had been erected in 1861 in honor of the impending visit of the Duke of Edinburgh (who never came). Carnival balls had been held there since 1867. The first actual show seems to have taken place in 1922.

The shift from private ball to public show coincides with the emerging success of the colored middle class in appropriating Carnival for nationalist purposes. The shows were both controlled displays and publicly accessible. The 1922 show was a major theatrical spectacle in which fancy and elaborate costumes were showcased. It was held on Carnival Monday. This particular show, known as the "Les Amantes Ball," was held in this venue until 1948. In 1948 the city council offices were moved to the Prince's Building after a fire destroyed their structure. The ball was displaced across the street to the Queen's Park Savannah, a massive park situated in the northern half of downtown Port-of-Spain, where there was an open, outdoor stage surrounded by bleacher-style seating. Now a far greater number of Trinidadians had access to the stage shows, and people came who might not have been able or permitted to see such spectacles in the past. The middle class was opening up Carnival according to their own principles yet doing so in the name of the "nation." The result was the creation of a new public culture that preserved elements of the working-class Carnival dressed in middle-class costume.

Prizes were offered to individual portrayals, usually of historical or mythological characters. There were *tableaux vivant* that depicted scenes from English history, especially focused on the monarchy, Greek mythology, Shakespeare, and tales from European folklore. In 1959 George Cabral, a well-known masquerader, enacted a story entitled "Venetian Glass," a sort of Pinocchio meets Pygmalion in glass.[19] The sheer magnitude of these fancies cannot be overemphasized. Reports of giant wine glasses in which an orchestra was seated, turreted castles with flying banners, Greek temples replete with massive columns, and spinning human chandeliers were all presented at these affairs as designers tried to outdo each other in order to win prizes offered by the competition administrators.

The portrayals that won the most admiration were not only spectacular, they represented middle-class fantasies of European culture. These elaborate masquerades were still based upon European themes, Grimm's fairy tales, English history and literature, and so on. After independence the thematic elements would certainly shift again, with a greater emphasis on local folklore, native music, and dance and (after black power) homages not only to Africa but to other "cultures of the world" in a Carnival version of what Frantz Fanon has described as the postcolonial singing of "praises in admiration of each other" (1967: 169). Carnival as theater motif would be readily adopted by local artists and intellectuals alike in an attempt to forge a national culture (Hill 1972).

Carnival resumed in 1946, after having been banned in 1942 for the duration of the Second World War. It was in this year that the Dimanche Gras show officially began with performances and entertainments meant to add to the pageantry of the selection of Carnival Queen. These Carnival Queen events were in essence beauty pageants in which young "white" girls competed for the coveted title.

It is worth discussing the Queen competition briefly because in it we see the roots of the kind of Carnival-oriented showcase that has now become the norm in Trinidad and abroad. The Carnival Queen competition was also a point of some controversy in that it was, for many years, the most highly promoted aspect of Carnival and by far the most lucrative for its contestants, being sponsored by corporations both local and international. At the same time it was perhaps the least representative of the "culture of Trinidad." The competition, like most of the competitions held at Carnival time, was a part of the middle-class effort to co-opt Carnival by cleaning it up. The standard middle-class line was that Carnival had the potential to be an exemplar of the talents and ingenuity of the Trinidadian people but, without the proper moral guidance, was merely a forum for potential violence or moral transgression.

The goals of Carnival reformers were various. Among them, surely was the genuine belief in the mission of morally improving the lower orders. This coincides with what has been observed as the (predominantly colored) middle class's devotion to the ideals of the white upper classes. On the other hand, this same colored group could not have been blind to the position into which they were forced by the white and often foreign agents of colonial rule. Often holding contradictory views, being frequently divided against each other, and being the unfortunate victims of a constantly shifting and capricious history of colonial policy toward their number, the colored middle classes, at some level, transplanted the seeds of many of the contradictory feelings that surrounded them into the fantasy of their masquerades. Carnival today and Carnival-related shows still bear out these concerns as evidenced by the King and Queen competition covered in chapter 5.[20]

By 1958 growing nationalist sentiment in Trinidad had led to the abolition of the Carnival Queen show as part of the Dimanche Gras spectacular, but the popular performances and "cultural shows" persisted with an increase in the appearances of traditional masquerade characters. This transformation signals an important shift in Trinidadian national and cultural consciousness, for it ushers in the self-conscious replacement of European cultural forms and values with local or native ones. It marks the attempt to develop a clear-cut local identity and separate the country's public culture from Euro-colonial forms. Performances such as the Queen of Carnival and other Dimanche Gras contests, which were almost exclusively performed by the European segment of the population, had to be substituted for others of more local flavor. Their replacements came in the form of African-derived masquerade forms that had existed in their own worlds on the margins of public culture and as threats to it. Characters from the J'ouvert celebrations that were also in existence at this time began to figure prominently in official environments. Masquerade performances held by the urban black poor in Port-of-Spain at this time largely took place in the barrack yards, those enclosures created by the rear façades of the housing units whose fronts faced the streets. It was here that the masquerade balls of the white upper classes were parodied and African-derived forms of performance and music flourished (see below in discussion of sailor mas'). Nationalist politics and the coming of independence provided the perfect setting for the coaxing of formerly antagonistic masquerade forms into the white-hot lights of the Savannah stage.

The mining of formerly despised masquerade forms for national cultural material is fraught with pitfalls. This is so primarily because an ambivalent situation arises with the appropriation of marginal forms. Because these masquerade practices were beyond the aesthetic or intellectual experiences of the middle classes—because they were often openly hostile to reform and were considered degraded, unclean, and dangerous—they had to be reshaped or purged of their offensive qualities. The initial strategy of the middle class was to eliminate such forms all together. But this was done during a time of insecurity vis-à-vis Carnival. Once the festival was securely in the hands of the middle class, its next step was to nationalize the content over and against masquerade forms such as the Dutch women and milkmaids mentioned above. Thus the middle classes sought forms to replace the overtly European ones from the

African-derived traditions. They chose, however, the kinds of masquerades that were no longer of relevance to the classes that produced them. In selecting costumes such as bats, clowns, sailors, midnight robbers, and blue devils, the middle classes were exhuming the practices of the working classes that were moribund. This was at once a safe strategy and yet one that produced frustrating results. Because these forms were no longer salient, they were not played any more. Yet the middle classes railed against the population for not taking them up and accused the masses of forgetting their traditions. In order to exhort the recalcitrant populace to remember their roots, it is common in Trinidad for the middle class—the state-sponsored guardians of culture—to produce enormous amounts of cultural narratives and histories. Through public education, the popular press, radio, and television, narratives of Carnival are spread. Yet to call this the "invention" of tradition is to oversimplify the case. The narratives are rooted in the desires and experiences of the middle class. They are not pure fabrication, although they focus on the elements of their own choosing. Furthermore, the narratives have become part of the consciousness of all the classes. The mission to preserve culture, remember one's heritage, and be loyal to the nation are serious matters and are enthusiastically taken up by many, from all walks of life.[21] The narratives generated by the middle class have become relatively common currency, yet, as we shall see, they also produce some interesting and unintended consequences. For the moment, however, I wish to investigate a particular case of middle-class cultural resuscitation. The sailor mas' yields a very good example of this trend.

History of the Sailor Mas'

By tracing the historical development of the sailor masquerade it is possible to witness the on-going attempts by the middle classes, since independence, to harness the cultural forms of the working classes—such as the sailor, the steelband, and the calypso—in the service of the creation of a national culture. Many of the tactics employed in the early days of middle-class incursions into Carnival continue today in remarkably unchanged form. In the previous section I detailed middle-class intervention with regard to the history of the Dimanche Gras performances. The dominant feature, historically speaking, of such interventions had been the attempt to strengthen middle-class legitimacy with the masses in the name of nationalism over and against foreign, Crown Colony rule. The control and political manipulation of Carnival in the name of the polity had been the strategy to disguise basic class interests under the guise of national interests.

With regard to the sailor one can see the same principles at work. The fate of the sailor mas' illustrates the shift from middle-class animosity to middle-class nostalgia and co-optation. The relatively limited aims of the movement against Crown Colony status gave way to a movement toward complete independence from England, especially in the post–World War II era. After independence in 1962, however, middle-class reform of Carnival did not cease. Eric Williams himself, although seemingly ambivalent about Carnival, encouraged the continued focus on Carnival development but with different goals in mind than his predecessors. Since that time and in the current instance, when independence from the Crown is no longer the goal, the emphasis has shifted toward the country as a sovereign nation. Akhil Gupta's conception of sovereignty as being a nation's ability to control commerce as well as culture is of primary importance as both culture and commerce become conceived of as synonymous. I will return to this in later chapters.

We must go back to the middle of the nineteenth century in order to find the first reported naval themes in Carnival.[22] In 1859 a band called "The Veterans of Sebastopol" took to the streets with a large canoe, mounted on wheels as a kind of float. The portrayal resulted in a struggle with the police in which the canoe was taken away and "a canopy [was] viciously destroyed" (Hill 1972: 93). In 1860 a band of some years in existence, called "A Man-o-War's Men," was reported in Port-of-Spain (Crowley 1956b: 217). In Carnival of 1886 a "full-scale naval masquerade" appeared, drawing its participants from the wharves. Called "Naval Masquerade," the players were all dressed as officers and exhibited a large "fully rigged ship, which was mounted on wheels" (Hill 1972: 93). The real turning point, however, in the popularity of naval masquerades seems to have come in 1907, when the U.S. Atlantic Fleet visited Trinidad (Hill 1972: 94). The early twentieth century was a time of great transition in Carnival. The period of the jamette or underworld Carnival was passing and the middle classes were finally beginning to exercise a definitive influence over its organization and structure; no one group seemed to control the streets. One reporter at the 1907 Carnival claimed that it was marked by a "degeneracy in character as well as in song" and he bemoaned the "presence of numerous bands of stickfighters," those combatants who squared off against each other brandishing batons of wood with which they skillfully dueled. At the same time, advertisers and opportunists were aware of the captive audience they had during Carnival days.

The presence of American sailors on shore leave created quite a stir. The Carnival of that year produced a number of Yankee sailor bands that copied the American uniforms down to the caps, which were often snatched from unsuspecting sailors as they cruised the streets looking for women and rum. There was even a replica of the American ship *Alabama* in the parade (Hill 1972: 94). This would not be the last time that an American or British naval force would grace Trinidad's shores, and soon the sailor band would be firmly fixed in the Carnival masquerade repertoire.

Between 1907 and World War II, sailors grew and developed as a masquerade form. In the 1920s there appeared on the streets what came to be known as "All-About" or "Knockabout" sailors. These were also sometimes called "bad behavior" sailors and were characterized by soiled uniforms, feigned or real drunkenness, and the habit of beating onlookers with inflated pig's bladders. The sailors often wore simple masks to cover their faces, which were made from cloth and worn either as a face mask or an entire head covering with holes cut out for the eyes, a false nose, often fake rosy cheeks painted on, and a mouth opening. Sailors were known to carry corn cob pipes, calabashes, and even chamber pots from which they drank. The body dress was a traditional white sailor costume complete with bellbottoms (often exaggerated) and a jumper with the standard collar and neckerchief. The original "bad behavior sailors" were an outfit from Hell Yard, a notorious section of Port-of-Spain, from which some of the greatest steelbands would emerge. They were fond of "roll[ing] in coal dust to dirty their uniforms" and would then proceed to scare off masqueraders in pretty costumes.

In the 1930s innovations in the sailor masquerade began to take shape. The long, false noses of the traditional sailors became the focus of much creative and comic attention. Jason Griffith reports that one great innovator, Jim Harding, who had been involved with creating the original masks worn by sailors, was always experimenting with these mask forms. On one occasion an ice cream vendor happened by his house as he was sitting in the gallery. He noticed the children running about with the cones and the idea came to him to use the cone shape for a nose (Griffith Interview 1993). From the initial cone nose there appeared various creatures and embellishments, which were placed on the nose in humorous fashion—everything from warts and spiders and flies to little airplanes and ships. The development of the nose gave rise to further expansions in which the noses were substituted for whole headpieces, which portrayed some kind of comic or menacing scene. At the same time some sailors were elaborating upon the basic sailor garb itself. By attaching fanciful insignia, braids, and other indications of rank and status, these sailors distinguished themselves from what were known as the "floor member" sailors, the rank and file. Such elaborations created a new class of sailors known as "King" sailors and later "Fancy" sailors.

The emergence of the Fancy sailor comes at a very interesting time in Carnival history; a time during which the middle classes were strengthening their dominant position in the administration of Carnival and furthering their general project of taming the event for political purposes. The Fancy sailor, while still a solidly working-class form, enjoyed a peculiar relationship to the older, bad behavior sailors, in the sense that it represented a "pretty mas'" version of a masquerade that was often openly hostile or contemptuous of pretty masquerade forms. The Fancy sailor was not in and of itself an attempt to appeal to the middle classes, but it did eventually develop in part as a way of competing with large pretty bands for prizes. The pretty aesthetic, however, was not instituted into the sailor mas' by or for the middle classes, just as the fancy and ornate warrior bands were themselves not conforming to the middle-class pressure. However, it was their "prettiness" that ensured their survival and codification. In 1930 the Summary Conviction Offenses Ordinance had attempted to curtail the grosser misconduct of the sailor bands by prohibiting the carrying of bladders and chamber pots. The Ordinance allowed for the immediate arrest of persons misbehaving as "drunken sailors." The costume was left intact, while the behaviors associated with the costume, so vital to its portrayal, were denied.

There are several reasons as to why the sailor bands became the "grassroots" mas' extraordinaire. From a pragmatic standpoint, the costume was easy to make, inexpensive, and could be used year after year. But for that matter so was a soldier's costume, and furthermore a jab molassi or blue devil was about the least expensive costume one could imagine, comprised as it was of tattered shorts and grease, mud, oil, or blue paint with some horns and a tail. In addition, poor Carnival players were not always concerned about expense, often saving large amounts of money to spend on the construction of far more elaborate costumes such as wild Indians, red Indians, dragons, and other characters whose outfits required an investment in materials. Clearly economic considerations were only part of the formula.

The presence of American sailors on the streets of Port-of-Spain played a vital role in establishing the sailor as a powerful symbol for working-class African Trinidadians. The large-scale presence of whites whose behavior was disruptive, violent, and immoral must have been a great source of amusement to a group whose main contact with whites and light-skinned people would have been one marked by condescension and moral superiority.

It has been mentioned elsewhere and often (Stuempfle 1990; Crowley 1956b; Hill 1972; Liverpool 1993) that the sailor mas' came about as an imitation of white, especially American, sailors on shore leave. However, very few of these accounts indicate why such a presence would resonate so deeply within the African Trinidadian community. When American soldiers first came en masse to Trinidad during the Second World War, it was the first opportunity that many black Trinidadian men had to see whites performing manual labor. The impact was profound and contributed to a sense of America and Americans as representing another social order. At the same time Americans segregated their soldiers, and white American soldiers and sailors were often openly and brutally racist. These factors produced a kind of ambiguous attitude toward American soldiers and sailors within the African Trinidadian male community. "The automatic deference to a white face became a thing of the past" (Brereton 1981: 192). They enjoyed their cavalier and often rough behavior, their free spending, and the willingness on the part of the American military to hire and pay good wages to locals, and at the same time resented their racism and their success with local women.[23]

Such an impact, which really began with the American presence after 1907, must have produced rather mixed emotions on the part of the already disenfranchised black youths of Port-of-Spain. On the one hand, it was comic and undoubtedly an everyday occurrence, ripe for lampooning. On the other hand, parodying white misbehavior had a many-layered power to it. Sailors were admirable in that they demonstrated a kind of public freedom from recrimination, an insouciance, an arrogance that appealed to young men "from the hill" (and continues to do so). Bravado marks the creative endeavors of the calypsonian, the steelbandsman, and the masquerader who plays warrior, sailor, Indian, devil. The aesthetic considerations are intimately interwoven with essential features of the masquerade being played. Thus, it is not so much who the warriors and soldiers and sailors *are* but what they *do* that matters. The working-class masquerade is very different from the middle-class masquerade in that the working-class masquerade is marked by a desire for freedom to act with authority, with a sense of power, while the middle-class masquerade is marked by disguise or freedom from the constraints of their own moral codes or by a desire to forget the responsibilities that result from having power. The poor masquerader, especially the male masqueraders that dominated the working-class Carnival until relatively recently, used masquerade as an adoption of a persona that befit his personal conception of himself, "to cultivate and uphold that spirit of rebellion and warriorhood" (Lovelace 1979: 73).

The middle-class masquerader already held a position in society that allowed for a general feeling of enfranchisement but was restricted by codes of moral conduct, propriety, and appropriate behavior. This was especially true, as Barbara Powrie notes, before World War II (1956: 106). Carnival was and is a time for the expression of desire, but specific desires are specific to one's social position. The general incommensurability between these two kinds of mas' is marked by the sailor's attacks against the pretty mas' bands of the middle classes. This is not to say that working-class costumes and portrayals lacked beauty but that they lacked an idea of beauty that could be conceived of as an independent concept from the quality and character of the portrayal. Thus it was beauty in the service of a powerful mas'; one might say that, more than beauty, it was *glory* that was sought.

Fig. 1. Fancy sailor with centipede headpiece.

The fancy sailor was as glorious a portrayal as could be imagined, rivaled perhaps only by the spectacular Fancy Indian and Fancy Clown costumes. The Fancy or King sailors exemplified the appropriation and absurd exaggeration of military status and hierarchy. It was a tribute to power and a mockery of it simultaneously. In fact the "fanciness" of the costumes took on a life of its own. Fanciful ranks and decorations gave way to masses of beads, braid, mirrors, pictures, swansdown, and other ornamentation that left even the basic structure of military decoration far behind. Similarly, the headpieces grew to staggering proportions, with massive representations of fanciful creatures, space flight, undersea life, and mechanical objects such as cameras and television sets. Such displays have prompted bandleader Peter Minshall on more than one occasion to label the Fancy sailor as Trinidad's own autochthonous surrealism.

Up until the middle 1960s, before the advent of mobile disc jockeys and sound systems and before the development of mobile brass bands, most masqueraders played with steelbands. The steelband provided the masquerader with an organizational structure in which to play. The masquerades most associated with the steelbands were military or naval. Sailors were a common portrayal as they were conducive to the spirit of militant neighborhood rivalry that had marked the street Carnival throughout its history. Early steelbands were often combative, with rivals battling it out musically and physically in the streets of Port-of-Spain. The sailor and military portrayals thus accentuated the antagonistic nature of the early steelbands. Many of the oldest steelbands in existence today took their names from popular war movies, which served as a major source of popular entertainment during and after World War II. For instance, Desperadoes, Tokyo, Renegades, Casablanca, and Invaders all hail from this period. The steelband masqueraders generally comprised the largest number of players. Other kinds of masquerade bands, such as historical or biblical bands, commanded much smaller numbers and generally attracted a different class of masquerader. In addition, very few ole mas' masquerades were ever organized into bands that reached the proportions of the sailor bands. Although there were large and elaborate devil bands such as those mounted by the famous "Chinee" Patrick (also known as khaki and slate bands) and Indian bands, which were "the most popular bands after sailors" (Crowley 1956b: 203), such masquerades never reached the level of popularity that military and especially sailor bands achieved at their height. In addition, sailor bands became intimately associated with the steelbands (Stuempfle

Fig. 2. Sailors on the road, 1950s postcard.

1990: 78–79) and thus with a mass cultural movement. A steelband on the road might have over 2,000 thousand revelers, while a historical band might only have 300 to 500. Thus for many Trinidadians within a particular socio-economic class, the sailor and the steelband *were* Carnival.

The steelband and the sailor mas' proudly took to the streets in massive numbers from such blue-collar enclaves as Belmont, Newtown, St. James, and the even poorer areas of Laventille, Hell Yard, John John, East Dry River, and Gonzales. The steelbands incorporated the very same working, unemployed, and under-employed populations that would make up the vast numbers of Trinidadian emigrants to the United States in the middle 1960s. This was the Carnival image that many such people carried with them in their youth when they left their homes to work and settle in Brooklyn.

The Rhetoric of Loss in the Story of Carnival

What Carnival was dominates the contemporary official discourse, because these conceptions are all not only histories but pleas to recapture a "golden era" of mas'. In the following pages and by way of conclusion, I would like to outline the basic elements that inform the rhetorical practices of the official guardians of culture. Overall there is a great deal of consistency in this type of discourse.

However, one can identify two basic forms. The first is perhaps the most common and is what I will call the bourgeois narrative of Carnival's meaning and importance. In this version the threat to Carnival is seen as a threat to the vitality of the nation. The loss of cultural identity is linked to the victory of the mass media and especially American culture over indigenous forms. There is a basic cultural-imperialism thesis embedded in this type of discourse, yet it is replaced by a focus on the development of indigenous industry derived from the preservation of national heritage. The second derives from the artistic class fraction of the middle class and takes a slightly different approach to the meaning of Carnival, one more concerned with the festival's form and content. Here some of the concerns are the same—the welfare of the nation, the resistance to foreign commercialism—however, there is a greater focus on Carnival as art and on the loss of true creativity in the festival and a general resistance to commercialization or commodification in any form. In investigating these narratives I will draw most of my examples from discussions or comments about the sailor costume.

What both types of discourse have in common is an underlying sense of urgency or panic having to do with the imminent disappearance of a treasured cultural heritage. This fear has everything to do with the management of culture and the future of national sovereignty, especially for the middle class. In a recent publication, one of the most eloquent spokespersons of Trinidad's artistic community, Peter Minshall, has written that "mas' offers the participant an opportunity for transformation, to transcend the conditions of daily existence; and the opportunity to be a part of a transient but highly charged community of people, to be a part of something larger than oneself" (1995: 50). What is at stake here in the contemporary Carnival is just what that "something larger" is to be. In the call for mas' appreciation and salvation, that something larger is the nation, administered benevolently by the middle-class guardians of culture.

Typical of the rhetoric of loss is the following by Pat Bishop, an important artist and composer in her own right and an extremely insightful commentator on all aspects of Carnival. Her dissections of the festival, which have appeared over the years, are well known within Trinidad, and she has lamented the growing commercialization and superficiality of the spectacle of mas'. Her criticisms are couched in a lament for cultural forms past. In this comment on the Dimanche Gras of 1987, Bishop relates what for her was the only real highlight: "Indeed one of the most delightful and persuasive of the Dimanche Gras offerings of 1987 came from a presentation of small costumes derived from the traditional masques of Trinidad. This is the heart of the mas' in this little procession of human-scaled individuals . . . and for a moment time stood still in this capsule of history for a multitude whom, I suspect, knew little and cared less for this display of the wellspring of the mas'" (Bishop 1987: 26).

Her sentiments are echoed by Minshall as well as by Trinidadian scholars such as Errol Hill. In an issue of *Caribbean Quarterly* devoted to Carnival, Hill produces a statement on the importance of preservation complete with a program for developing moribund Carnival characters. The justification for preservation lies in both the salvaging of history and the connected benefit of commercial development. This feature of a profit-making corollary in conjunction with the construction of heritage industry is one distinguishing characteristic of the bourgeois discourse on culture. The creation of an industry of Carnival dolls, a portfolio of authentic Carnival drawings that typologize the various characters, slides, costume exhibits, videos, and the like are all created in the spirit of a marketable "museumification" or perhaps "exhibitism" (Hill 1985: 16).

The bourgeois discourse is not restricted to the private sector. There is a continuum between the private sector of culture brokers, cultural spokespeople, academics, and the government. In 1972 the Ministry of Education and Culture produced a report entitled "Report of the Working Party— Chaguaramas Secondary School Conference 1972" that outlined the role that culture was supposed to play in the development of an indigenous educational system. In that report many of the themes discussed here emerge. Citing "constant external pressures from some of the developed countries," the report recommends that an educational policy must be developed to "counteract these influences" (Ministry of Education and Culture 1972: 6). The report makes a direct association between national unity and cultural development and makes the "discovery" of collective identity the imperative in forging relationships with other peoples of the world as "the world grows smaller and therefore nearer to us through the great advance in communication" (1972: 32).

The narratives produced by the artistic fraction contain many of the same elements. In general, however, there is expressed a hope that Carnival arts will be fostered and that they will be considered alongside "serious" or "high" art. In considering the fancy sailor Minshall has expressed his admiration for the form, comparing sailor costumes to Chagall, meanwhile lamenting, much like

Pat Bishop, that due to a lack of "understanding, or appreciation of ourselves, we don't even see it yet.... It was just the most extraordinary format and it was done totally unconsciously" (1985: 20). Views such as these necessarily contain contradictions. That is, what is celebrated is the unconscious, autonomous, and autochthonous expressions of "the people" or "the nation" and therefore the proper source for national art. (Errol Hill's view of the Trinidad Carnival as a mandate for a national theater is one example.) At the same time the act of preservation, of development, of "interference" by the outsider, bourgeois class threatens the forms themselves. And yet as further a complication, apparently the only class that can perceive the importance of these forms is this outsider class itself.

Conclusion

However contradictory such views are, they occupy an important position in the development of identity in Trinidad and in the transnational experience. Growing out of the independence movement, middle-class ideas of fear and loss are expressed in the ongoing project of resisting European hegemony, of eluding the grip of a powerful Western culture gone global. In that sense such narratives have a distance from their European progenitors and are productive of new meanings. Romantic preservation projects in Trinidad are, ultimately, different than their counterparts in Europe, North America, or even Japan (cf. Ivy 1995). They play an important part in the national and transnational imagination in ways that are unintended yet fruitful. Although the state, the artistic community, cultural entrepreneurs, and culture brokers within Trinidad have different goals, as do the mas' makers and players and their counterparts in Brooklyn, the circulation of standard narratives and metaphors of Carnival link them all together in a community of imagination.

2

The Brooklyn Carnival

Mandate for a Dual-Sited Ethnography

My discussion of dual-sited ethnography begins in the airport, that limbo of the transnational subject. It is 1995 and about a week before Carnival. I am with a large group of passengers and we are all waiting to fly out of John F. Kennedy Airport to Trinidad. But I, like the few tourists who are also waiting, am suddenly a foreigner on American soil. Most of the rest of the passengers waiting for the flight are Trinidadians, and this is their plane and their gate. There are friends recognizing each other, as well as strangers discussing Carnival and the new crop of calypsos. The "standard" English adopted by many Trinidadians in their lives as American citizens or residents falls away here, in this context. When the flight attendants announce that seating will proceed by rows, everyone, regardless of seat number, rushes the podium and jockeys for position, seemingly oblivious to the fact that their seats will be reserved for them. Music is playing somewhere, people are eating food from home, and many wear t-shirts or caps or sweatshirts with some reference to Trinidad emblazoned boldly across the front.

This tiny corner of the airport has ceased to be the indifferent space of international travel. It has begun to look a bit more like Charlotte Street in Port-of-Spain.[1] But there is another noticeable feature to this group of travelers: many of them are dressed in clothing, carrying boxes and bags or holding items that cannot be found in Trinidad or are beyond the means of relatives or friends still living on the island. This is not a Trinidadian crowd from Charlotte Street that happens to be in a New York airport. These are New Yorkers, many of them longtime residents, voting citizens, home and business owners. They are, however, on their way "home." They may not live in Trinidad and some, like an acquaintance of mine in Brooklyn, have never been back in the twenty years since their emigration, yet it is still home.

In this chapter I give some background to migration from Trinidad to Brooklyn in order to situate the migrant experience. It is within the context of the massive migration from Trinidad and the West Indies in general that cultural and social forms begin to take on a special sort of meaning. Their presence within the lives of the migrants help constitute what I will be calling the transnation. In this chapter I will be discussing the implementation or continuation of cultural forms from home in the Brooklyn setting, with special emphasis on Carnival. Such forms are transformed in their reterritorialization but still rely on their rootedness at "home." Changes to forms such as Carnival take place at a very self-conscious level but also, as a matter of course, by necessity or by chance. Taking account of transplanted cultural forms gives an idea of the negotiations migrants make with both the host society and their memories and attachments to home. In later chapters I will examine how transplanted cultural forms must change to suit pressures in the new locale, specifically by looking at the power of New York City's brand of ethnic politics as well as the general unfamiliarity with the Carnival tradition. I will also suggest ways activities at home in Trinidad affect Carnival in Brooklyn and how Brooklynite Trinidadians contribute to state-sponsored strategies that use nostalgia to consolidate their authority of national cultural production. For now, however, I will focus on the formation of the Trinidadian transnation and the prominent role Carnival has played in its development.

Transnational situations lead the social scientist into complex and layered cultural dialogues. If Trinidadians bring Carnival to New York, then New York changes Carnival. If Trinidadians go home, they bring New York to Trinidad. Trinidadians returning home draw upon that Carnival as from an authentic source, drawing inspiration from but also in part rejecting its power. They return to New York and reinvest Carnival there with new meanings. Trinidadians who are involved in the administration of Carnival at home see in the New York festival potential for developing interest in the original festival and in Trinidad in general. They are also concerned with the role of Carnival at home and its development locally for two reasons: first, Carnival, as part of national culture plays a role in the dissemination of nationalist mythologies of multicultural harmony; second, Carnival is an important component in the development of a national cultural narrative to be mobilized *internationally*. Trinidadians in New York draw upon cultural narratives and developments in Trinidad but mobilize these factors in response to local political is-sues. In doing so they actively construct public identities, which become part of the identity of the transnation in general.

The Caribbean: A History of Migration, a History of Transnationalism

Following Carnival developments, the student of transnationalism is treated to a lesson in the complexities of attempting an analysis of both local and global phenomena. Be that as it may, the Caribbean region seems a logical place for such complexities to have developed. Many studies of the Carib-bean in many disciplines have focused on the importance of migration and movement to the history of the region. Caribbean culture and society are the product of massive movements of people into an area almost purely for eco-nomic exploitation. From very early on and many years before the Industrial Revolution, the organization of certain labor practices and production in the Caribbean were "modern." The plantation operated on a sophisticated time schedule and required efficient coordination of workers and machinery. The scale of production was enormous and drew upon the massive slave trade and, later, indentured labor from Asia. "Said in today's tormented language, the modernization of Caribbean people took place in the constant presence of multicultural Others" (Mintz 1994: 295). In addition, the Caribbean was the heart of Europe's colonial enterprise for centuries before either India or West Africa entered the picture. In that sense the Caribbean has been part of the European world system longer than many other places that are now en-compassed by it.

What this has meant for Caribbean scholars, as Michel-Rolph Trouillot has indicated, is the necessity of using "multiple units of analysis" as a way of tying "their immediate unit of observation to the wider world" (Trouillot 1992: 34). The wider world has always been a factor in the history of the Caribbean, and current trends toward local/global articulations are well served by examining the Caribbean example (Robotham 1998). It is for this reason that I decided to utilize a dual-site ethnographic approach. The effect that such an approach has is to delineate the intimate connections between kinds of identity across dis-tant spaces and through time. The dual-site ethnography is indispensable to an anthropology of transnationalism because it understands implicitly that loca-tion and culture are not primordial, mutually dependent, and reinforcing re-alities but are themselves subject to external pressures and influences.

For example, the state in Trinidad has concerns at the local level (say ethnic disharmony) and at the international level (say national sovereignty, economic independence). Developments in one area will profoundly affect another. In dealing with these issues the state must define itself "nationally" in the sense that the state as a governing body must legitimate itself as the proper authority for the nation. Certain problems of nation-state disunity, such as can be found in Eastern Europe, wherein a state, which controls some territory, contains within it members of a collectivity that does not define itself as part of the nation and therefore is not legally subject to the state's rule, is not the main problem in the Trinidadian case (Verdery 1994).

This is true over much of the Caribbean, where primordial ethno-national sovereignties are not historically defensible. Rather, the case in the Caribbean, and in Trinidad in particular, is that the goal of the state is to shape and disseminate national culture as part of its duties in the interest of gathering a multiethnic constituency under the "umbrella" of national culture (Segal 1994; B. Williams 1992). Similarly, none of the ethnic groups in Trinidad attempt to lay claim to territory as might be done with indigenous groups or with ethnic groups claiming historical rights to land.

This feature of Trinidadian nationalism ultimately has a profound impact on the form that Trinidadian identity takes in diaspora. Because the state is attempting to articulate a national culture that will unify ethnic groups within the country, Trinidadians abroad have a steady stream of "official" culture upon which to draw for their own purposes. The focus of both of these culture-forming endeavors on Carnival makes it an especially rich subject for a dual-sited ethnography.

The dual-site approach allows one to begin to trace interactions between the world and Trinidad and between Trinidadians "at large" and their fellow citizens "at home." Where I want to push the transnational approach, however, is in its conception of imagination and the "invention" of tradition. Such concepts underlie much transnational scholarship and, as noted in the introduction, only recently have been interrogated (see especially Segal et al. 1996). "No nation now but the imagination," Derek Walcott once wrote, and his words cut to the heart of this project. There is a tension that underlies the investigation of transnational cultural processes, especially when such investigations have as part of their aim undermining essentialist or primordialist assumptions about ethnicity. But what is often left out of the equation is the role that such essentializations play in the active construction of identity. That role is the one I wish to examine throughout the remaining chapters.

Caribbean Migration to New York City

New York City is and has long been a destination for West Indians coming to the United States. The lure of better employment opportunities, the growth and development of Harlem as a center of black culture, and the relative proximity to the West Indies have all been significant to this process. Although peoples from throughout the Caribbean have had a history of migration to this country, I want to focus here primarily on the massive migrations from the English-speaking islands beginning in the mid-1960s, with special emphasis on migrants from Trinidad and Tobago. Immigration statistics prior to 1950 lump Trinidadians into the category of British West Indies along with Barbadians and Jamaicans. The total from these three former colonies for the years 1941 to 1950 was a mere 15,801.[2] From 1951 through 1960 the figure for Trinidad and Tobago alone is 1,074. But with independence in Trinidad in 1962, the closing of the UK to immigration in the same year with the Commonwealth Immigration Act, and the opening of U.S. immigration policy, Trinidadians, like their counterparts in the rest of the former British West Indies, began to stream to America and New York City. Since 1961 some 10 percent of the population of Trinidad and Tobago has emigrated northward, settling primarily in Brooklyn.

The vast majority of Caribbean migrants to the New York metropolitan area began arriving in the mid-1960s. Prior to the 1960s the majority of migrants from the English-speaking West Indies had settled in Harlem, but as the 1950s came to a close, migrants began to seek out opportunities in Brooklyn, where unique housing options existed (Kasinitz 1992: 59; see chapter 3 for more detail). As Brooklyn became the center for West Indian migration the neighborhoods began to reflect the West Indian presence with the emergence of shops and markets that sold West Indian goods and with the growth of West Indian nightclubs, dance halls, and recreation centers. In 1964 the West Indian Parade moved from Harlem to Brooklyn.

The following year (1965), the American government changed its immigration policy. This new legislation, the Hart-Cellar Immigration Reform Act, did away with the national quota system that had been in place in one form or another since 1924. Prior to Hart-Cellar populations seeking to migrate to the U.S. were forced to bypass the tiny national quota allotments by claiming their rights as British citizens. After Trinidadian independence in 1962, a quota of 100 legal immigrants per year from that country was put into place (Kasinitz 1992: 22–24). Thus the reform of the immigration laws in the United States opened the door for a nearly unlimited number of people from the Anglophone West Indies to enter the United States. Kasinitz cites the change in government attitude toward Caribbean migration as stemming from advancements made during the Civil Rights movement. Social and political progress made during those volatile years impressed upon the Johnson administration the untenable position of its inherited immigration policies. The government, however, had no idea of the degree to which Caribbean people would seize this new opportunity (Kasinitz 1992: 27). One possible explanation for this can be found in the concurrent modification in British immigration law. Relatively open-door policies in operation since the 1950s in England were reversed after 1962. Suddenly, a significant source of employment for West Indians disappeared, and the United States loomed as the next best possibility. A combination of factors over the next ten years resulted in an enormous swell of Caribbean migration from the Anglophone West Indies to New York City, such that by the early part of the 1980s approximately 50,000 legal immigrants from the Anglophone Caribbean were entering into the United States every year.

To fully appreciate the relationship that Carnival in New York has to its home country and to the populations of Trinidadians and others who make up this Caribbean transnation, some of the factors that engendered such an enormous and continuing movement of populations must be noted. With fully 5 to 10 percent of Anglophone West Indians living outside of the West Indies, Caribbean migrants constitute the largest group of migrants in the world in terms of percentage of population. These migrants differ from their European predecessors in their ongoing and active relationship to their countries of origin as well as to the social and political institutions of the city. As Constance Sutton has noted, "The dual-place orientations and identities resulting from the active ties Caribbeans maintain to their homelands while becoming New Yorkers has resulted in a transnational sociocultural system coming into being" (1987: 21). Whereas the cultural transformations of Caribbean populations in New York have been ably examined (Kasinitz 1992; Sutton 1987), fewer studies have explored cultural factors in the reverse—most often, they choose to focus only on economic and political effects. This has led at least one scholar to conclude that returnees do not have a major cultural influence on their home societies (Chaney 1987: 12; for an exception see Olwig 1993).

Reasons for Migration

The standard explanations for Caribbean migration to the United States apply only partially to the Trinidadian situation: heavy capital investment in the West Indies, a rising cost of living, a booming economy in the States, the entrance of more and more American women into the workplace—these are just some of the factors that account for the waves of Caribbean migrants after 1965. In Jamaica the discovery of bauxite meant an increase in foreign capital investment but not an increase in employment due to the nature of bauxite mining, which requires a relatively small but skilled labor force. Capital investment may also lead to a loss of jobs by helping to eliminate local competition in a particular economic area (e.g., the case of international food franchises pushing out smaller establishments). In other commonwealth Caribbean nations a growing labor force and chronic job shortages produced a population in desperate need of economic options. Statistics showing the breakdown of jobs taken by immigrants throughout the heavy migration period show a high percentage working as "service industry" employees, which often meant working in the homes of American families caring for children or maintaining the household. Service positions however did not account for all of the jobs filled by West Indian workers. In addition to "blue collar" employment, both skilled and unskilled, many professionals migrated to the United States bringing with them high levels of education and experience. Amounting to what scholars have termed the "brain drain," the flight of professionals from the West Indies, especially Jamaica, created a dire situation in sectors such as health care, upper management, technology, and the like.

Trinidad has been one of the largest contributors to the West Indian migration flow. However its role in this capacity must be treated somewhat differently from the rest of the Commonwealth Caribbean. Because of Trinidad's history of oil production and exportation, its economy took a different direction than that of its neighbors during the period in question. In 1973, in the midst of the implementation of a series of five-year plans orchestrated by the government of Eric Williams, the OPEC nations unilaterally began increasing the price of oil. Trinidad suddenly saw its revenues skyrocket. During this period the public sector increased its employment dramatically, and the unemployment rate in Port-of-Spain, which had hovered near 10 percent, dropped to 4 percent. Yet during the same period emigration continued and increased and the rate of unemployment stayed relatively stable for the nation as a whole, indicating that the "Oil Boom" was beneficial primarily to the capital city and to the oil-producing regions of the country. On the one hand, the rate at which emigration proceeded from Trinidad accounted for a smaller percentage of the population than in other Commonwealth Caribbean nations, amounting to 10 percent as opposed to 18 and 17 percent respectively for Barbados and Jamaica. Thus there was not as great a need to leave as there was in those nations. On the other hand, there was still a significant increase in emigration relative to the patterns established before the oil boom. There are several possible explanations for this, the most important being the transformation of U.S. immigration law that facilitated such moves in the first place. In addition, the Oil Boom brought with it an increase in imports, curtailed expansion of the local production of basic goods, and an attendant rise in the cost of living. For those not in a position to benefit from the Oil Boom there were still plenty of economic reasons to emigrate.[3]

Cultural motives added to the economic motives for leaving. The growing dependent relationships that West Indian economies were realizing during the 1960s and 1970s also produced a stronger cultural relationship to the United States. In Trinidad massive governmental investment in infrastructure was generated by the Oil Boom. The construction of new roads, schools, telecommunications networks, electricity, and running water all facilitated a more "upscale" lifestyle for the average Trinidadian. More homes had televisions and a greater access to images of foreign lifestyles and to foreign cultural goods. Daniel Miller has noted that a preoccupation with foreign—especially American and British—culture was not new to the Oil Boom years, but had a history in Trinidad due to contact through both British colonialism and the presence of American soldiers during the Second World War (1994: 204–5). Yet the sudden prevalence of these images and items certainly had an unprecedented impact on the way in which Trinidadians began to think about standards of living. Speaking primarily of Indo-Trinidadians, but with a general application to all members of society, Miller notices a "close association of lifestyle and place" such that North America becomes the place where, "even if one has less money, at least that money can be translated into goods which are of the requisite quality befitting the kind of person one has become" (1994: 272–73).

The period of greatest migration, then, can also be seen as the period in which ties to the north become most pronounced at every level. In Trinidad the growing intimacy in relations with North America led some members of society, especially those members of the cultural elite—publishers, culture ministers, and educators—to worry about the impact such ties were having on local cultural forms. One frequently encounters in academic literature, the popular press of Trinidad, and the official rhetoric of the state a stance toward this phenomenon that is marked by a growing fear of the loss of "authentic" culture (van Koningsbruggen 1997: 200–202). Miller notes in these pronouncements a sense of "decline in the knowledge of traditional folklore, attached to agricultural labor, medical diagnosis and treatment, the supernatural and traditional folktales, as well as traditional foods and customs" (1994: 205). The general sentiment among the educated elite is at best an ambivalence toward the country's association with things foreign. Certain influences constitute an unambiguous good, including technologies, medicines and treatments, foods, and manners. A kind of worldliness is invited, while the "loss" of local cultural forms is lamented. This ambivalence does not seem to be shared by the classes to whom these features of local authenticity properly belong (Miller 1994: 206). The specifics of the response to foreign influence will be discussed in a later chapter, however the dynamic interplay between home and host generated by mass migration should be seen here as taking place on multiple levels. That is, the phenomenon of migration does not merely produce a population "in exile" but emerges out of global transformations creating conditions in the home society that necessitate movements of people. Yet, at the same time, the political and economic situation is not the only area affected in the home country. The migration from Trinidad (as well as from other parts of the West Indies) was not always undertaken out of duress. In traveling to England, for instance, many West Indians as "English people" were eager to dwell in the "motherland." It was fashionable to migrate. In the North American case many who left were of an educated and upwardly mobile class, eager to fill posts in more cosmopolitan locales (Gmelch 1992: 41–61).

In any case, the attractions that drew West Indians away were part and parcel of the global processes that brought images of foreign locales to their doors as well as unemployment to their shores. There were multiple reasons for leaving. The state's response, especially in the case of "brain drains," was to lament the loss of West Indian culture and society and to blame the siren song of the Western world. Yet most West Indians who left did so with the idea that they would return. Although family members were often sent for and settlement often occurred in the new country, many wanted to return and did so. If retirement to a quiet house in Tobago or in the pleasant suburbs of Port-of-Spain could not be attained, then temporary visits were made. The traffic at holiday times, for instance, is enormous on British West Indies Air, the main carrier for the region. The mobility of the Trinidadian population in America, their constant travel, creates an environment of cultural cross-pollination. It also facilitates the creation and maintenance of a market for Trinidadian goods abroad. A significant trade in Carib beer, roti skins (a kind of Indian bread used to wrap up the curry stew known as roti), calypso CDs, and other items has grown up to serve the transnational community.[4] A network of remittances from the United States helps sustain family and friends at home and is augmented by the revolving credit associations known as *susus*. The neighborhoods in which Caribbean migrants have settled have been transformed physically into approximations of their Caribbean urban counterparts, complete with open-air shops, music, vendors, and even a version of the "maxi taxi" system of minibuses carrying passengers along set routes through parts of Brooklyn. The greatest public manifestation of West Indian life in New York, however, is Carnival or the West Indian American Day Parade. Its very title contains an awareness of the dual identity that marks the transnation.

Carnival in New York

On a cold February evening in 1957, people began arriving at the Rockland Palace Casino in Harlem shortly after eight o'clock. As they stepped into the brightly lit hall they discarded their drab, heavy winter coats and revealed costumes that gleamed brilliantly under the chandeliers. It was the tenth anniversary of the Trinidad-American Club's Carnival Dance, an event started just after the Second World War and one of many such cultural activities sponsored by benevolent associations and clubs across Harlem for the benefit of residents from the British West Indies. On this occasion in 1957 the Carnival dance at Rockland Palace Casino was only the first of a series of dances and balls organized or coordinated by the Carnival Dance Promoters League. That evening there was a steel orchestra competition, competitions for costumes and for Calypsos. "Caribbean Islanders" emerged victorious for their costume portrayal of the "King and I," just beating an ensemble dressed elegantly as "Poodles." Later that week the festivities would continue at the eleventh Calypso Ball held at the Park Palace Ballroom on 110th Street, sponsored by the Club La Douze and the ubiquitous Carnival Dance Promoters League.

Events such as these, in one form or another, have been staged by West Indians in New York City since the early 1920s when the first waves of immigration from the Caribbean were at their highest. According to a WPA research paper, by the 1930s Caribbean-run churches were sponsoring "such ceremonies as . . . Island-type Harvest festivals, Christmas and New Year celebrations, Emancipation Day ceremonies [to] help soothe the nostalgia for the homeland and assist the churches in financing themselves" (Watkins-Owens 1996: 60). Originally such festivals and celebrations were held at the time of year customary to them. There were Carnival balls and celebrations held in February or early March to coincide with Ash Wednesday and the beginning of Lent. Carnival, however, was not generally viewed in religious terms, even back home. Many of the participants were not themselves Catholic, although those who were often took the period of abstinence following Carnival quite seriously. Such celebrations continued through the Second World War, and in 1947 Jesse (or sometimes Jessie) Waddell, a Trinidadian immigrant to New York, organized the first outdoor Carnival in Harlem. Although this festival grew enormously, especially in terms of crowd attendance, it did not supplant the festivals held at Carnival time. Such galas continue even today.

My focus here, however, is the rise and growth of the Labor Day Carnival in Manhattan and its subsequent move to Brooklyn in the 1960s. It has been suggested that scheduling the festival over Labor Day facilitated the participation of West Indians of all religions (Kasinitz 1992: 141), however, to my knowledge, its traditional pre-Lenten time has never seemed a barrier to the participation of non-Catholics in Trinidad or elsewhere. Carnivals held in Toronto and London made their politics overt by scheduling the event over the August Bank Holiday "in order to correspond with the day on which Emancipation is commemorated in the English-speaking West Indies" (Kasinitz and Friedenberg-Herbstein 1987: 315). In New York the choice of Labor Day allowed organizers to both facilitate an outdoor presentation in warm weather and to situate Carnival close—but not too close—to Emancipation Day (Hill 1981: 33). The event was duly covered each year by the various organs of the African American community but largely ignored in the "mainstream" press. The Trinidadian (and West Indian) relationship to New York City's black community and to its political, social, and economic institutions have all had a profound effect on the formation of the Trinidadian transnation. The following account of the development of Carnival demonstrates the public dimension of the transnational imagination and shows how, in addition to cultural politics, the relationship between what can be imagined and displayed as "culture" is always restricted by external forces from without the community. The main point, however, is to suggest ways in which developments surrounding Carnival signal changes in Trinidadian ethnic consciousness.

The Harlem Years

Carnival was originally planned to take place every year on Labor Day Monday in Harlem. Harlem had been the established place of settlement for West Indian immigrants since the turn of the century. In the space of thirty years (1900–1930), close to 40,000 immigrants had arrived to live and work in the emerging African American community. Harlem was a growing and thriving enclave of African American and foreign-born black entrepreneurship, artistic production, and politics. Within this community there lived a broad spectrum of people of African descent. In the 1920s and 1930s about one-sixth of the black population in Harlem was foreign born, and most of these were from the British West Indies. British West Indian adjustment and adaptation to New York City life inspired the formation of various organizations whose purpose it was to provide a place where nationals from the same islands could meet and to provide financial assistance to recent immigrants or established persons who found themselves in difficult financial situations. These benevolent associations, as they were called, had their roots in the northern migrations of southern African Americans at the end of the nineteenth century. The Caribbean versions were largely modeled on these institutions. In addition to providing financial relief, benevolent associations helped local leaders or aspiring leaders earn "social distinction" (Watkins-Owens 1996: 65). Finally, such groups often took an active interest in the political developments of their homelands and generally supported independence movements. Benevolent associations persist today and are still important in the development of Caribbean transnationalism, although in some cases these organizations have given way to other kinds of institutions, most notably educational and cultural clubs (Basch 1987; Bonnett 1981; Basch et al. 1994). Not only did these groups provide much-needed financial support, they "facilitated the individual's adjustment to American society" as well as "reinforc[ed] and strengthen[ed] a sense of common ethnicity" (Basch 1987: 169, 174). Here, then, were institutions that were not "from home" yet which fostered a sense of "homeness." Benevolent associations, then, provide good examples of the kinds of purely local (here meaning New York–based) phenomena that help develop the transnation.

As indicated, the promotion of national or island identity went hand in hand with the provision of financial and spiritual help within the associations. In order to raise money, social events were sponsored that often had national cultural themes. Thus Barbadian organizations held Crop-Over balls, Bahamian groups celebrated Jonkonnu, and Trinidadian associations promoted Carnival. As the West Indian community grew so too did the number and frequency of such events. African American newspapers from the period record dances, balls, and gatherings especially at times coinciding with traditional events back home. It was not until 1947 that the idea and implementation of an actual "imitation" of the Trinidad Carnival came into being. The "brain child" of community leader and activist Jesse Waddell, Carnival was intended to promote harmony between the African American and African Caribbean communities in Harlem.[5] To this end Mrs. Waddell founded the West Indies Day Committee, the precursor to all subsequent Carnival organizations. By 1957 the West Indies Day Parade was a firmly established fixture in the African American calendar and was eagerly anticipated by African American and West Indian communities both within and outside of New York City.[6]

The parade's organization, in certain fundamental ways, has remained relatively intact to this day. The numbers of participants and the crowds of spectators have grown immensely, but the parade is still marked by costumed groups, music, competitions, and the ubiquitous presence of local politicians. In the 1950s the parade was routinely patronized by Hulan Jack, a prominent local Democrat originally from Guyana. Jack rose through the party machinery to become borough president of Manhattan in 1953. He held the post until 1960. His presence encouraged the participation of other local leaders, including notables such as Adam Clayton Powell.

The parade route was relatively short, from 110th or 111th Street to 142nd, via Seventh Avenue. In the early days the parade's more spectacular sights were the commercially sponsored floats. By way of example, in 1951 there were floats entered by a flower shop, Blumstein's Department Store, the A & J Bottling Co., Ming Garden restaurant, and Schenley Inc. The themes ranged from Chinese dancing girls to a floating hospital to an open car with girls dressed in French costumes.

The turnout from the late 1940s until the late 1950s was quite remarkable. In 1951 close to 250,000 Harlemites witnessed the parade. Photographs of the procession show decorated cars and open trucks, an enormous pirate ship and bands of women dressed in "exotic" Eastern costumes. Throughout the course of the 1950s, however, both participation and attendance began to wane. Newspaper accounts from the period record a steady decline. In 1958 attendance was estimated at 165,000. This was still a sizable crowd, but not nearly the throngs of just a few years earlier. One possible explanation for this can be found in the growing number of West Indians who were moving to Brooklyn, either from their homes in Harlem or directly from the West Indies themselves. The growing number of Caribbean migrants to Brooklyn would have a profound impact on the African American community in Harlem and, more directly, would change the shape of Carnival forever.

The influence of the Brooklyn West Indians began to be felt on Carnival as early as 1960, when the *New York Amsterdam News* reported a decline in participation and unrest in the parade, quoting Harlem officials who blamed the trouble on "the Brooklyn West Indian group" (1960: 32). Others interviewed by the paper felt that the parade officials themselves had allowed the event to flounder. The following year the first record of substantial violence was recounted as the *Amsterdam News* headlines blared "West Indian Parade Becomes a Brawl" (1961: 1). On a day of stifling heat and humidity a steelbandsman and a spectator struggled over a "drum," which the musician subsequently used as a club. The "riot" resulted in ten men being held on a total of $45,000 bail and growing trepidation on the part of the city about continuing to allow the revelry to proceed. In 1964, reports Donald Hill (1994), a bottle-throwing incident resulted in the revoking of Jesse Waddell's parade permit. Lionel "Rufus" Gorin, a Trinidadian who had been "playing mas'" since he was a boy in Harlem, took the initiative to move the parade to Brooklyn. In the same year Mr. Gorin created the United West Indian Day Development Association (UWIDDA) and masqueraded in the few blocks surrounding his home. The parade drew modest participation but attracted a devoted coterie of masqueraders and costume makers. Gorin moved Carnival to Brooklyn just as that area was beginning to develop a large West Indian presence. This demographic shift indicated not only a search for opportunities to purchase housing but a shift away from an association with Harlem in general.

The golden years of Harlem as an African American community were behind it by the early 1960s, and West Indians were beginning to develop the sense that they needed to forge an identity separate from native African Americans. Primarily, and like other groups from the Caribbean, the shift was an attempt to counteract the negative effects of "blackness" with the positive affects of cultural differentiation (Stafford 1987; Sutton and Makiesky-Barrow

1987). Carnival provided an excellent forum for the promotion of ethnic identity.

The remainder of this section will focus on the development of the Brooklyn Carnival from the migration period and Oil Boom years up to the present. The close relationship that exists between Carnival in Trinidad and Carnival in New York must first be seen in the light of the historic and political-economic ties that have been established during this period.

Brooklyn Carnival: 1964 to the Present

When Rufus Gorin brought Carnival to Brooklyn from Manhattan in the early 1960s, he had a very small contingent of participants and masmen who in the early days would parade around the streets in Gorin's neighborhood. Gorin then founded an organization entitled the United West Indian Day Development Association in order to facilitate the administration of Carnival. The event began to attract spectators—especially West Indians, who were beginning to pour into Brooklyn in the mid-1960s.

In 1967 Carlos Lezama, a young Trinidadian born in Venezuela who had migrated to the United States to work as a machinist, took Carnival one step further and brought it onto the Eastern Parkway, a magnificent thoroughfare that cuts a broad swath through Brooklyn, lined with museums and proud homes and culminating in the Grand Army Plaza with its heroic arch facing the undulating expanse of Prospect Park. Renaming the organization the West Indian American Day Association (later to become the West Indian American Day Carnival Association or WIADCA) Lezama managed to secure another permit to parade. The early organization had thirty-six members from many backgrounds and with a diversity of interests, such as Marie Austin, who worked many years as the business manager and treasurer in addition to her regular work.

WIADCA is a relatively small body for such an enormous affair, yet they have managed to handle the growing complications of mounting Carnival with a certain degree of aplomb. There have been, however, a fair share of disagreements, tensions, and adverse situations that have marked the history of Carnival and WIADCA.[7]

Although the "parade" started small, it has grown steadily both in participants and in spectators. The resulting strain put on both the organizers and the city has been, at times, overwhelming. Carnival is generally a peaceful affair, but crimes ranging from petty theft and pickpocketing to shootings and stabbings have been known to occur. Despite the fact that these hazards exist in any kind of large crowd situation, members of WIADCA as well as mas' makers and spectators have often complained about the enormous police presence at the event. In 1994 the *Carib News*, a local organ of the West Indian community, reported that the city had deployed as many as 4,100 police officers along the parkway (*New York Carib News*, Sept. 13, 1994: 26). There is a general sense that such a force smacks of racism, given that events of equal size in other communities are not often attended by so much law enforcement.

In addition to the police presence, there is the issue of insurance, which parade officials must secure before they can be issued a permit. The costs of this insurance have increased enormously according to WIADCA president Lezama (Personal interview 1995). From $1,000 in the early years the insurance bill climbed to $6,000 twenty years later, a nominal increase. After Crown Heights, the premium soared to a reported $67,000. WIADCA appealed to the governor, claiming the parade would have to cease if something were not done. The insurance was reduced to $20,000, still an enormous burden.

Finances are always claimed to be a source of anxiety by the WIADCA. Getting sponsors, prizes, band fees, and government grants are always a top priority and always difficult. The WIADCA is nonprofit, so all money earned is tax exempt. Suspicion seems to infect many of the relationships between WIADCA and other Carnival-related groups such as the bandleader's association and the steelband association. Finances are generally kept private, so there is never any certainty or accountability with regard to the acquisition or dispersal of funds. This has contributed to a general but apparently not crippling feeling of mistrust. It was my experience in interviews that people in the world of Carnival, whatever their feeling about one another, were very careful to speak with respect and tact when it came to "internal" matters. Yet many bandleaders complained of prize money being delayed or being unfairly apportioned. One interviewee maintained that prize moneys, which were often donated by sponsors, were purposely held for a period after the event in order to collect as much interest on them as possible. There is no way to corroborate these kinds of accusations, but they serve to illustrate the ways in which the organization maintains a certain distance from the mas' makers themselves.

Don Hill, writing of these interactions in the Brooklyn Carnival, has stated that "the masqueraders and the steelbandsmen had a fundamental conflict of interest with the Association" (1994: 51). Moreover, the masqueraders and the steelbandsmen had conflicts among themselves. The "class- and interest-based differences between members of the Association, steelbandsmen and masqueraders were played out in almost routine disagreements" (Hill 1994: 51). These disagreements were due to the natures of the various groups themselves. Steelbands often were (and still are) sponsored by businesses whereas masquerade bands try to operate as small businesses. The steelbands try to provide payment for their musicians, many of whom are working class, while mas' band leaders tend to be from the middle class. These groups often come into conflict over prize money and over funds generally granted to the Association.

The 1970s: The Struggle for Control

In 1969 the West Indian Day Parade made its debut along the Eastern Parkway. The WIADCA began to consolidate its control over the event but suffered growing pains. Throughout these years local papers reported a decline in the festival, although there does not seem to be much indication that the festival did anything but grow in popularity and in visibility, making it an extremely potent political forum. It was through the decade of the 1970s that Carnival acquired its position as a venue for politicians aiming to capture the West Indian and African American vote. At the same time controversy over the nature, aim, and scope of the event was everywhere trumpeted by the New York West Indian and African American press. Complaints about the way in which the WIADCA was handling the event culminated in 1982 with the Manhattan Basin Festival affair.

Perhaps the first public challenge to the proprietorship of Carnival occurred in 1974. The *New York Amsterdam News* reported a rift between the (then) West Indian American Day Association (WIADA) and "rival faction" New York Carnival Council Incorporated (NYCCI). The latter body had been formed by former WIADA members, who pushed for the transference of the festival to Fifth Avenue in Manhattan. Their stated aim was to "reap the benefits of media coverage, business sponsorship of bands and greater police control of crowds that hamper the visibility of the costumes" (as quoted in *New York Amsterdam News*, September 7, 1974: A-1). The NYCCI's attempt to negotiate separately with the city for a permit to parade up Fifth Avenue failed. Herman Hall, who was at the time the public relations officer for WIADA, claimed the reason the rival group was turned down was "because the City recognized us as the sole and legitimate sponsor of the parade" (*NYAN*, Sept. 7, 1974: A-1). NYCCI's main interest was to represent the masmen and steelbandsmen and their hope was to be able to attract more outside business support in an official Fifth Avenue setting. The police department attempted to mediate the conflict by proposing a joint committee made up of members from both organizations. That suggestion was rejected by WIADA.

In October of 1976 another group appeared to offer an alternative voice to WIADA's in the administration of Carnival. The National Council of Caribbean Artists (NCCA) was formed in order to represent the bandleaders in Brooklyn. Submitting proposals to WIADA outlining changes that could be made to Carnival, the group claimed to have secured the interest of major business sponsors. Again WIADA held fairly firm to its position as sole leader, rejecting or modifying NCCA's suggestions. In response there was a call to boycott Carnival. This attempt never got off the ground (*New York Daily Challenge*, Aug. 8, 1977: 4).

In 1977 "Rufus" Gorin retired from the Carnival scene after having been there from its inception. In an interview granted to the *New York Daily Challenge*, Gorin lamented the decline of the parade. He cited the growing violence, the poor attendance, and the general disrespect given to bandleaders by the association. Ultimately for Gorin the symbol of the parade's demise could be found in the growing relationship Carnival was developing with politicians: "All they [WIADA] are concerned about is the rubbing of shoulders with politicians and not give a damn about the youths nor the cultivating of one of the finest cultures in the world" (*NY Daily Challenge*, Aug. 24, 1977: 4).

With dissent and conflict attending Carnival year after year, a concerted effort was made in 1982 that posed the greatest challenge to the (now) WIADCA hegemony over the festival. In that year a coalition of Trinidadian business leaders and promoters attempted to launch their own Carnival in Manhattan. This affair was meant to serve as a respectable alternative to Brooklyn and would, claimed the organizers, establish "something Caribbean people could be proud of (Hall, *Everybody's* 1982: 14). Carnival in Manhattan was meant to showcase Caribbean products, to emphasize the Caribbean as a tourist destination, and to stage professional entertainment in a professional manner. The Manhattan Basin Festival (MBF), as it was known, was meant to appeal directly to the city and to non-Caribbean people. It was culture turned outward, with all consideration given to an audience that had no notion of Carnival.

The MBF shows that Carnival events are not only held in the interests of gaining city recognition, although they are usually about ethnic display. Herman Hall, in an extensive article on the subject of the Manhattan Basin Festival, drew comparisons between Brooklyn and Trinidad. In Trinidad, Carnival and what was the Carnival Development Committee, now the National Carnival Commission, had the basic support of the government. Funds were provided by and losses absorbed through the government. No such safety net exists in Brooklyn, with promoters responsible for producing the majority of the pre-Carnival events and handling any profit or loss. The WIADCA is only responsible for the shows held at Dimanche Gras at the Brooklyn Museum, the proceeds from which, in the eyes of the organizers, barely make a dent in the organization's expenditures. Because of these basic financial problems Carnival is frequently beset with controversies and dissatisfaction from patrons and participants alike. It was, in part, as a response to this that the MBF billed itself as a professional, business-like operation.

Held on Pier 88 along the Hudson River, the festival was touted as a sort of high-gloss version of Carnival in Brooklyn. With support staff working full-time, a lineup of well-known Calypsonians, and the support of business leaders and politicians, the leadership of the MBF was all set to steal Carnival from Brooklyn using a formula of American-style hype, polish, and promotion. The MBF, then, also shows that cultural politics and the focus on display events as conduits for self-conscious, ethnic advertising are not only for acquiring ethnic identity status in New York City. Other interests are at work, often simply the quest for commerce. Yet the promise of profit is seen as deriving from successful cultural display as well. The presence of the Manhattan festival in 1982 serves as just one example of the power and promise of an ethnic spoils system in New York City, in which the stakes for ethnic self-promotion are indeed high. This theme will be taken up again in chapter 4 in an examination of what I call bureaucratic multiculturalism.

In the long run the Manhattan Basin Festival failed (no one showed up) because it ignored its constituents. Outsiders want to see insiders enjoying themselves. Outsiders want authenticity. The MBF example highlights an important paradox in the relationship between the promoters of Carnival and outside observers of the event and Carnival participants. Promoters, such as the team of businessmen in the MBF, see the success of Carnival in terms of its outward appeal. For instance, can Carnival reflect well on the community? Can it be used to heighten awareness of Trinidad and Trinidadian culture? Can it be a "springboard" to the sale of other Trinidadian products? Such businessmen are hoping that they can duplicate the fantastic success of the Trinidad Carnival in terms of participation. They want numbers and exposure. Yet in their efforts to attract outsiders, they routinely ignore the features of Carnival that attract "insiders." The professionalization of Carnival is undertaken in the effort to demonstrate how efficient its promoters can be, but little effort is made to appeal to the Carnival-goer him- or herself (the features that attract West Indians to the festival will be discussed further on). Yet it is precisely local participation that outsiders come to the event to see. Without them, there is no Carnival. Carnival, the MBF experience indicates, may provide a forum for ethnic self-fashioning and the imagination of community, but the form of Carnival alone holds no guarantee. In other words, people will not attend just any event billed as "a Carnival." The fact that over the course of the three days of scheduled events no one showed up revealed a deep misconception on the part of the MBF promoters, a misconception that would be repeated again in Trinidad itself thirteen years later (see chapter 5). The imagination is not built solely on "forms," although forms are the primary concern with ethnicity politics. In chapters 3 and 4, I take a closer look at exactly what constitutes the transnational imagination and why certain forms succeed and others do not. This is a theme that will also be taken up in the final chapters as we examine the failure and success of different Carnival competitions.

Parading Politics in the 1980s

After the Manhattan Basin Festival's poor showing, the WIADCA's leadership over Carnival was solidified. During the 1980s attendance grew, the problems associated with enormous crowds grew, and so did the visibility of the parade. Although the press relating to the event could be negative and tensions between the Hasidic community and the Caribbean community often flared, the increased attention brought with it an unprecedented political presence. As already noted local politicians such as Hulan Jack and Adam Clayton Powell in Harlem had been involved from early on, and although as early as 1977 in Brooklyn Rufus Gorin could lament the ubiquity of politicians in the parade, the West Indian American Day Parade really came of age in the 1980s as an important arena for courtship of the West Indian and African American electorate.

According to sociologist Philip Kasinitz, in 1984 "the WIADCA lost its political innocence," after local Hasidic leadership challenged the staging of the event. The WIADCA were backed in their efforts to retain Carnival by state senator Martin Markowitz,[8] and responded to challengers by naming Mr. Markowitz Grand Marshall in 1984 and in 1986. This helped solidify Markowitz's positive association with the West Indian and African American community in the face of an important upcoming Democratic primary. In addition the WIADCA emerged as an important "ethnic leadership group" (Kasinitz 1992: 143) and demonstrated its ability to confer recognition by the community as a whole.

In 1984 an appearance by Jesse Jackson in the parade highlighted tensions between African American political leadership and West Indian leaders. During a speech to the assembled Carnival-goers on Labor Day, Jackson made a rather generic speech, ignoring the specific West Indian nature of the crowd. WIADCA officials were "furious at what they regarded as a snub" (Kasinitz 1992: 155), primarily because Caribbean distinctiveness was ignored. In general, as Kasinitz points out, Caribbean identity was too often lumped in with African American identity by African American leaders as well as by other local politicians. Although the WIADCA promised not to allow politicians to speak at future Carnivals, the following year it was clear that Carnival had become a major opportunity for political hopefuls to get their messages across to the Caribbean crowd. Marching in the parade became de rigueur for any public figure hoping to make an impression on one of the fastest growing ethnic communities in the city. It was during the 1980s that Carnival's potential as both signature ethnic display event and public forum for political action was realized.

Carnival in the 1990s

If Carnival became political in the 1980s, its politics reached a level of maturation in the 1990s. Not only was the tradition of political leaders marching continued, but Carnival emerged as a self-conscious expression of a Caribbean identity whose political rights were rooted in ethnic distinctiveness itself. Although this is dealt with more explicitly in chapter 4, some explanation is warranted here.

Everybody's Magazine, a popular journal published by and for the Caribbean community in New York, could confidently declare in 1990 that "the annual Caribbean carnival on Labor Day weekend in Brooklyn, New York is now an institution. After twenty-three years of bargaining for concessions, Carnival . . . is now held in high esteem and enjoys the popularity associated with the Irish and Columbus Day parades on Fifth Avenue in Manhattan" (*Everybody's* 1990: 4). Indeed, by 1994 the competing events on Labor Day—Wigstock and the Labor Day Parade—were moved or had disappeared, respectively, leaving carnival as the major attraction on Labor Day Monday.

Given the high profile of the event, the increased media coverage, and the potential for controversy, the Brooklyn Carnival was catapulted squarely into greater New York's public view. In 1992 the *New York Times* ran a feature article, while the *Village Voice*, *New York Newsday*, and other newspapers began to routinely mention the parade and perhaps show the obligatory photographs of costumed dancers or bikini-clad women "wining" on police officers.

Carnival 1994: The Rosh Hashanah Controversy

Carnival in 1994 was in part dominated by fears that the city would not grant a permit for the parade. A letter written by Hasidic leaders to the deputy mayor asking that the parade be re-routed because of the coincidence of Rosh Hashanah with Carnival that year, was met with outrage by the Caribbean community. The fact that the permit was subsequently delayed added fuel to the fire, even though there was no real correlation between the two events.

The letter, written by Rabbi Joseph Spielman on behalf of the "Crown Heights Jewish Community Council," was sent to Deputy Mayor Fran Reiter with a list of fourteen demands. The demands called either for re-routing the parade or for the city to provide transportation and a corridor of passage between the Jewish enclaves in Crown Heights, the airport, and the Montefiore Cemetery in Springfield Gardens where Rabbi Menachem Schneerson, the messianic Lubavitcher Rabbi, is buried. The letter also demanded that no liquor be sold except on Eastern Parkway.

The letter received instant reaction from mas' makers, Caribbean leaders, and, on Labor Day itself, irate Carnival-goers. Yvette Rennie of Hawks International, a major Carnival, band called the letter "a serious form of harassment," while Anthony Dowdy of Borokeete USA opined, "Even as their leaders seek peace in the Middle East the Hasidim are trying to engage in cultural repression here" (*New York Carib News*, Aug. 2, 1994: 3). The pressure built as the week passed, with article after article speculating on the fate of the parade permit. City councilwoman Annette Robinson, through whose 36th District the Eastern Parkway passes, emphatically stated that she opposed any re-routing of the Carnival procession. All across the Brooklyn political scene people were issuing statements, controlling damage, showing agitation until an article appeared in the *New York Carib News* on August 16 that put their fears to rest. The permit was officially approved as the deputy mayor, with a sort of baffled casualness, wondered publicly what all the fuss had been about, claiming that "the community was reading into things that are not there. I wish somebody had spoken to me, then all this anxiety and uncertainty would never have come up" (*New York Carib News*, Aug. 16, 1994). In attendance that year were a host of dignitaries vying for the recognition of the Caribbean community. Among them were Mayor Rudolph Giuliani, Mario Cuomo, Rev. Benjamin Chavis of the NAACP, Fran Reiter, Comptroller Carl McCall, Kings County Democratic chairman Clarence Norman, Rev. Al Sharpton, Una Clarke, John Hartwig of Guinness Imports, the fight promoter Don King, city councilman Rev. Lloyd Henry, state senator Marty Markowitz, assemblyman Nick Perry, Jamaican scholar Rex Nettleford, and a host of other, lesser-known local figures. The dignitaries generally march at the head of the procession and are generally forgotten as soon as they pass. Giuliani was booed, however, as he marched by Sharpton followers who dogged his every step down the Parkway.

The climate of the parade, at least at this level, is one of campaign jostling, reputation building, and general glad-handing. This does not, however, constitute the entire event nor does it begin to describe the experiences had by mas' makers and participants. It is this understanding of the event that is addressed in chapter 4. However, the political dimension of the parade does underline some crucial issues current in the Caribbean community. Noteworthy events within the community are often addressed within Carnival, either in the form of celebration through calypsos, band themes, or steelband tributes or in the form or criticism and "social commentary." Furthermore, in multiethnic Crown Heights, public social and cultural strife is often mediated by goodwill appearances in the parade. The following chapter discusses the role that Carnival played in the 1991 Crown Heights "riots." Carnival occupied a central role in helping smooth over a highly volatile situation while solidifying its position as a central ethnic display event, which, as we saw in 1994, would cast it into the center of controversy.

Conclusion

Carnival was established early on in the migration experience. It has played many roles and changed dramatically since its inception, yet it has grown to occupy a major place in the struggle for Trinidadian and West Indian recognition within New York City. As the Trinidadian migrant community has come into being through global forces that precipitated large-scale dislocation, so too has a transnation emerged, also in conjunction with these forces.

Carnival in New York grew out of the Trinidadian and West Indian experience of migration and was at the heart of the transnation as it formed. What is often evoked, especially during times of conflict or during times when the existence of Carnival is threatened, is the preservation of culture. Carnival must continue to exist else it will signal that a significant blow has been dealt to West Indian culture. The fear is that a loss of Carnival will be a loss of heritage. The struggles over control of the festival and its structure (i.e., Carnival vs. parade) have been concerned with gaining the authority of the Trinidadian and even West Indian voice within the city. The mobilization of cultural forms, histories, and narratives from home lend authenticity to the project, even as they are actively constructed there by authorities who find themselves with similar problems of legitimation on their hands. But it is the adoption of these various narratives that makes the transnation a viable entity through the work of reproductive imagination. In the previous chapter we were able to see the gradual appropriation of the Trinidad Carnival by the middle classes. From that emerged Carnival narratives and the ability of a proprietor-class to produce and control such narratives both for the production of national culture internally as well as externally or globally. Those histories of Carnival became useful in the construction of ethnic identity in New York. Thus the construction of identity in New York becomes of paramount importance. It is in the environment of ethnic politics in New York City that Carnival narratives get put to new uses. In the next chapter the focus shifts to the men and women who make use of and transform these narratives specifically. From official spokespeople to bandleaders and craftsmen to the "rank and file," the narratives metamorphose into lived practices and experiences. Some of these reinforce the dominant line, others do not. As we shall see, however, in many cases the narratives become internalized and naturalized.

3

Mas' Camps and Masqueraders

Perspectives on the Production of Carnival

The West Indian American Day Parade has emerged as a political forum in what one writer calls "the institutional sense" (Fraser 1989: 166). In other words, the parade/Carnival provides a space for official political maneuvering and the promotion of both political and cultural platforms. However, there is also another political dimension that exists alongside the first. In this chapter I will suggest ways in which the practices of individuals, whether they be masmakers or Carnival participants, respond to, embrace, reject, and modify the received discourse of cultural identity espoused by community leaders, the Trinidadian state, and other organs of "officialdom."

By focusing on the masquerade camp (mas' camp), where much of the work for Carnival bands is undertaken, as well as on what masmakers say about their work and evaluations of Carnival bands by players, it will become apparent that the politics of recognition is always at risk of erosion from within. The nationalist emphasis on stasis versus culture is often adopted by groups seen by masqueraders to be in opposition to themselves, the "ordinary" West Indians. This leaves such rhetoric open not only to overt criticism, or partial acceptance, but to obsolescence in that what it describes is rarely isomorphic with what is happening. I will begin with a look at the workings of a mas' camp to demonstrate how this vital "institution" within Carnival works, how it is instrumental in producing changing ideas about Carnival, and how it has become the focus of culturalist "museumification" strategies by New York City and by cultural organizations.

I follow this with an investigation of the middle-class Carnival in its current incarnation as seen through the eyes of some of its enthusiasts. Their opinions about which Carnival bands are the best to play in give us some idea about how common practice diverges from official discourse. What they value about the festival is quite different from what many community leaders, culture brokers, and, to a lesser degree, New York City administrators value. What I also discovered, by coming to an understanding of their motivations, was that their pursuit of the good liming situation actually helps preserve the more Carnival-like atmosphere in Brooklyn. In an effort to keep their party going they resist the "paradification" of the event and extend Carnival into their neighborhoods, off the official route. Thus, where those agents of official, preservationist discourse see the middle-class Carnival as destructive, I suggest that it has productive qualities related to its relevance to a specific population.

Next, offering a different perspective, Kevin "Fuzzy" Davis provides insights into both the masmaker's art and the older masquerader's ideas concerning Carnival's meaning. Davis, like many who left Trinidad in the 1950s, places a much greater emphasis on the meaning of the costumes themselves. And therefore his thoughts may be contrasted with the middle-class position. Carnival's beauty and power lie, for Davis, in the effective portrayal of characters and themes. Davis laments the passing of the old ways in Carnival and the disappearance of quality masquerades, noting that he has not seen a steelband on the road in years in Trinidad. His sentiments, shared by many older Trinidadians I interviewed in New York, foreshadowed actions taken in 1996 when the National Carnival Commission instituted a steelband competition that encouraged steelbands to come out on the road during the Tuesday Parade of the Bands in Port-of-Spain. That competition proved to be an enormous success due, in part, to the large numbers of New Yorkers who returned to participate. Examples such as this one demonstrate that opinions such as Davis's work very well in helping support the official promotion of old-time Carnival, even though the motivations for doing so might be quite different from each other.

Parade versus Carnival

Although I have already touched briefly upon the difference between the parade form and Carnival form, it requires further elaboration in the context of the practices of Carnival players. The celebration is different from other sorts of ethnic parades in the city such as the Puerto Rican Parade or the St. Patrick's Day Parade in that it is based on an existing festival that has its own structure (or lack thereof) already in place. Taken from its Trinidadian model, Carnival in Brooklyn has tried to capture the spirit of its Caribbean parent by emphasizing a lack of order. This has been difficult to achieve in the New York setting because there does not exist a fundamental city- or nation-wide collective understanding of Carnival tradition. In Trinidad, even if one does not choose to participate, one must acknowledge the presence of Carnival and the preeminence of Carnival on the days of its celebration. In New York, as a Trinidadian journalist put it, on the next street it's "business as usual." Most of the city, until recently, had no idea of or interest in Carnival. And even today, with interest growing, many of those present at the festival in Brooklyn are purely spectators.

In Trinidad, except for certain judging and spectating venues, most of the people on the street are in Carnival in some way or another. In Port-of-Spain, Trinidad's capital, there is no clearly set route for any of the bands to follow. Although they must pass in front of three judging venues, they need not proceed to them in any particular order. For the most part Carnival bands control their destiny within the city. Oddly enough, in Port-of-Spain, very few streets are officially closed or cordoned off, though there are parking restrictions and certain streets have special traffic laws for the days of Carnival. There exists a general understanding that during Carnival driving would be a folly. In New York, conversely, there is an official set route, although, as we shall see, in some neighborhoods bands have countered these restrictions by roaming about relatively freely. In general though, the Eastern Parkway from Utica Avenue to Grand Army Plaza is the current pre-set route for the Brooklyn Carnival.

The Carnival Process

Carnival in Trinidad serves as the model for Caribbean-style carnivals in North America and in the UK in more than just performative ways. The basic organizational and procedural principles are relevant as well. Carnival in Brooklyn follows the same general "map" as the Trinidad Carnival. So, what I will describe for Trinidad, unless otherwise noted, is also the case in Brooklyn. In Trinidad Carnival is not merely a festive event spanning a two-day period, Carnival Monday and Tuesday. Prior to these days, which are technically the days of the "pretty masquerade bands," there is a whole host of activities including competitions, fetes, and Carnival shows to be attended. In the early fall (midsummer in New York) Carnival season opens with the launching of the various masquerade bands. A masquerade band is not a musical outfit but a group of costumed participants who pay a fee and receive a costume and the rights and privileges associated with "playing" in the band. The term "playing" means participating in a band. Participation basically involves a member of a particular masquerade band "jumping up" or dancing in the streets and "liming" with friends. When one plays in a masquerade band (simply called a band), one goes "on the road" with that group on Monday and Tuesday.

To join a band a person must register. The way one chooses a band is to visit the various mas' camps scattered about Port-of-Spain or, in Brooklyn, mas' band headquarters such as restaurants, cultural associations, or bars after their official launchings, when the drawings of the band's costumes are posted up on the walls. The bandleader or administrative head of the band, either independently or in conjunction with a committee that includes a professional designer, will choose a "theme" for the band for that year. Themes range very widely and have also changed over time, often being centered around current events or trends within Trinidadian society. Particular kinds of themes enjoy a vogue and then may fade from popularity. In the 1940s and '50s, for instance, after World War II, it was extremely popular to play as a sailor (see chapter 6). However, any theme that provides the designer with many colorful sub-thematic options is acceptable.

The bands are divided into sections. Each section will portray some element or aspect of the general theme. If the theme is "Gems of the World," for instance, a section may be called "Jade" or "Diamonds," with the costumes in each bearing the colors or features of those gems. As it stands currently, many of the designers and bandleaders produce rather generic costumes whose foundation is a bathing suit upon which are heaped various beads and tassels. In addition to this masqueraders will receive a headpiece and a collar and a standard. There are exceptions, of course, and these can be quite dramatic. For the most part though, no matter how simple, the costume will have some features recognizably associated with the costume's subject matter. The choice of band for the average reveler these days is made less for the costume than for the lime, the social group involved with the band. You play with your friends.

The section pictures are drawn by a designer who is contracted by the bandleader or who may be the bandleader him- or herself. The pictures are posted at the mas' camp, and patrons come in and decide whether or not they would like to join and, if so, which section they would like to play. They then register with the band and put down a deposit on the costume. The band will make the appropriate number of costumes for each section according to the registration.

Obviously, some sections will be bigger than others, and if a section is not terribly popular it may be canceled altogether.

The band launchings are festive affairs. The bandleader(s) will organize a "fete" or large party with live music, disc jockeys, beer and rum, and so forth. The designs for the band will be unveiled and the public can officially begin to register with the group. Many bands will have loyal followers and so the theme from year to year is of little importance. However, even a well-established band can lose supporters if its designs become markedly poor. The masqueraders can be very fickle and are certainly vocal about their approval or disapproval of designs. Mas' players bring a wide range of criteria to bear upon their choice of band. The acts of evaluating and choosing rely heavily on the choice of lime. This appears to differ from the older Carnival in which the masquerade itself played an important role in the choice of band. There is a markedly different age and gender makeup in today's Carnival versus Carnival of the late 1950s and early 1960s, when many of the first migrants made their way north. In those days Carnival was still primarily the male, working-class festival it had been since emancipation.

Carnival in New York as well as in Trinidad is mostly made up of women, and the costumes are predominantly variations on a bikini with colorful beads, headpieces, and standards to complete the ensemble. These outfits have very little in common with the fancy portrayals of the past in their use of materials and even in their choice of theme (see below). Once the choice has been made a Carnival participant can enjoy all of the other features of Carnival that are not directly related to what is known as "pretty mas'" or the fancy bands. Carnival season is replete with options and events. There are the fetes; there are the calypso tents, which showcase the season's calypsos and calypsonians; there are the panyards in which steelbands practice their tunes for the Panorama steelband competition in the Savannah on Carnival Saturday night. These activities begin with the launchings in the fall and build in frequency and intensity through Christmas and Old Year's Night into Carnival. Most of the events, again, are characterized by liming (see below). Although people come to watch the shows, they tend to last a long time, with significant lulls between performances in which people can eat, drink, and lime.

In the last week before Carnival Tuesday, the preliminary competitions, which have been slowly weeding out contenders for the various titles in Carnival, come to their conclusion. There are competitions for Calypso Monarch, Steelband champion, King of Carnival, Queen of Carnival, Soca Monarch, and

Extemporaneous Calypso singing. Each of these competitions has its "play-offs" with their elimination rounds. The weekend before Carnival, the winners in these categories are determined. Saturday night is the Panorama and Sunday is Dimanche Gras, which determines the King and Queen of Carnival as well as the calypso champion. A committee selected by the National Carnival Commission undertakes competition judging. The judges come from many different parts of society, and different judges sit for different competitions. In recent years a Carnival Judges Association has offered Carnival judging courses, at the end of which participants receive a certificate. This does not guarantee their selection as judges, however.

Criteria for judging are exceptionally vague. Categories such as "visual impact" for masquerade bands receive points, and the points for all of the categories are tallied at the end of the competition. For Carnival 1994 a judge was selected who had been a florist because he had had sufficient training in aesthetics. Other Carnival judges have been noted masmen and well-known musicians, but in the main judging remains vague and hotly contested.

After midnight on Sunday, at approximately 2:00 A.M., J'ouvert starts (see introduction). J'ouvert is the official opening of Carnival, when the Merry Monarch is officially given the keys to the City. In Brooklyn, over the last twenty-five years, most of these features of Carnival have been established. There is now a Panorama, a Dimanche Gras, and a Calypso Monarch competition, as well as a Jouvay celebration.

This is the basic organization of Carnival both in New York and in Trinidad. On a superficial level the celebrations have much in common. Perhaps the greatest difference lies in the nature of what in Trinidad is Carnival Tuesday and what in Brooklyn is Labor Day Monday. These are the days of the "parade of the bands." In Brooklyn Carnival is much more strictly parade-like. All the bands are required to follow the same basic route from Utica Avenue to Grand Army Plaza down the Eastern Parkway. In Brooklyn there is only one judging venue and the bands pass by it in order as they proceed down the Parkway. There is, in addition, a strict time limit to the parade.

This situation in Brooklyn has evolved slowly over time. Initially the organizers of the event wanted the same random, nonparade-like quality that existed in Trinidad. As the event grew larger the city grew more apprehensive about the event's supposed lack of organization. Furthermore, this supposed chaos was damaging the event's public-relations image. To many outsiders Carnival seemed dangerous. Some younger leaders within the Caribbean community argued, with the city, in favor of a more parade-like atmosphere to promote a better image of Caribbean culture (see my discussion of the Manhattan Basin Festival in chapter 2). The Brooklyn Carnival is distinctly more parade-like now than it has ever been, as the younger leaders' point of view has won out over the desires of some other organizers to preserve a more Carnival-like atmosphere.

Mas' Camp Lime and the Masquerade Camp

The "mas' camp" in the Brooklyn Carnival production process plays a unique and specific role. Not only does the mas' camp provide the conditions and the labor for the production of Carnival costumes, it also provides a singular space for a special kind of social interaction that Trinidadians refer to as "liming." Liming is the term used for general socializing and casual "hanging out," and it is especially important at Carnival time. Liming in the mas' camps serves as a counterpoint to the increasing regimentation and ordering of Carnival in the streets that comes as a result of New York City's policy toward the festival.

Carnival is the supreme liming time. Thomas Hylland-Eriksen describes liming as "entirely contingent on the shared meaning that can be established spontaneously" (1990: 24). It is hanging around, socializing, talking, laughing, and a great deal of reminiscing—and can be extremely productive. Another venue for liming is in the mas' camp. Opinions get aired through the mas' camp lime, of course; more importantly, however, relevant topics of interest to the lime and the limer's community are made manifest. The liming situation establishes a forum for its participants, and through this the parameters of the group's world are partly established. The mas' camp lime frequently focuses on issues within Carnival. The camp itself provides the venue and the seemingly endless opportunity to discuss Carnival.

The camps, places in which costumes are assembled and constructed, can be anywhere. In Trinidad they are usually in a separate building that also serves as the band's headquarters and registration site. In Brooklyn bands cannot afford to rent out such spaces and so camps are scattered about the neighborhood and the City. A camp during Carnival season might be somebody's living room, back yard, garage, or basement. In exchange for working in the camp people are fed and given drinks and are sometimes compensated with a free costume or two, a paid phone bill, even money for bail for someone. Generally people come to the camps after they have finished work. They bring with them news of the day, gossip, politics, sports, soap operas, and news about

Carnival. Frequently included in these discussions is the relationship of the city to the festival and the ways in which Carnival is damaged by government interference.

The liming that goes on in the mas' camps offers an alternative to and a forum for remarking on the changing of Carnival. The mas' camp is not entirely within the purview of the city because it does not count as part of Carnival; it is not categorized as part of the performance but as backstage. The mas' camp is not backstage, however, in many ways. It is integral to the constantly changing nature of Carnival from year to year because it is here that Carnivals are in part created. In recent years there has been an effort on the part of local museums, community activists, WIADCA, and the city to promote interethnic understanding and multiculturalism. As part of this effort, displays of mas' camp activity, both in the museum setting and in the neighborhoods, have been proposed and implemented. In replica mas' camps or as stops along walking tours, the mas' camps have become more and more visible as part of Carnival experience. The impact that this will have on the role of the mas' camp and on its day-to-day function remains to be seen.

Life at Borokeete, USA

In the summer of 1991 I made my first trip to a mas' camp. I had read about them and seen pictures of them from Trinidad to Toronto to Notting Hill. In all of the photographs each camp had seemed different from the others. Some were cramped quarters in someone's basement, while others seemed to occupy cavernous spaces. My first experience was in Scotch Plains, New Jersey, in the garage of one of the creative directors of Borokeete, USA, one of the largest and most popular bands in Brooklyn. As it turned out, this location was only one of many such operations all coordinated in the service of bringing out that year's band. Ray Morris, the man in charge of much of the day-to-day production of the band, had to be on top of a disparate number of craftspeople all working in scattered locations from New Jersey to Brooklyn. Morris took the designs for the band, drawn by Neville Hinds, a well-respected Trinidadian costume designer and bandleader in his own right, and made certain that they came alive for Carnival day. Morris also oversaw registration for the band, sourcing materials, construction of most of the section costumes and countless other tasks, all the while operating as a graphic designer with his own business to attend to. Morris had a great deal of talent around him, including Kevin "Fuzzy" Davis. Davis has won a roomful of trophies during his many years in Carnival in New

York. All of these men and women have other jobs, other lives, other responsibilities, yet they tackle every Carnival season with a fresh passion.

When I arrived at Morris's home in New Jersey that rainy July night, he was out in the garage assembling headpieces. The children of the neighbors were helping him. It seemed as though anyone was welcome to join in if they wanted to stick some braid, or cut some fabric. It was another two years before I was able to see Morris at work again, and this time I was there to help. The main camp is located at the home of Morris's sister in Brooklyn. The theme in 1993 was "The Four Seasons." Neville Hinds had again drawn the designs for the band and Morris was coordinating their realization. The mas' camp consisted of a yellow tarpaulin stretched over the backyard and was surrounded by fencing. Benches and tables were set up upon which volunteers could work. Pepta Pierre, Morris's sister, and her family kept the camp running by providing food and drink for the workers. Most camp workers could only come after their own jobs were over for the day. Thus the camp, which got into full swing usually at

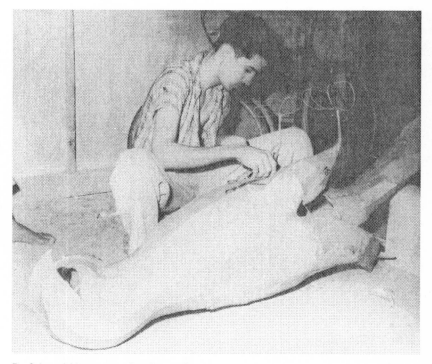

Fig. 3. Joseph Vieira at work in his mas' camp.

the beginning of August, for a Labor Day deadline, did not begin to be very active until around five or six in the evening. There was always music and beer.

Work in the mas' camp can be very tedious and time-consuming. There are many details to attend to, which must be duplicated hundreds of times over all of the pieces of all of the costumes. The point, then, is to socialize while maintaining a good level of work. Although the atmosphere is casual, a mas' camp cannot tolerate those who are only there to lime. The Borokeete mas' camp, as with many of the camps across Brooklyn, is not centralized. During the course of my visits I had the occasion to travel around with Morris as he checked up on the progress of other sections being constructed or assembled in the homes of friends in other parts of the borough. Morris was only responsible for the sections he supervised. Under agreement with the band leadership, a person or committee may bring out a section if they feel that they can deliver the product on time and can get people to play in their section. The band will get them materials and help in some ways, but the success of the section is largely the responsibility of the section leaders themselves. Bringing out a section in a band is one way for younger, aspiring bandleaders to get the training and the cultural capital they will require when they eventually split to form their own bands. In Carnival, most successful bandleaders can claim a pedigree that leads them back to a famous "ancestor" such as George Bailey or Harold Saldenah.

Most of the volunteers in the mas' camp that I spoke with were there to see friends, share gossip about "home," and perhaps work toward a free costume for their troubles. A surprising number of participants were not from Port-of-Spain, where Carnival is the largest, but were from smaller cities such as Arima and San Fernando. Furthermore, many of them had never played Carnival, let alone worked in a mas' camp when they were in Trinidad. In this way Carnival was a revelation, a source of "culture," of which they had not been aware, that had not impressed itself upon them when they were at home, immersed in it. Carnival only began to take on an added resonance in their situation of "exile." "It's like home," many told me, although clearly not a home they themselves had ever been part of. The camp workers who said this tended to be older, further removed from their former lives in Trinidad.

Labor in the mas' camp was informally divided along gender lines. Most of the people doing the piecework were women. Women were also generally responsible for providing food, while men supplied beer, shandies (beer and ginger ale), and other beverages. The food and drink was paid for and supplied by the mas' camp itself. Men took the roles of operating the power saws, painting, and other jobs that required a degree of technical specialization. Women were entrusted with tasks that required delicate skills and required many hours of concentration. This was also the work that I primarily performed, although I was encouraged, as a visitor, to try all of the tasks.

To pass the time during the hours of gluing braid and sequins, people conversed. Topics ranged widely but were focused on developments in family and personal relations, work, and television, especially soap operas. People also talked about the latest calypsos, about other Carnivals, and especially about Trinidad Carnival. If anybody had returned that year for the event it was discussed in detail.

Toward Carnival time the camps begin to work much later into the night, sometimes through the night. A feeling of excitement, a sense of purpose permeates the camp. Not too far from the Pierre household/mas' camp lies the headquarters for Borokeete, usa, a social club of sorts, complete with bar and dance floor. The headquarters are utilized all year round, but it is Carnival time when the place seems to awaken. In the basement of the club is the registration area where interested parties can put down their money and reserve a place in their favorite section. The process is now computerized to ease the burden of keeping track of hundreds of costume buyers. Upstairs the large, colorful drawings of the costumes, seductively imagined and conceived by Neville Hinds, are displayed "in action" as it were with shapely, idealized dancers showcased on the walls of the club. The drawings are an extremely important part of the process, serving to attract potential masqueraders to the band. People will make their decisions concerning whom to play with that year based on the quality of the drawings and how the costumes are depicted.

In 1993 Borokeete, usa, was playing the theme "The Four Seasons." Costumes were designed to try to evoke not only the four seasons proper but many different elements within each season. Thus, within autumn there were costumes depicting the changing leaves as well as costumes depicting Halloween (a tradition not observed in Trinidad generally, but gaining in modest popularity due to its introduction by Trinidadians returning from the United States). Similarly, with summer there might be sub-themes relating to the sun and the heat along with portrayals of activities that might be pursued in summertime, such as sailing. For each of the many sections (anywhere from fifteen to twenty in the larger bands) the costumes require special materials. Costumes are often designed along similar lines to facilitate the overall production of patterns and headpieces without having to dramatically retool, as it were. The more elaborate outfits will fetch higher prices and may utilize more material and labor-intensive techniques or more specialized techniques.

Nights at the mas' camp usually begin in the early evening and seem to gain momentum as the night wears on. Volunteers filter in slowly, saying their hellos over the constant volume of soca music on the radio. Soca is Carnival music (a somewhat recent musical form that emerged in the late 1960s and early 1970s as a kind of fusion between soul and calypso; hence "so-ca"). Existing alongside more traditional calypsos, soca tunes command the lion's share of popular radio time during Carnival season. By the time Labor Day arrives in Brooklyn, people are mostly acquainted with the crop of soca hits that were produced in Trinidad.[1] Thus Brooklyn recycles Carnival songs from Trinidad from earlier in the same year. The most popular songs are played continually. One hit can spring a calypsonian or a soca band or can launch them into the public eye, but might it might not be enough to sustain them. As a Calypsonian you are only as good as your current offering.

The Borokeete camp on Church Street comes into being about a month or so before Labor Day. Before the yellow tarpaulin is tied into place the mas' camp is a concrete backyard, populated by some plants, a bit of greenery, the toys of many relatives' children, a barbecue grill. But come August, roof securely overhead, work tables—scarred by many cuts of the scalpel-like utility knife—settled into place, round tables and chairs for gluing, the smell of paint, curry, shandies, rum, and beer, the yard is a camp. Into the night, every night, the work proceeds.

When I arrived I was immediately seated at a work station, introduced as the student of Carnival, and given a stack of collars to adorn with gold braid. The talk went in waves, a tide, ebbing and flowing, carrying us from topic to topic. I was told repeatedly that I could never be a masman, never understand mas' until I was "up with the morning dew," had stayed up all night. I took this to be an invitation and decided to make that great leap into "acceptance." I found myself at four in the morning utterly alone, gluing braid onto collars.

One early morning, at about three, a truck arrived carrying a shipment of large wooden dowels to be used for the standards carried by the masqueraders on Carnival day. How such a delivery was arranged remained a mystery. The sleepy driver still had other deliveries to make and slowly drifted his truck like a barge down the misty roadway, turned and headed for some other shining backyard, standing out in the Brooklyn night. I was reassured that Carnival did indeed inspire vigilance, sleeplessness, dedication.

As the season wore on the camp became more and more frantic. There simply seemed to be no time to complete all of the costumes. Registration was long over, yet people continued to try to secure costumes. Deals were made through the chain-link fence. People were turned away. Some were disappointed, they had traveled all the way from the Bronx, they said, they had been assured.... In the camp the leaders were generally unmoved. There was already too much work. I was taken on rounds to see the other, smaller camps that comprised the network of satellites revolving around this main camp. Progress was being made. People were working, for no pay, on their own time, often until very late. There were, of course, problems, especially with materials. Materials ran out quite frequently, were wasted or mishandled by the inexperienced. Glue and glue guns were at a premium. It is amazing what can take on value, inspire greed or subterfuge, and glue sticks seemed to be the object of desire at one stage, with no amount of them being enough. "You see these?" I was asked, perhaps warned, "These things are expensive and rare." Glue. I learned how to conserve glue by squeezing out a small dollop onto the fabric and then pulling it along the area where the braid would go.

I returned every year to the Pierre household, even if only for a day or two to help out and get the latest word on Carnival. What were the topics, favorite calypsos, who had been back home. In the meantime I had spent nearly a year in Trinidad and had gained a much better picture of what people were talking about when they named places, calypso tents, local politicians, and such. In 1995 a heated topic of discussion was the curfew imposed by Mayor Giuliani and the subsequent problems this posed for enjoying a true Carnival experience.

Mas' Camp Strategizing

It is in and around the mas' camp that I found that discontent about Carnival was expressed. One basic reason for this was that the mas' camp is one of few places where Trinidadians (and other West Indians) can find others who understand and care about the issue of Carnival. The other reason is that the work being performed is in the service of Carnival and so Carnival is on everyone's mind. I found that many bandleaders and masqueraders alike were dissatisfied with the way Carnival had been transformed into a parade. In the words of one longtime masman, "Carnival is not Carnival now. It is a parade. Until the administration changes its attitude toward Carnival it will deteriorate" (Davis interview 1995). Opinions, of course, were divided about Carnival. Subject position played a significant part in the opinions held, with age, gender, and class being noteworthy but not determining the response. I contrast two very different views of Carnival that arose in my discussions and suggest ways in which the ideas held and the practices engaged in by these different groups have differing and in some ways unexpected relationships to "official" discourse about Carnival.

Views from the Mas' Camp

Carnival in practice is extremely fluid. It can be "objectified" in discussion and commodified in various ways, and each of these practices attempts to secure an understanding of Carnival in an act of exchange. The casual conversation about Carnival, the interview about Carnival, the presentation of an "official" discourse on Carnival—all seek to objectify the festival in the interests of some form of interaction marked by exchange, whether it be a relatively simple exchange of information or an exchange of cultural identity for access to political power. Carnival has a dynamic form and is polysemic, which leaves it open to many kinds of objectification. A friend of mine said to me recently, "There are so many versions of Carnival; they are all equally valid."

Thus, Carnival may take place at a certain time of year and have structural features that are similar from year to year, but Carnival is nothing from year to year but the aggregation of individual experiences that happen within it. It is fleeting, personal, and immediately relevant. Very little of the actual content of Carnival endures. The songs are topical, the costumes disposable. Carnival's power for the individual is its open promise of something new and exciting but fleeting and transient. You will be allowed great joy and indulgence, but you will not be held accountable from year to year either for your actions or to recreate Carnival in any one way. Carnival seems to belong to that Caribbean "criollism" marked, as Gustavo Perez Firmat says, by its "rootless, unearthy, movable, translational rather than foundational" qualities (quoted in Harney 1996: 21). However, as Peter Minshall, the veteran and celebrated masman says, "There is something . . . liberating, about a work [a masquerade band] that sparks to brilliant life but once, to extinguish itself in the ashes of a festival that, phoenixlike, will re-emerge in the next season in new and different form" (1995: 53).

That liberation has to do with what can be imagined within Carnival. Carnival has often been linked with rituals of inversion and with the disruption of everyday hierarchies of authority. Although there is general agreement on this aspect of Carnival, there has been a traditional divergence concerning the implications of this inversion. Some, such as Mikhail Bakhtin, see inversion as a liberating and critical strategy undertaken on the part of the disempowered to attempt the disruption of the social order (1986). Others see Carnival as merely a "steam valve," an illusion of change to preserve the social order throughout the remainder of the year (Eco et al. 1984). Carnival, in this view, is ultimately repressive. Yet often these claims are made without examining the actual practices of specific people or groups of people within specific Carnival traditions. Perhaps the most satisfying treatment of actual Carnivals in this regard can be found in Roger Abrahams's work on the St. Vincent Carnival (1983). Here Abrahams dispenses with the steam-valve theory, noting that the "anti-social" behaviors of Carnival time are not necessarily restricted to that time and are often performed by the very people who are prone to that sort of behavior year round. In that sense the work also shows the inadequacy of facile "inversion" theories. What are most useful about Abrahams's insights are that they are concerned less with constructing generalizations about Carnival and more with performing close analyses of individual behavior in relation to specific Carnivals.

In my own interviews I found over and over that people were interested in either perpetuating the identities they held throughout the year or in using Carnival to assume identities that would be valorized by society. I do not claim that this has always been the case in the Trinidad Carnival. It seems much truer of the newer, middle-class Carnival and reflects that group's general preoccupation with status within the existing social order. In the older, working-class Carnival the portrayal of fantastic, splendid personas (as detailed in chapter 1) reflected the disenfranchisement of that community. In both cases, however, the masquerade offers one the chance to be seen in or to act out an idealized role. Another point of differentiation between the middle-class Carnival and the working-class Carnival is that players in the former tend to be concerned less with the actual theme of the band and more with who is playing alongside them. Thus, any sense of inversion or social transformation in Carnival in Trinidad has to be seen in relation to the specific masquerader. Let me illustrate this point with two examples. In the first example a group of young, professional, middle-class women give their reasons for joining the popular, somewhat elite band Poison. In their statements one can see the role that status plays in the middle-class Carnival and the relative lack of interest in the themes being played. In the second example an older male masmaker deplores the passing of vibrant, meaningful, and somewhat literal portrayals in favor of the new, more abstract themes of the contemporary festival. In both interviews a unique discourse about Carnival emerges; an objectification of the event. Yet these narratives are not alike, nor do they exactly mirror official discourse.

The Poison Lime

On one occasion in 1994 I had the opportunity to interview a number of women in Trinidad who routinely played in the band Poison. Poison is a large band that attracts mostly young, attractive, middle-class women and men (see below). The women, however, far outnumber the men in the band. Poison's costumes are usually very minimal, with a bikini as the basic garment. Added to this, generally, are a collar-piece of sequins and braid, a headpiece, some-

Fig. 4. Midnight robber headpiece shaped like a monument.

thing for the shins or ankles, and bands for the wrists. Masqueraders are also given a standard, which is a long wooden or fiberglass rod with some emblem attached to signify the section of the band. Poison attracts one of the largest followings, with bands in recent years swelling to over 4,000 people. That Poison is an "elite" band demonstrates the changing demographics within Carnival itself, as the average masquerader is now more likely to be a young, middle-class, perhaps suburban woman.

As with almost all the bands these days, no masqueraders actually construct their own costumes. The work is performed at the masquerade or mas' camp. The profile for the typical female Poison player articulates a whole series of social positions within Trinidad. These women are often well educated, having gone to one of the prestigious convent schools, but may not be university bound. If they are not at the University of the West Indies or at school abroad, then they are typically working in white-collar professions such as a bank or other financial institution, an insurance company, advertising agency, or marketing firm. There is also the chance that they are BWIA (British West Indies Airlines) flight attendants, a post commonly believed to have the most beautiful women.

In one respect or another none of the five women I interviewed from this band fit the typical Poison configuration. They all seemed to agree on the above criteria for Poison players, but did not include themselves entirely within that description. Some did not go to convent, did not have the right connections or the right job. All of the women mentioned that special sections were reserved within the band for the women who looked the most "with it" and that they refused registering some people in Poison, the implication being that they were too overweight or did not have the right look.[2] The special sections had separate costumes and were often featured on top of the music trucks. I asked how such women were selected and was told that "if a woman comes into the mas' camp and she looks like a Coca-Cola bottle, then ..." None of the five women were in this select group and even seemed to disparage the practice. I asked them why they had joined this band in particular. In addition to the lime (their friends were playing in Poison), they all mentioned the music. Giselle[3] noted that she had switched from another band called Hart's because the music was not as appealing, even though the costume was pretty. The music was considered better because it "got the crowd involved, they would carry on and they would get you involved." The band's role, if it is to be successful, is to provide a context in which a good lime can continue unabated for long

Fig. 5. Poison girls.

periods of time. The supreme marker of this in Poison is the fact that the group has its own theme song. Monica noted that the theme song "really sets the crowd mad, I mean you could be chipping and after you hear 'if you think that your sexy' [lyrics to the song] and people are like 'Oh God' and they start jumping up . . . that's their song."

Finally, the band Second Imij, long associated with Poison, is cited as an attraction because its lead singer Tricia Lee Kelshall embodies the ideal Poison woman. From an old and well-known Trinidadian family, she epitomizes the light-skinned (white), well-to-do, well-connected young elite that Poison would like to have as its clientele. Poison attracts these women, even as they are critical of some of the band's practices and members, because it provides them with an opportunity to see themselves as members of the most privileged group. They are allowed to celebrate their position and, it is hoped, maintain or even improve that position. There is a subtle combination of "playing yourself" and playing who it is you want to be or want to continue to be. It was agreed by all of the women that Poison had ugly costumes that year, but it was not enough to deter them from playing in the band because that was where the lime was.

Kevin "Fuzzy" Davis

Kevin Davis, or Fuzzy Davis as he is known in Carnival world, is a Carnival costume builder living in Brooklyn, New York. He lives in a comfortable two-story home in the Flatbush/East Flatbush section of Brooklyn. The kind of home he lives in has been described by Kasinitz in *Caribbean New York* as one of the many housing developments created to accommodate the thousands of West Indian immigrants who moved to that area in the 1960s and '70s. Each house is separated from the next by a long driveway at the bottom of which is a garage. The houses have yards and are nicely kept. It is a sedate and tree-lined neighborhood off of hustling Utica Avenue only a few blocks away. In addition to the dining-room and living-room furniture sets and decorations, there is a collection of tropical birds, including a "semp" from Trinidad. Its cry reminds him of afternoons back home. There is also a collection of large plants, almost a makeshift greenhouse using the front windows as a kind of solarium. Crowded together on almost every available surface in the living room are Mr. Davis's trophies from his career in Carnival. He has received awards for everything from band titles to individual titles (as has his wife for the portrayal of Carnival queens). He has received an award for his contribution to West Indian culture in the United States.

Davis is originally from the Woodbrook section of Port-of-Spain, growing up on Kitchener Street near the celebrated mas' camp of George Bailey and his brothers. ("Exactly, that's where my schooling came from, from George. I started in nineteen fifty-something, nineteen fifty-six, fifty-seven. Around there.") It is an area with a long and celebrated history in Carnival and is currently the site of the band D'Midas run by Davis's longtime friend Stephen Derek, himself an award-winning designer, bandleader, and wire-bender. Davis grew up in a barrack yard housing complex, a common living arrangement in parts of Port-of-Spain. The barrack yards were courtyards formed by low, one- or two-room apartment buildings that formed a square. The doors of the dwellings opened out into the common yard where cooking and cleaning were often done. Barrack-style houses are not nearly so prevalent as they once were.[4] Davis's family lived near George Bailey's mother. He also grew up next to Terry Evelyn, another well-known masman. Terry brought out a Fancy Indian band. Fancy Indians dress in elaborate war bonnets, some from twelve to fifteen feet high. They are covered with braid, sequins, and all manner of decorations. They are modeled after North American Indians, but taken to a fanciful extreme.[5]

In those days, recalls Davis, there were very few big bands. He started out helping with papier-mâché molds, clay molds, wire, beading, feathering, and other costuming skills. At that time many of the largest bands were those of the steelbands: Invaders, Rising Sun, and (Destination) Tokyo. Harry Basilon, Solomon Hackshaw, Terry Evelyn, and Errol Payne were some of the designers he worked with as he learned the trade. Davis himself has been in Carnival for close to forty-five years. George Bailey, one of the most celebrated of masmakers, started bringing out a section (producing one portion of the band) with the Invaders steelband. There was a dispute with the leadership, however, as often happens in Carnival mas' camps. Bailey struck out on his own and brought out Timor's Leopard Kingdom. He was an instant success. He then produced Back to Africa, which made an even bigger impression. Davis and Terry Evelyn stayed with Bailey until 1968, his last band being Fantasia. Davis subsequently left Trinidad and came to New York in 1968. The old masquerades were labor-intensive and required a wide range of skills to produce. There was metal work, in which wire was bent or copper beaten into masks, helmets, and breastplates for warriors or knights in armor. There were clay molds, which were shaped by hand, after which grease was poured over the surface. The artisan would then layer paper and cement over the mold and place it in the sun to cure. Large skull-shaped heads used in the band Back to Africa were made by this process. Chicken-wire frames are now used more commonly and wire workers such as Cito Velasquez and Geraldo Vieira have become undisputed masters of the art.

Fig. 6. Geraldo Vieira with flowers.

George Bailey's bands had from 500 to 600 people, a very large number for a fancy band at the time. His portrayals were extremely popular with the crowds as they were some of the most elaborate displays in Carnival history. Performing such themes as Merrie England, Bailey dressed his players in ermine, silk, and heavy brocade. His kings had ornate crowns and his queens majestic scepters. Yet although the fancy bands were popular, not everyone could afford such elaborate costumes, and although Bailey's bands were ample at 500, steelbands commanded numbers in the thousands. It was the steelband that dominated the road when he was younger, yet Davis had not seen a steelband on the road in years in Trinidad; especially bringing out their own mas.' For him this was a great shame (see chapter 6 for more on steelbands).

I was curious to hear Davis's opinion about the current Carnival. Having noted that the costumes were not as elaborate as they had been, he stresses that they were better done in New York, now, than they were in Trinidad. I was surprised to hear, however, that his evaluation did not rest on skill alone. It was the way the theme was brought to life by the costumes. Thus, while the theme could encompass many things, it had to make a visual impact and it had to be something people could readily identify. He is not taken with Carnival bands that have sections entitled "molasses" with some cloth and a bikini. There is no representation of molasses there. I inquired about Peter Minshall's portrayals, which were often very elaborate in construction, sometimes literal and sometimes abstract. Davis replied that for him Minshall had lost sight of what Carnival really was. Taking the position that Carnival is not about the abstract portrayal of themes but depends upon the depiction of a particular subject, he opined that costumes should be recognizable while at the same time imaginative.

The trend toward the portrayal of abstract concepts or concrete elements in an abstract manner Davis calls "commercial." He likes some of Minshall's work but tends to be attracted to those bands that have recognizable costumes. Davis feels that Carnival is about visual impact, not about a "show," which he says is for Queen's Hall (a performance venue in Port-of-Spain). He recalls the great Carnival portrayals in the past, Merrie England, Titanic, Back to Africa, and emphasizes that the spectator and the participants could see exactly what was being portrayed. The abstract or symbolic representation of good versus evil, something that Carnival artist Peter Minshall is fond of doing, is decidedly not Carnival for Davis.

But that does not mean that there is no place for the symbolic in the festival.

"Carnival has to have an element of mysticism, aligned with a supreme being, portray this anyway you want. There is a spiritual element in Carnival, masons, Kabbalah, Baptists, salt in their shoes, clove in the mouth, lavender, etc. Serious element in mas'." Although Davis does not get involved with that—he wants it to be fun—he understands the seriousness of the competition and the spiritual side of the masquerade.

Fuzzy Davis holds that the meaning of Carnival lies in the masquerade. The players' ability to inhabit a costume, to be the warrior, sailor, Indian, queen, or maiden, relies as much on the artistry of the costume as it does on the imagination of the player. The spiritual element emerges when both costume and reveler join *and* when that embodiment is successfully conveyed to an audience. There are dangers to this process. Stories abound surrounding the ill-fated efforts of George Bailey to produce a band on the relics of ancient Egypt. Workers on the project had accidents, floats disappeared; the band itself would not move on Carnival day until it was blessed by a priest. One worker who was involved with the painting of the hieroglyphics went mad and could not hold a job after Carnival. Many people attribute Bailey's death to his tampering with Egyptian mysteries. Yet at the same time, his skill as a masman created a portrayal so vibrant, so potent, that it was able to provoke the wrathful effects of ancient Egyptian curses.

The practice of defending oneself against spirits and other dangers during Carnival is directly related to the power of the masquerade to transform the masker, to remove him- or herself from the corporeal plane. That is the seriousness of a Carnival mas' well-played. This danger in masquerade recalls the Trinidadian tale of the Soucouyant, an airborne, vampiric demoness whose form of locomotion is as a ball of flame. The Soucouyant transforms into this creature from her human form by peeling off her skin and hiding it at the base of a silk cotton tree. The way to defeat the Soucouyant is to find her skin and sprinkle it with salt. The salt prevents the demon from returning to her human form, which she must do before daybreak or else die. In the early morning you can hear her crying out, asking, "Jouvay? Jou paka ouvay?" Has the day broken? In J'ouvert celebrations masqueraders dressed as Soucouyants would roam the streets in the early morning hours crying out in the same fashion. The soucouyant has a metaphorical relationship to masquerade in which there is a danger of transforming into a demon successfully—so much so that one's safe return to human form is in jeopardy. Witness the poor fellow in George Bailey's band who, Davis told me, "never returned" to sanity. What is lacking in the contemporary Carnival for Davis is any sense of the theme being portrayed. There is no concern for the masquerade, only for abstract themes. Yet while it is true that the portrayals of Davis's era have been relegated to stage shows and official parades, the act of "playing" a mas' remains albeit in a newer, altered form. The young women of Poison play their fantasies of suburbia, of being elite, of being beautiful, admired, and in the "in" crowd. They may not enter into the dangerous world of demons, spirits, and ancient legends, but they play at entering a world of material gain, luxury, and status.

Taken together the statements of these informants demonstrate the transformation of Carnival over time, from the Carnival Davis describes, at its height in the late fifties, to the Poison lime that is part of the contemporary festival. Yet what is also of interest is that the older masmaker lives and works in Brooklyn now. He is representative of the Trinidadians who left Trinidad when the working-class Carnival was still alive and of the kinds of returnees who come back to play the sailor masquerades discussed in chapter 6. Furthermore, he is much more likely to agree in principle with the government's attempts to bring back Ole Mas' or the old-time Carnival characters and traditions. The younger players, on the other hand, have very little interest in those portrayals because they have no relevance to their contemporary experiences and do not have even nostalgic value. People like Fuzzy Davis, who experienced an older Carnival and who place a value on the older masquerades as objects of potential power and resonance, are more likely to applaud the government's desire to preserve those elements within Carnival, not because the result has any power or skill but because it resonates with their understanding of what Carnival should be.

The younger, female masqueraders, however, are much more the norm than the older male or female ones. They are the ones who give Carnival its real life and the ones to whom most Carnival bandleaders must cater in order to realize a profit. Although their Carnival is decried by the guardians of culture, both in Trinidad and in New York, their actions have transformed the event. Sometimes disparagingly referred to as suburban, brown-skinned girls playing themselves, they nonetheless are the heart of the mas'. Their pursuit of the perfect lime helps to undermine the official rhetoric of Carnival. Their contribution to the "destruction" of Carnival challenges the commodification of nostalgic Carnival as national culture, even as it commercializes the event as spectacle and tourist attraction. In New York the emphasis, over and above all else, is the lime, the party, just as it is in Trinidad. In New York, as in

Trinidad, the majority of players are young women in "skimpy" costumes. Yet despite official moans about their presence and their apparent lack of concern with the presentation of "culture," their more pressing desire to socialize, reinvigorate networks, and greet friends and family means that they are the most resistant to the parade form. It is their influence that starts the parade earlier, that continues it around the streets of their neighborhoods, that eludes the official geography of the festival.

Conclusion: The Future of the Mas' Camp

Mas' camps are, of course, not the only places to hear opinions about Carnival, but they do provide a place where ideas can be aired, positions solidified, and debates argued out. The mas' camp does not produce consensus, but it does foster discussion of issues that often come to it from the outside. In the case of the paradification issue, discussion centered on how to keep Carnival going outside of the parade route. Those concerns come directly from the priorities for Carnival held by participants such as the women from Poison. Similarly, Fuzzy Davis's attitudes about the decay of Carnival, aired in his home/workshop, generate actions that, as we shall see in chapter 6, partly support forms of official discourse.

The mas' camp has recently, but only slightly, become part of the city's view of Carnival culture. There has been talk of including the camps on walking tours of West Indian Brooklyn, and simulated mas' camps have also been established in the Brooklyn Museum. What effect this will have on the production of Carnival remains to be seen. But the impulse to objectify the mas' camps is part of the larger culturalist enterprise in which features of ethnic or national culture are increasingly commodified. Yet commodification does not necessarily mean the end of "culture" unless we consider culture to be somehow compromised by any and all involvement with situations of exchange in the capitalist sense. However, using the notion of culturalism I have proposed—following Appadurai—whose definition emphasizes the presentation of identity for political purposes (1996: 14), we end up broadening our understanding of the exchange process. For once culture and identity are expressed in order to gain something, such as recognition, we must include them as examples of exchange, albeit for other forms of capital. I propose that commodification is only one step in a process that leads to forms of cultural negotiation. The results of such negotiations will be covered in the last two chapters.

Culturalisms also have their place in identity politics. In chapter 2 I described the historical development of Carnival in Brooklyn and suggested that the festival has played a role in the politics of recognition in New York. In the next chapter I provided a detailed example of this phenomenon, setting the Crown Heights disturbances of 1991 against the backdrop of New York's ethnic political structure.

4

Bureaucratic Multiculturalism and West Indian American Day

Becoming a Tile in the Gorgeous Mosaic

> Identity—it's a psychic sense of place.... And it's a way of knowing that no matter where I put myself, that I am not necessarily what's around me. I am part of my surroundings and I become separate from them and it's being able to make those differentiations clearly that lets us have an identity.
>
> Ntozake Shange, *Fires in the Mirror*

> Ethnic identity and difference are socially produced in the here and now, not archeologically salvaged from the disappearing past.
>
> M. P. Smith, "Postmodernism, Urban Ethnography and the New Social Space of Ethnic Identity"

On Labor Day 1991, the motorcade of the Grand Rebbe Menachem Schneerson pulled out of the World Headquarters of the Lubavitcher Hasidic sect on Eastern Parkway in Brooklyn, New York. The car was mobbed by throngs of well-wishers and supporters eager to get a glimpse of the man thought by some Lubavitchers to be the Messiah himself. An unmarked police vehicle led the Rebbe's car as it attempted to make its way to a cemetery in Queens where the Rebbe's wife and father-in-law are buried. Suddenly the motorcade jerked to a halt. Towering over the cars, swaying lightly in the breeze, were the sun and the moon.

The sun and the moon, in this case, were two masqueraders from the West Indian American Day Parade. The impasse was reported in the *New York Times*, a symbolic moment that capped a two-week period of ethnic violence and tension between the West Indian and the Lubavitcher Hasidic communities in the Crown Heights section of Brooklyn.

This chapter traces the events of this two-week period in 1991, with special emphasis placed on the role the Brooklyn Carnival played in the aftermath. As I have noted, Carnival has long been a point of tension between the Hasidic community (especially the Lubavitcher sect) and the Caribbean population. The leaders of the Hasidim had complained of difficulties in celebrating their holidays when Carnival was being held. They had petitioned frequently for a change in the venue, a change of the dates, and even the cancellation of the festival. The West Indians, the vast majority in the area, had frequently complained of the preferential treatment given to the Hasidim by the city of New York. Their leaders were given police escorts, special parking was made available, and in general, it was claimed, they had a greater influence on the city council than their numbers would merit.

The events of late summer 1991 provide a context within which to examine the relationship not only between these two communities specifically but between the "ethnic performance" of a transmigrant community and the structure of a kind of "ethnicity" or "identity politics" in New York. As this chapter will show, the very way in which Carnival becomes positioned within the city's political-economic framework is in part determined by the expectation that participants be fully determined as "ethnic" to be considered within that framework. That is, Carnival, especially to those in leadership positions within Carnival's administration as well as members of the Caribbean cultural and political elite, takes on a new significance that is in part determined by the city's attitude toward events like Carnival.

Identity politics cannot be completely divorced from other kinds of political activity, of course, and this chapter will highlight some of the ways Carnival, which makes West Indian "culture" explicit and publicly available, serves as a kind of magnet for city politicians who can recognize the community as a significant player in city politics. The ethos that informs city politics in New York is here exemplified by a phrase used by former mayor David Dinkins when he described the city's multiple ethnic groups as forming a "gorgeous mosaic." The mosaic image is more than a colorful piece of speech making. As a rhetorical device it speaks to the heart of a political philosophy that sees the city divided into marked and bounded cultural territories that city administrators must negotiate, especially with regard to the allocation of resources.

Thus, the outcome of Carnival of 1991 was of dire importance, because it was something of a test case for the possibility of the West Indian community's political success. If it could come off without more ethnic violence then it could remain a positive symbol of West Indian solidarity and commitment to peace. If it disintegrated into more violence, it was feared that the festival would lose any of the political clout it had gained painstakingly over the years.

These were, it must be stressed, primarily the concerns of local Caribbean leaders, many of whom see the event as a legitimator of what they perceive as their "largely invisible community" (*New York Times*, Aug. 30, 1991: B-1; see also Bryce-Laporte 1972). For these leaders Carnival plays an important role in their bid for a share in the city's ethnically based political and economic spoils exemplified by such bodies as the mayor's Ethnic Advisory Council, which was responsible for community grants and other aid to communities.[1] I will demonstrate, however, that what is known in anthropology as a "resource competition" model of ethnicity is largely imposed upon the community through the contextualization of the festival vis-à-vis other groups and their relationships to city hall.

The Discourse of Bureaucratic Multiculturalism

Part of what I want to discuss here is the special emphasis on a universalized discourse of culture and cultural models that both the city administration and the culture brokers mobilize within the ethnic politics of the city of New York. Such models of culture emerge from a generalized idea of culture, which requires that an ethnic or national group have clearly identifiable, bounded, and marked cultural features in order to (a) prove their ethnicity and (b) take part in the kind of ethnic spoils system institutionalized in New York through, for instance, the Mayor's Ethnic Advisory Council. In short, I want to look at the impact that the politics of recognition has on Carnival. As Linda Basch has written, "Ethnic structuring in New York City ... focuses attention on ethnicity and encourages groups to organize around and thus reproduce their ethnicity" (Basch 1987: 173). My contention here, partly in keeping with the work of Brackette Williams (1991), is that ethnicity is not itself a preexisting social fact or positivity into which groups retreat or to which they latch on for political reasons, given the right circumstances. Such a position implies that ethnicity is already "out there." I feel it is more accurate to say that the nature or the shape of ethnicity is, at least in part, determined by frameworks imposed upon a group through a dominant discourse of what ethnicity is (not to mention the geographical restraints imposed upon ethnic groups across the city's terrain). The model at work in New York, which I will call "bureaucratic multiculturalism," imposes restrictions upon the practice of Carnival and the Carnival experience while helping to restructure the form itself. Bureaucratic multiculturalism operates within the general ideology of the politics of recognition but adds to this the dimension of social control. By employing a universal model of culture the city facilitates its ability to administer to diverse populations within its borders.

The nature of this universal cultural model is that it privileges bounded, expressive cultural forms especially those that are "familiar." Thus cuisine, music, marriage and kinship patterns, festivals and celebrations all become signposts for recognizing Otherness, for familiarizing difference. Such cultural signposts, especially festivals, need to take a manifest form that is readily understood and manageable by the city. The city shapes ethnicities, which are represented by agents concerned with the kind of culturalisms mentioned previously in chapter 2.

A recent example of the rhetoric of such city policies can be found in the language former mayor Dinkins used when describing the city as a "gorgeous mosaic." The metaphor is apt in many ways and speaks to an underlying assumption about ethnicity held by city administrators. This assumption sees ethnic groups as "tiles" held in place, in neat juxtaposition to each other, set apart by clear boundaries, distinguished by different colors, and forming a unified and harmonious whole. The mosaic's wholeness depends on the stasis of the tiles and their colors remaining constant. More concretely, inasmuch as each tile represents a distinct ethnicity, their legitimacy depends on their being neatly separated and historically and culturally static. That is, it becomes difficult to recognize a cultural group whose cultural forms change over time. Furthermore, each "tile" must be clearly demarcated by its color—that is, Irish versus West Indian versus Jewish, for example, but categorically the same as tiles/ethnic groups. Along with rhetoric, administrative bureaus such as the Mayor's Ethnic Advisory Council reward ethnic groups that can represent themselves as legitimate and therefore worthy of grants and other funding and special services. In order to determine who gets these benefits the council must rely on who fits the model of a genuine ethnic group, and leaders of communities must represent themselves along ethnic parameters. It is this group of locally elected officials, journalists, and cultural leaders who stand to benefit from city patronage that I have referred to as culture brokers. This policy is what I mean by bureaucratic multiculturalism, and its yield is culturalisms such as Carnival.

The Crown Heights Incident of 1991

On the evening of August 19, 1991, the motorcade of Menachem Schneerson was heading out along Utica Avenue on its way to the cemetery for his weekly visit to the grave of his wife and father-in-law.[2] Passing across President Street, the car rushing to bring up the rear of the motorcade allegedly went late through the intersection, was sideswiped, jumped a curb, and killed Gavin Cato, the seven-year-old son of a Guyanese immigrant and injured Cato's seven-year-old cousin, Angela. A crowd of local African Americans and Caribbean Americans soon surrounded the vehicles. Yosef Lifsh, the twenty-two-year-old driver of the car, got out, he claimed, to help the children. He was immediately set upon, beaten, and allegedly robbed. The police arrived and a few minutes later a private ambulance from a Hasidic company rushed into view. The police hustled Lifsh into the Hasidic ambulance—for his own protection, as they later stressed—and, as the van raced from the scene, a city ambulance came to care for the children. The crowd perceived this as yet another example of members of the Jewish community getting preferential treatment. The crowd became angry, then violent. In addition to setting upon Lifsh, the crowd attacked the Hasidic ambulance drivers and the police. The crowd grew thicker as people emerged from a nearby B. B. King concert. Within a few hours there were reports of looting and general destruction of property. Members of the local media were assaulted as they tried to photograph the scenes of violence. Three hours after the accident a gang of approximately twenty black youths attacked Yankel Rosenbaum, an Australian student conducting research in New York. Rosenbaum, not a Lubavitcher but an ultra-Orthodox Jew, was stabbed. Police rushed to his aid and the gang of youths scattered. The authorities apprehended Lemerick Nelson and, after finding a bloody knife and three bloodstained one-dollar bills, brought him to a local precinct where he allegedly confessed to the stabbing. He was later acquitted. Rosenbaum was taken to a hospital where two of his wounds were treated. A third wound went unnoticed and he bled to death.

Over the next three days a storm of protest and devastation raged across Crown Heights. Crowds of African American protesters stood outside the Lubavitcher world headquarters and shouted anti-Semitic slogans such as "Hitler didn't do his job."[3] The violence would have seemed extreme if it were based solely on the accident that killed Gavin Cato. However, the long history of smoldering animosity between the two groups contributed greatly to the magnitude of the ensuing clash of that week in August 1991. Perhaps the greatest contribution to the tension between the groups was that West Indians traditionally believed the city to be more responsive to the needs of the Jewish community than to their own. A report in the *New Yorker* magazine explained some of the West Indian grievances toward Hasidic Jews (Logan 1991). Chief among these was the desire of Lubavitchers to live as close to the Rebbe as possible. Lubavitchers often tried to secure homes for their families by pressuring their black Caribbean neighbors to sell out. The Hasidim also had a reputation for being clannish, even to other Jews, and they continue to operate their own private, heavily armed security forces.

Jews and West Indians in Crown Heights

The Lubavitcher sect of Orthodox Jews, founded in the mid-eighteenth century, moved almost en masse to Crown Heights from Poland in 1940. At the time the neighborhood was largely Eastern European Jewish and Italian. The massive migration of West Indian blacks began in the early 1950s and increased steadily through the 1960s. "White flight" marked the 1970s in Brooklyn, with the exception of the Hasidim. Within a relatively short span of time, Crown Heights, and the adjacent Flatbush and East Flatbush sections of Brooklyn, became largely African West Indian enclaves. West Indians, who in the earliest migrations had settled in traditionally black neighborhoods such as Harlem, now avoided such areas. There may be several reasons for this, including an aversion to what was perceived as ghetto living and, as Kasinitz has pointed out, architecture (1992: 57–58). The areas most preferred by the new West Indian immigrant populations offered small family homes for purchase rather than rentals from unscrupulous landlords. The purchase of homes by West Indians was often what ensured the capital base to provide for their children and the accumulation of more capital (Kasinitz 1992: 58).

As the core Caribbean population has grown in Brooklyn, so have the external manifestations of this new "ethnic" presence. Now comprising approximately 300,000 people in this area alone, the main market strips along Flatbush Avenue, Utica Avenue, and other streets have developed a strong Caribbean quality. As mentioned, roti shops, Caribbean music shops, travel agencies run by and for West Indians, and markets with West Indian goods are now common sights. The centerpiece of this strong cultural presence in Brooklyn is the West Indian American Day Parade. This great flowering of the West Indian community surrounds the Lubavitchers almost entirely. For the greater part of the history of these two communities, there has been a general acceptance of and peace between neighbors. Disputes have often been handled by local community boards, the Bureau of Ethnic Affairs or other bodies established by the city in conjunction with local leaders.

Reconstructing Carnival in Brooklyn

The parade-like route of Carnival is one restriction that Brooklyn West Indians have had to work with. However, the leadership of Carnival, the West Indian American Day Carnival Association (WIADCA), has always stressed their desire to try to avoid the parade feeling to which such structured routes contribute. They have tried to approximate not just the Parade of the Bands, as it is called in Trinidad, but the whole complex of Carnival activities that make up the four main days of Carnival. Toward this end they have reassembled the various parts of the Trinidad Carnival in New York. There is a Panorama Steelband competition, a Dimanche Gras competition in which the elaborate Kings and Queens of Carnival vie for prizes, and a Calypso Monarch competition. Perhaps the most impressive element in the Brooklyn Carnival is the J'ouvert. It is the most unrestrained and purely ecstatic part of Carnival in Trinidad, and it has managed to flourish and grow in Brooklyn with the general cooperation of the police and the city.

The many facets of Carnival mean that it is not merely a parade or an ethnic showcase. Much of what happens is not directed outward but inward, toward the community. Carnival spans most of Labor Day weekend, culminating on Labor Day itself. The day of the parade of the bands is obviously the most visible feature of Carnival, and it is here that the event comes closest to being an ethnic parade. Within the community the participation in and enthusiasm for the event are enormous and wide-ranging, cutting across national boundaries and class divisions. It is cited by many as the "centerpiece" of West Indian identity in New York City. It is the one major occasion during which Caribbean peoples, especially from the English-speaking regions but also including Haitians, Martinicans, and others, pronounce their significant presence in the city. The unique position of Carnival as a forum for the presentation of ethnicity, along with the growing size of the Caribbean community, has ensured that Carnival will become the focus of intense political activity. Of the many different types of political activity that surround Carnival, the one that draws our attention in this chapter is the role of the festival in the complex arena of identity politics. As mentioned, by the middle of the 1980s both Carnival and the community were attracting serious attention from city politicians. The West

Indian vote could no longer be ignored, and the event and the community were established as permanent fixtures in the city's ethnic array.[4]

Resource Competition and Ethnicity: Some Background

The literature on ethnicity in anthropology was for some time dominated by the resource competition model (Despres 1975; B. Williams 1990; Eriksen 1993). This position holds, at one level, that a kind of political ethnicity results when disempowered groups create informal, culturally based associations in order to participate to greater effect in the political-economic process of the larger political unit (especially the nation-state). Resource competition as a way of explaining ethnicity certainly has had advantages. Chief among its contributions to understanding ethnicity, the resource competition model encourages scholars to abandon primordialist conceptions of ethnicity and distances the relationship between ethnic identity and culture.[5] In this regard we might see it as related to, but not identical with, some of the same theoretical impulses that spawned anti-essentialist, "invention of tradition" works in that all of these trajectories share a desire to separate identity from primordial, essentialist, bounded, cultural traits. Furthermore, by calling into question primordial identities, resource competition requires us to situate ethnic identity squarely in the realm of human activity. "Definitions [of ethnicity] based on notions of shared culture wrongly imply that the maintenance of ethnic boundaries is unproblematic" (Eriksen 1993: 37). Thus the task of the social scientist is to explain the *processes* of ethnic identity formation. In some cases, as in the invention-of-tradition literature (see especially Hobsbawm and Ranger 1983), advancing an anti-essentialist agenda means seeing group identity as the product of the actions only of the powerful or elite. The "process of ethnic identity formation" in these cases is the processes of self-conscious, possibly cynical, construction.

In place of culture, then, the resource competition model substitutes political economy. By focusing on ethnicity as the product of political/social relationships, the resource competition model highlights what Frederik Barth calls "boundary maintenance" between ethnic groups (Barth 1969). That is, ethnic groups exist in relation to other groups in situations where select differences are brought to bear meaningfully in/for political action. Abner Cohen's work on ethnicity emphasized the organizational dimension of ethnicity (Cohen 1974). Cohen acknowledges the meaningful side of ethnicity, that is, its capability of explaining a group's origins and its deepest shared values, yet none of these issues becomes really salient without the political side of things. Despres's work in Guyana expands on Barth and Cohen by adding that any understanding of interpersonal cross-cultural relationships in a multi-ethnic society will have to take into account the institutional framework of the society (Despres 1975). It is only here that one can begin to understand how and to what degree ethnic identity is communicated or acted upon in any given situation.

Williams notes that such theorists failed to take into account the larger ideological foundations upon which the nation-state is based and therefore missed important elements that would determine the structure of "ethnic" associations. Williams also points out that resource competition models fail to address the presence of nonethnic resource competition groups. She indicates that resource competition models do not "address the knotty question of how individuals or even immigrant cultural groups identify and rank their interests" (1989: 409). And to this I would add that such models do not seem concerned about the kinds of interests such groups might identify. In other words, resource competition does not fully explain "ethnicity" if it foregrounds economic interests over cultural ones. It does not always demonstrate the relationship between economic necessity and the social construction of a cultural group. For example, does the charge that Hasidim in Crown Heights get special treatment on holy days speak to their successes with economic or cultural benefits? It seems clear that the two are intertwined. The question is: why should this be the case? For if it is true that the presentation of a distinct ethnic identity tends to yield greater access to goods and services within New York City, then the presentation of ethnicity must operate at both cultural and economic levels simultaneously. What both of these things have in common, however, is a sense of ethnicity as self-conscious difference.

Culture and Ethnicity in West Indian Brooklyn

It is largely the perception of the West Indian community, as expressed through its cultural and political leaders as well as through its editorial pages,[6] that a responsibly presented West Indian identity—through Carnival and the increase of voter registration and political participation—will lead to a much more advantageous position for West Indians within the city's ethno-political hierarchy. In that regard, a self-conscious understanding of the power, if not the constructed nature, of ethnicity is routinely made manifest. As an editorial comment in a widely read Caribbean travel magazine stated, "The single thing that unites West Indians in this country is our Carnivals. Our leaders must now use the leverage provided by these circumstances to build and consolidate our political muscle and agenda. No more nice guys." In a thinly veiled reference to the Hasidim the editorial continues, "Our lesson can be well learned from the very people who annually threaten this event. Politics and only politics is the means by which 4 percent can dictate to 96 percent" (*SYGTC* 1995: 95).

The imploring quality of this editorial is echoed by other publications. Carlos Lezama, president of WIADCA, has written that a sense of community is "critical to us in maintaining our existence within the wider sphere of other ethnic groups" (cited in Kasinitz 1992: 149). A major factor in the under-representation of West Indians in New York City politics has been the lack of voters registered from West Indian backgrounds. Although Una Clarke, a city council member originally from Jamaica, states that one-third of all recently naturalized citizens are Caribbean and that a greater number of Caribbeans are participating in the electoral process, the nature of the Caribbean community may still be called transnational in a very specific sense. From 1965 to 1975 the Caribbean population in New York doubled. Although the size of the population increased the concerns of the immigrants, most tended to stay focused on their home countries. Frequent trips home, remittances, and retirement to the Caribbean prevented many from investing both mentally and physically (if not financially) in their adopted country.

The events surrounding the Crown Heights unrest of 1991 brought into relief many of the issues outlined above for local Caribbean leaders and activists. The highly organized and seemingly coherent Lubavitcher community stood in contrast to what was criticized as the loosely organized, under-represented, and politically apathetic West Indian community. The culturally coherent Lubavitchers could rally around their undisputed leader, the Grand Rebbe Schneerson, while the West Indian community was fractured along nationality lines and, within the larger black populace, ethnicity lines (i.e., American versus West Indian). This view of a unified Jewish front is not completely accurate because within the spectrum of ultra-Orthodox and Hasidic groups there are a number of important distinctions and divisions. On the other hand, many of these distinctions seem to lessen when the general group is faced with "outside" pressure.

Let us return, then, to our previous dilemma—namely, how do we understand the limitations of the resource competition model of ethnicity in a situation that seems to support such models? The benefits bestowed upon ethnic groups in New York are largely dependent upon the ability of the collectivity to prove its status as a "group." The government of New York has, like much of the rest of the country, responded to pressure to "maintain and preserve" ethnic heritages in the implementation of state and federal programs. Bilingual education, access to city services, and influence in city decision-making are examples of "rewards" available to the visible ethnic groups. There is no better way to become "visible" than through conspicuous displays of culture. It is the manipulation of overt cultural features that end up being the signposts of a viable ethnicity. What emerges, then, is a situation in which ethnic groups petition, in one way or another, for recognition by the city until they are considered sufficiently "ethnic" enough to be legitimate. The result is that recognition becomes a city service in itself. Culture/ethnicity becomes something that the city has within its power to bestow. In this sense there seem to be a number of "culture-criteria" to which groups must in some way conform. I am not making the argument that the fulfillment of these criteria in the public sector necessarily reflects on actual practice. Often practice is ignored or downplayed when it runs contrary to the kinds of official culture promoted by a group's own spokespeople. Innovation, assimilation, and the creative manipulation of cultural forms in the immigrant setting are often frowned upon by representatives of the ethnic group because it creates the illusion of there being no culture there at all. Yet it is exactly such manipulation that keeps the cultural form alive and relevant to the majority of practitioners.[7] Thus, changes made to Carnival are always contested for many different reasons.

It is here that Williams is again useful. She stresses that one ignores the larger ideological underpinnings of the state (or in this case the city) at one's peril. In the case of New York, the power structure rewards cultural presence in digestible forms such as ethnic parades. The importance of Carnival to the West Indian community lies in its ability to impart ethnicity to West Indians. Their own public comments on Carnival begin to revolve around the festival's power to confer political clout on the group. Although other factors are present in many individual West Indian's descriptions of the value of the event, public rhetoric is shaped by the ideological constraints of the larger polity. It is ultimately the city that is imposing a resource competition model upon the "gorgeous mosaic" of New York. The successful accomplishment of this ethnicity bestowal requires the active compliance of leaders within the West Indian community.

The importance, then of the West Indian Carnival's survival is clear. Although Carnival is not easily pressed into the service of political agendas (of which more later), it remains a visible act of expression by a large group of West Indians and therefore is the perfect location for the superimposition of identity rhetoric. It is possible to suggest at this point that Carnival is not really the fount of West Indian identity in New York, but rather that West Indian identity is required of, laid over, the festival. However, this too would be overly deterministic. The idea of Carnival as being a source of Caribbean identity, as an expression of Caribbean culture, ultimately shapes the way in which Carnival is organized and the manner into which it is entered by participants. The rhetoric does not just hover over the event. To the degree to which it has influence over individuals, it helps shape the event as well.

It is also clear that Carnival's survival after the Crown Heights disturbances began to rest heavily on its ability to "patch things up." The great unifying potential of Carnival was finally put to the test. Two weeks after Crown Heights, leaders of the Lubavitcher community were asked to march as guests of the West Indian American Day Carnival Association as a sign of goodwill. Carnival went off peacefully. In the wake of the event, both sides promoted efforts to contribute to greater cultural understanding between the two groups. In 1994 Carnival fell on Rosh Hashanah. As part of the ongoing efforts by both groups to avoid conflicts of the same magnitude, various meetings and symposia were organized.[8]

Also in 1994 a Korean cultural group was asked to join the parade in the wake of conflicts between West Indians and Korean grocers. The case of the Jewish, the Korean, and even the African American community within Carnival illustrates the precarious position that the festival plays in relation to West Indian identity production/reproduction and the resolution of local ethnic conflict. On the one hand Carnival is a Trinidadian–become–West Indian affair, meant, at one level, to serve as a way of bringing together different members of the West Indian community and providing an "authentic" cultural event, an ethnic display event. It also wants to be, in the mind of Carlos Lezama, its chief organizer, a way to build bridges to other communities such as African Americans (most importantly), Jews, and Koreans.[9] Other active members of the West Indian community have noted the economic benefits Carnival has for the city. But as stated above, for most of these benefits to emerge from the event it has to be a West Indian affair. Most of the money spent by spectators, be they tourists or city dwellers, West Indian or not, is to experience not just a parade or a festival but a West Indian festival.

The resource competition model, coupled with a multiculturalist ethos, together dominate the raison d'être of Carnival for some of its organizers, leading some Caribbean leaders to carry with them the burden of requiring cultural "purity." The event must continue to be "we thing," as many Trinidadians say, while at the same time not provoking animosity from other groups. It is difficult terrain to negotiate, because actions of ethnic groups are often perceived to be exclusive and can have divisive repercussions, while, on the other hand, fluid cultural boundaries can give the appearance of an intangible or weak cultural presence. It would seem the "gorgeous mosaic" ideology of Mayor Dinkins's administration has been a catalyst to strict sectarianism amongst the city's ethnic groups, albeit inadvertently, even as it stressed multiculturalism.

The relationship between a notion of identity as a means to an economic and political end and Mayor Dinkins's provocative metaphor of the "gorgeous mosaic" ends up being of key interest here. The mayor is clearly avoiding the problematic metaphors of the past to describe the coexistence of many cultural groups together under one administrative unit. That is, the "melting pot," "salad," and "stew" metaphors all have come under fire for their various descriptive shortcomings. The mosaic has the advantage, presumably, of emphasizing the importance and beauty of cultural difference as each culture adds to an overall, unified "picture" that, upon "stepping back," is fully revealed. The mosaic metaphor implies the presence of neatly defined "tiles" placed cheek by jowl in the service of a grander order that no one tile may accomplish alone. The interesting aspect of this metaphor, as opposed to the others I have mentioned above, is its unique emphasis on spatiality and, what is more, its reification of those spaces. In the mosaic tiles have special places reserved for them, in positions firm and fixed. It is the perfect metaphor for the kinds of essentialized identities required by an administrative bureaucracy such as New York City's that allots goods and services upon the basis of ethnic identity.

Stasis and Identity Politics

The current literature exploring space and identity is growing with great rapidity (e.g., see Keith and Pile 1993; Lash and Friedman 1992). Doreen Massey (1993) has contended that prevailing implicit or explicit dichotomies of space and time are inadequate. She claims that temporal metaphors and temporality in general have been given precedence over spatial metaphors and spatiality.

Furthermore, time has been defined at the expense of space, as presence to space's absence. Space has been generally conceived of as stasis and temporality as progress, with the possibility of an emancipatory politics being privileged in the temporal realm.

In New York the mosaic metaphor resonates with the idea of space as stasis. City policies are reflected in this metaphor in the sense that New York distributes it goods and services based largely upon ethnicity. The mosaic metaphor implies that a governable ethnic population is dependent upon recognition and therefore upon static principles. The metaphor seems to elicit comfort in the same way that city planning in other contexts does. The comfort of the grid, of numbers intersecting, of places conforming to a predictable pattern is constantly threatened by the pirating of public or private spaces by the unruly minions of disorder. The ethnic group, moving into a space and transforming that space into a usable living space—into a place, if you will—potentially undermines the authority of the metropole at large. The mosaic gives the impression that all is in order, static, easy to locate. What constantly belies this image is the relationship of the "tiles" in the system. If the system is meant to impart "presence" or give definition to identity only in relation to others, then such a system equally depends upon a notion of reified ethnic identities that persist through time, which fundamentally cannot change or else risk becoming meaningless. The mosaic requires tiles that not only sit in their assigned places but do not change color, as it were. That is, the "tiles" do not change what is perceived to be their fundamental character, their essence.

But the West Indian community is not marked by "cultural" attributes over which it has no power. The West Indian community is made up of individuals who must have an active relationship to their "culture." Caribbean culture exists in New York because people make it so. But the actions of these many thousands of individuals, whether it be in Carnival or kinship relations, are not necessarily the same as what various interested parties claim those actions represent. Anthropologists may be sensitive to praxis and the performance of culture, but the city of New York and the various culture brokers and leaders of the Caribbean population cannot found a relationship on the uncertainties inherent in praxis-oriented approaches to culture. Such approaches de-essentialize culture, and that makes the mosaic fuzzy.

In many ways Carnival's peacemaking role lends legitimacy to Caribbean leadership. It signals the presence of a responsible, coherent West Indian community, and it indicates that West Indian identity exists without being a threat to the social order. These are essential qualities in becoming a tile. But there exists a tension in the constant shifts and changes that occur every year in the way in which Carnival is actually undertaken.

How, then, do we theorize the relationship between city policy and the shaping of ethnic identity? "Identity" in this case is predicated on the official recognition of who one is in relation to who one is not. It is, therefore, a determination based upon principles of differentiation that all groups must share. In that sense it must be done through the close examination of a series of features or a checklist of characteristics. The features utilized in the construction would conform, categorically, to some more universal or absolute model of what it means to be an ethnic group, such as dances, festivals, costumes, and cuisine. These criteria would hold true for all groups purporting to have separate identities, for example Dominicans, Irish, and Jewish. Furthermore, in determining the "true" nature of an ethnic group there must be "authentic" ways of doing things as opposed to inauthentic ones. There is then a sense of "we don't do it (cook, worship, marry, sing) that way, we do it this way." The authority to determine authenticity is one of the goals of culture brokerage.

By way of example, consider an incident that occurred in 1993 as I was preparing to go to Trinidad for fieldwork. I had been conducting research in Brooklyn, visiting mas' camps, taping interviews, and helping to make mas' when I found myself in discussion with Ray Morris, a member of the Borokeete USA organization. I was operating a power saw and carving the blade through Styrofoam in order to create the headpieces worn by masqueraders on Carnival day. We began to discuss Carnival. I made the mistake of calling the event a "parade," and my informant corrected me. In making the distinction for me he told me that Carnival was really what the festival was, but a parade was the name the city used: "The Trini name is Carnival. It's not like a parade, but all the Irish and Puerto Ricans and such make parade. The city likes the parade, but we are Trini. Carnival in Trinidad is not like so, with one street. It is all over, you will see. It used to be that way here, but you wouldn't find that again." I asked him what he saw as the difference between Carnival and a parade: "Anybody can do a parade. Look at all the parades in this town. Everyday is a parade. Only Trinis can do Carnival. Is we ting. Everywhere there is Carnival? There is a Trini. From the sky Trinidad looks like a little nothing, when you flying over it, but we can do Carnival, man. There would have to be a Trinidadian in charge for it to be Carnival" (Morris interview 1993). Another man working nearby added that he thought too many outsiders were involved now. He looked right at me and in a very pointed manner said, if "you people get a hold of Carnival it will be gone."

These statements belie a feeling that Carnival is something uniquely Trinidadian and yet something that can be taken over or "stolen." It is something that only Trinidadians can do, but something that exists independently of their doing it. Here we find the chief contradiction inherent in the "culture" as thing discourse that derives from politico-institutional sources. For as long as culture is perceived as a thing made up from an amalgamation of other things such as expressive forms, the actual practice of the event, even if done by Trinidadians, will run the risk of seeming illegitimate as long as such practices involve changing the event. The strategies available to the culture broker, then, include the promotion of nostalgic forms through museum exhibits and old-time Carnival shows and competitions or the staging of alternative Carnivals, such as the Manhattan Basin Festival, in which contemporary Carnival is showcased as a giant party. The latter strategy, we have seen, generally fails. The former strategy, as will become evident, may succeed.

Ideas of difference, whether they belong to negative ideologies such as racism or "positive ideologies" such as multiculturalism, emerge in conjunction with the development of a theory of a universalized human subjectivity.[10] These categories, however, are frequently made to appear natural in the discourse of culture. To my mind they help organize a kind of stereotyping of cultures frequently engaged in between nation-states or, on the smaller scale, between city administrators and ethnic groups. The subject of the naturalization of constructed ethnicity is a difficult one and has been taken up elsewhere,[11] but it raises the important issue of the role of the imagination in the "imagined community" and of invention in the "invention of tradition."[12] That the analyst can adequately assess or pronounce that certain traditions, practices, or basic features of a group's ethnic identity are constructions is frequently irksome to those members of the community who see their ability to speak for that community once again being undermined by outsiders. I return to this discussion below.

The Politics of Recognition

The treatment of cultural forms and ethnic boundaries as ossified acts as a kind of fetishization in the service of bureaucratic control, in what might be called the management of difference. This leads one to ask: how is it that culturalisms arise under multicultural bureaucratization? Back to Carnival. Recently Mayor Giuliani enacted a 6:00 P.M. curfew on the parade in order to keep the bands moving at an even more rapid pace. The curfew effectively limits the time one can spend, as a masquerader, on the road. Joining a band, which is expensive, becomes a waste of money for the amount of time one gets to enjoy oneself on the Parkway. These new restrictions on the Parade's form also prevent the bands from stopping and restrict the ability for old friends to find each other, socialize, and "play mas'." These restrictions, imposed both for ease of policing and for their likeness to other ethnic display events within the city (such as the Puerto Rican Day Parade or the St. Patrick's Day Parade), transform the festival itself, not because they limit Carnival in certain ways (Carnival has long been called a parade and there have always been limits) but because the city has taken further steps to impose a recognizable structure on the event that renders it available as both a marker of identity and as a forum for political activity.

Conclusion

Carnival has a role in the actual day-to-day life of specific members of the community at large. This means that individuals are at work, changing their perceptions and practices in relation to new circumstances that confront them. In the previous chapter I demonstrated how this quality threatens the required "authenticity" and exclusivity upon which solid "ethnicities" may be built. Future research into Caribbean cultural change in diaspora must take into account the different pressures cultural forms negotiate as a clue to the processes of change the forms themselves undergo. These changes radically reflect the conditions of power within which the transmigrants themselves must exist, but they also illustrate responses to those forms of power that contribute to the shifting terrain on which the transnation must try to found itself. Using the conception of ethnicity as public culture within the constraints of particular social structures and contexts, we are able to see Carnival in the service of public cultural agendas.

5

Bringing It All Back Home

The Carnival King and Queen of the World Competition

> The world will say: Trinidad and Tobago is a place to visit; Trinidad and Tobago's Carnival is the most enjoyable Carnival anywhere; and Trinidad and Tobago is a country to buy things from. From regular goods and services to the full range of our art, crafts and our cultural skills.
>
> *Trinidad Guardian*, June 7, 1994

The next two chapters have as their focus the commodification of culture in the service of nationalism. I use two case studies of the state's attempt to commodify and "sell" culture; one that is successful and one that is not. In chapter 1, I traced the long relationship that the middle class and the state have enjoyed with Carnival and the image of Carnival they have tried to promote. At the center of this vision of national culture is a complex of highly visible, "recognizable" cultural "products" that, in keeping with an economic/state philosophy, can be controlled, coordinated, marketed—in short, easily manipulated for presentation on a global scale. However, in this first case study I will not be focusing primarily on the construction of nationalist culture per se but on what we might call a viable nationalism, a nationalism that works for the state. As Ernesto Laclau points out, a nationalist identity promoted by a ruling or dominant group must "show its ability to become a realistic alternative for the organization and management of the community" (1994: 16). In other words, in producing an objectified national culture the state must successfully present itself as the logical and natural administrator of that culture—not as its originator, but as its champion.

In Trinidad the state has taken to using a strategy of commodification. State agencies, culture brokers, and entrepreneurs have enthusiastically embraced this approach for different reasons, as detailed below. Caught up in this enter-

prise are Carnival costume makers, especially those who have long been involved in the production of costumes for Carnivals abroad. Their work has
been seized upon as a vital part of the commodification, promotion, and sale
agenda. I will suggest that control over national culture has followed a strategy
of commodification that objectifies cultural forms for the purpose of manipu-
lating their activities in a marketplace of culture, something that reinforces and
legitimates the sovereignty of the state. I conclude, however, that such attempts
are not always successful when they do not take into account the cultural narratives and expectations already at work in the society. Furthermore, what
emerges from an analysis of the contest is a better understanding of the high
level of fragmentation within the state.

The process of creating commodified cultural products is undertaken by
the state in the effort not only to produce a tangible group of Carnival items to
be bought and sold but to create a legitimate environment for the production
and reproduction of nationalist culture that the state can be said to operate.
The state's tactic takes the form of a mission to safeguard Trinidadian national
culture and can be seen as the production of a kind of nationalist/marketing
rhetoric. Organizations in the private sector are also eager to participate because the government's interest in things cultural has generated business opportunities. The prevalence of advertising and marketing techniques signal a
new approach to the construction of national culture undertaken by the state.
There is an underlying concern with the economics of culture that we do not
find, for instance, in the nationalist language of Eric Williams, who sought to
distance culture from economics for fear of creating what he considered a
humiliating and financially unsound tourist industry. Tourism, he noted,
was "harmful to the dignity of our people" if left uncontrolled. Williams saw
tourism as secondary to "promoting the Arts and Culture (especially Drama)
as part of the process of nation-building and achieving self-awareness" (1993:
309).

Compared to William's position, which stressed nurturing culture to increase the nation's sense of self and to build self-esteem after the passing of
colonialism, the current state's attitude reflects a much greater awareness of the
importance of external factors (global factors) and a perception of the necessary links between nationalism, culture, and economics. State power, resting
in part on the ability to foment nationalist sentiment, has responded to the
changing conditions around it. Thus, although the middle class has always had
a stake in influencing the direction of national culture, recently this concern

has shifted to a much greater emphasis on the promotion of culture as commerce, thereby yielding nationalist endeavors that are in and of themselves economically sound *and* patriotic. This has manifested itself as an interest in the export of culture.

Carnival's Export Potential

In searching for cultural forms to export, the logical choice for the state is Carnival. Although its position as a national form is continually questioned, it is the country's largest tourist attraction and is already exported by Carnival artists and promoters outside of the state. The Carnival King and Queen of the World Competition was devised in light of the commercial and popular successes of Trinidad-style Carnivals that have mushroomed in the United States and Canada, beginning in the late 1960s but really flourishing in the 1980s. Trinidad and Tobago–style Carnivals have also sprung up in Europe, especially in England (not only in London but in Manchester, Leeds, and Middlesex).

There are currently carnivals in Sweden and Germany with more proposed for Japan, India, and possibly parts of Africa. Trinidadian Carnival shows or Carnival-inspired spectacles have been included in the French bicentennial, the Olympic Games in Barcelona, and the World Cup in the United States (all involving the Trinidadian Peter Minshall). Within the United States alone there are nearly fifty cities currently boasting some form of Trinidad-style Carnival, even if included in a more general West Indian celebration. Canada can claim many Trinidad and Tobago–style Carnivals as well, with the largest, the Caribana in Toronto, attracting over a million spectators. The West Indian American Day in Brooklyn attracts over two million people each year and has recently emerged as the largest outdoor attraction in the city of New York.

Carnival has slowly crept up on Trinidadians as a potentially viable export commodity. In a symposium on Carnival's export potential in 1994 scholars noted that dominant economies are service economies and that Trinidad could develop a service industry based on the street festival. The service Trinidad would provide was termed "tension-release" and was to be facilitated by a sector of commerce devoted to "organized spontaneity."[1] The symposium organizers also noted that the export process had been going on for some time, citing the institution of Carnival celebrations in the 1950s by Trinidadians in Jamaica. Yet the "export" of Carnival has been going on much longer than that by Trinidadian transnationals (see chapter 1).

The devotion to export expressed by the state has more than merely economic motives (about which more below), but the economic motives have attracted entrepreneurs, culture brokers, and Carnival artists to support and increase export. Although tensions arise between these various groups—for instance, between administrators of foreign Carnivals, the National Carnival Commission (NCC), local masmen, and others—there is an attempt to come together to promote and facilitate export projects.

I have mentioned that Carnival and culture in Trinidad have benefited from Trinidad and Tobago–style Carnivals established by emigrant Trinidadian communities all across North America, Canada, and the United Kingdom. This has contributed both to the spread of Carnival and to the livelihoods of Carnival creators everywhere. The state has cautioned, however, that without some kind of firm, centralized control, Carnival is in danger of being appropriated by the world without proper acknowledgment of its roots in Trinidad (see the example of steelbands below). Carnival becomes merely "West Indian" or vaguely Caribbean, and this process is abetted because it makes greater political sense in a transnational situation to promote the event as pan-Caribbean (cf. Cohen 1982, for instance). In order, then, to effect greater control over the production and distribution of "national culture," the state and associated parties employ a strategy of historical admonition, with the state's version of the Carnival narrative serving as a cautionary tale of what can happen if the population, left to its own irresponsible devices, is allowed to carry on bastardizing, forgetting, and transforming a cherished tradition.

By centralizing the control of Carnival, the state creates an environment in which it is granted authority over the production and distribution of national cultural memory and, ultimately, practice. The state depends upon the successful objectification and commodification of Carnival and draws upon nostalgic versions of Carnival's history to appeal to Trinidadians in general. As we shall see in the next chapter, the use of nostalgic narratives has unintended consequences when such narratives are recontextualized by Trinidadians living abroad, yet even so they are actively and enthusiastically consumed. In any case, the state must legitimate itself and its authority over cultural production by incorporating and drawing upon the services of different groups within the society itself.

The solution is to increase control over licensing, marketing, and promotion of Carnival, to tighten the grip on the development of new Carnivals abroad, and to promote and extend Carnival season within the country of

Trinidad itself. The goal here is to increase the share of profit and actual participation (i.e., constructing costumes, providing music, or organizing fetes) for interested parties in Trinidad itself. This increase in participation would result from recognition by the world that Trinidad is the "Mecca" of Carnival. For example, the Carnival King and Queen of the World competition, as part of its promotional push, issued a magazine filled with short statements of purpose and historical notes all carrying didactic and programmatic appeals to save the nation by saving its culture. In one article, ostensibly a historical description of old-time Carnival characters that used to make their appearances on the streets of Port-of-Spain (such as jab jabs and bats and midnight robbers), the author stresses, "The characters in Trinidad's traditional Carnival are the repositories of very important features which distinguish Carnival Trinidad and Tobago style from other Carnivals. They add to the uniqueness of the national festivals [sic] which, with calypso, pan and above all else, the spirit, create a differentiation of the product as Trinidad and Tobago Carnival claims a niche in the world economic market" (Cupid 1994: 3). There is in this statement a clear sense that the preservation of "authentic, traditional carnival" is important for the formation of—or, in a sense, the continuation of—a unique national cultural form.

The form's uniqueness is important because its difference allows for immediate recognition and therefore easier marketability and control. At least part of the drive to recapture lost culture evident in this kind of rhetoric is to preserve what is considered to be the product differential and thereby its attraction. Thus, there is the implicit sense that aesthetic appreciation requires a "unique" form, not merely a form that can be said to be national in quality. It cannot be any Carnival that is the source of this beauty and popularity, but a Trinidadian Carnival specifically, with its specific identifying features such as the old-time Carnival characters. It is for this reason that such characters are treated as "endangered species" and showcased in a locked parking lot in front of the Queen's Hall auditorium and not out on the street. There arises, then, a link between the "mythopoetic metanarrative" inherent in the construction of a nationalist culture and the perpetuation and solidification of the nation's sovereignty as it is realized through effective control over commodity production and exchange.

I want to draw here a connection between state sovereignty and cultural commodification and export. I see the latter as forms of nationalism and therefore instrumental in the project of reinforcing sovereignty. In order to make these connections clearer I examine the 1994 Carnival King and Queen of the World contest as an example of the state's attempt to expand the marketing of Trinidad Carnival. Subsequently, I look into why the event ultimately failed. I suggest that the commodification of culture requires an audience with a desire to "purchase" such commodities. In chapter 6, by way of comparison, I describe a successful competition in which an audience actively consumed state-sponsored nostalgia.

The Carnival King and Queen of the World Contest

The issues that emerged during the planning and implementation of this contest highlight the turbulent relationship between the state, the professional Carnival community, foreign-based Trinidadian entrepreneurs, and those meant to consume the products generated by these groups. The King and Queen of the World contest seemed like a natural way for Trinidad itself to capitalize on the successes of the many carnivals around the world. It would be a way to attract capital and, what is more important in the eyes of some, a way to increase the visibility of the Trinidad Carnival and Trinidad itself as the "Mecca" of Carnival. Initially the idea was proposed by Dr. Max Awong, a gynecologist with many years of experience in the promotion and presentation of Carnival events in Trinidad. His original idea was to include the KQC as part of the string of Carnival-related shows that take place each year prior to the actual Carnival itself. His thought was to extend Carnival season, bring tourists down earlier, and increase the earnings potential of Carnival.

The idea was taken up by the National Carnival Bands Association, under the direction of Richard Afong, the leader of the popular band Barbarossa, a Carnival group that is, incidentally, often cited as indicative of the hedonist, middle-class Carnival. Along with other interested promoters, including some with a great deal of experience and expertise, the NCBA sought to hold the contest, not in February at Carnival time, but in September, when there were no other Carnivals taking place anywhere else and near to the annual celebration of Republic Day. The idea was to bring a measure of tourism to the island during this traditionally slow and difficult period.

From its inauguration at the Trinidad Hilton Hotel in August of 1993 until the actual event in the fall of 1994, things ran less than smoothly. There were immediate problems with raising the budget, initially projected at TT$8 million (about U.S.$1.5 million). Sponsors were hard to come by, or lost interest as the administration proved to be disorganized. Awong ultimately dissociated himself from the venture as he became more and more uncertain about the wisdom of a September event. He announced at the launching of the contest that he believed the project was doomed to failure. Not too long after his ominous prediction, many of the original organizers began to leave. Veteran advertising and marketing executive Val Rogers left because there appeared to be no financial backing. Geraldo Vieira, who designed a stage for the National Stadium, also quit for lack of funds. In June 1994 then culture minister Joan Yuille Williams spoke on behalf of the government and pledged full support of the show. Yet she also called upon business leaders to help with the funding. There was no response.

Scarcity of funding and inept management were only some of the criticisms leveled at the event. Many people I spoke to had not even heard of the competition until very close to the opening day and indicated that the timing for such an affair was wrong. Some informants suggested that there would be low turnout for the series of planned shows because it was September and most people had little discretionary income left after August holidays and outfitting their children for the upcoming school year. But by far the most oft-repeated criticism was that it was not Carnival time: "Trying to transfer that activity into this September mas' as it has been called has proven to be quite a difficult thing, not the least of which are the psychological problems involved with rekindling the feel that obtains during Carnival time. Because the national festival when it occurs is really mas' on the road with the kings and queens as a culmination. It is the end-product of a season of festivity that starts with the parang [a kind of Christmas music, sung in Spanish] season" (Joseph interview 1994).

By ignoring the very basic fact that Carnival is seasonal the administrators mistook enthusiasm for Dimanche Gras, an essential facet of Carnival, for enthusiasm for the costumes themselves. But without a Carnival season there is not the same gradual build-up to the grand event.

Synopsis of the Competition

The KQC ran from Saturday, September 17, until Saturday, September 24, 1994. The week-long schedule of events included a Soca party, a Caribbean music night, a "Talkalypso" competition, various cultural shows, and, of course, the King and Queen competition itself. The competition was based on the Dimanche Gras show that takes place each year during Carnival time. The Dimanche Gras, which is the Sunday prior to Carnival, is the time at which the largest and most spectacular costumes, the Kings and Queens of the respective bands, are judged (see chapter 1).

The King and Queen of the world competition was meant to capitalize on the sheer spectacle of Carnival, on its most visible and emblematic icons, the massive fancy costumes of the kings and queens. It was not meant to duplicate Carnival per se, but it was meant to generate income in much the same way that Carnival does. Because of the absence of any seasonal or temporal build-up, the KQC tried to stimulate Carnival-like enthusiasm from thin air, a conjuring trick that ignored what it needed from an audience, the desire to celebrate or the habit of doing so. In other words, the organizers of the King and Queen of the World contest were convinced that the attraction of the spectacular costumes, grand Soca shows, and Carnival-type fetes were enough to encourage participation and attract patrons from both abroad and at home.

The National Stadium in Port-of-Spain lies rather far from the city center along Wrightston Road. It is somewhat difficult to get to without a car for people outside the neighborhood in which it sits. The competition was slated to take place in both the stadium and in venues occupying the same "complex." When I arrived in Trinidad for the competition there was very little promotion of the event. I was told that all of the advertising money had been spent promoting the contest abroad (Joseph interview 1994). The local population, therefore, had scarcely heard of its existence, and those who had had heard about it on cable television, something only the relatively well-to-do are able to afford. Furthermore, the foreign audiences, especially the habitual Carnival-goers living in North America who are Trinidadians, were not the direct targets of the ad campaigns. Ads were placed in media markets not normally associated with West Indian consumption.

Although there was a weeklong schedule of events, I was primarily interested in the costume competition. This seemed to me to be the feature event, called, as it was, "The Final Glory." I was looking forward to seeing the entries from around the world and astounded by the contest flyers advertising entries from Italy and Brazil—places that either had no large Trinidadian presence or had their own Carnival tradition. Neither of those two countries had costumes in the show, as it turned out. On the night of the Final Glory I made my way to the stadium security office to pick up my backstage pass. There seemed to be many more people behind the stage in the stalls constructed to hold the massive costumes than there were audience members. The costumes

Fig. 7. Carnival king from 1994 competition.

were indeed from many different Carnivals (Italy and Brazil's absence notwithstanding). There were entries from Middlesex in England, Brooklyn, New York, St. Vincent, the Virgin Islands, Toronto, Notting Hill, St. Lucia, New Jersey, Ottawa, Washington D.C., and Orlando, Florida. All together there were twenty-four Carnival queens and twenty-two kings representing thirty-two Carnivals and eighteen countries. The first prize being offered in each category was U.S.$15,000. The competition was designed to be similar to the Dimanche Gras show, except the Dimanche Gras performance took place on the Savannah stage, an enormous runway between two sets of bleacher-style seating structures through which the costumes dance their way past spectators. Also, during Dimanche Gras, as in the Panorama competition, many people go down onto what is known as "the track," the strip of dirt road that leads on to and off of the stage. It is here that supporters of one band or another can get a close look at the costumes, talk to the artists, and lime. As with steelband, there are many hangers-on who help in one way or another by carrying costume parts, helping the person playing the costume to get into the frame (not an easy task with costumes weighing upward of forty or fifty pounds), and performing other minor tasks.

In the King and Queen competition all of the participatory qualities of the event were stripped away. The National Stadium carried a conventional stage set-up with rows of seats arrayed parallel to the stage-front and receding outward and upward as in a theater. The backstage area was not only re-stricted, it was blocked off by an enormous wall that, according to its de-signer, would "increase the visual impact of the costumes as they [came] onto the stage" (Vieira interview 1993). An enormous amount of work went into the design and execution of the National Stadium stage, but when the costumes were finally presented the dramatic effect of the stage wall, the lights, and sound system were lost. Barely 2,000 people were sprinkled across a stadium equipped to seat 17,000.

The show went on. Costume after costume paraded across the stage. They came with grand names meant to evoke distant lands, mythical themes, his-torical events or personages, such as "Jumbie Under the Sun," "Ami-Kumari, the Angel of Fire," "Light of the World," or "The Valiant Gladiator." There were references to Nefertiti, Sun Queen of Egypt, Cheyenne Indians, the Golden Hibiscus, the discovery of the Americas, the spirit of Jamaica, the spirit of Bar-bados, great masmen of the past, and more abstract renderings such as the spirits of light, fire, water, "the architect of the universe," and others. Many of the costumes were beautiful, some technologically astounding with lights, fire, smoke, and automated moving parts. In the end all of the prizes went to Trinidadians. This was a source of some embarrassment as at least one journal-ist confided to me before the event that it would be inconceivable for Trinidad to win all of the prizes. Such a development would surely discourage partici-pants from returning. But the same journalist later told me that he was not surprised. His position was that there was no money for the prizes and the only way to disguise that fact was to crown Trinidadians as winners, the idea being that it is better to control the effects of such a scandal when it is an internal matter than it is to try to avert an "international incident" (Joseph interview 1994).

In the long run the event highlighted tensions between the state and others who wish to have a say in the industry of Carnival. The National Carnival Bands Association ultimately depended upon the government for help with the costs. The NCC and the NCBA were never fully clear on who was in fact leading the operation. The government ultimately put in TT$900,000 toward a budget of TT$1.4 million, with the business community contributing little.

Preserving Heritage: The National Carnival Commission and the Middle Class

Surrounding both the export of Carnival and the export of other cultural goods such as the steelband (especially the actual drums or pans themselves), soca, and various foods (such as pepper sauce, roti, Carib beer), there is currently a kind of hysteria or "culture panic." The idea that the world will "steal" the country's culture if it is not rigidly controlled and monitored belies a more deeply held fear, on the part of the state, that the nation's economy and sovereignty is in fact at stake.[2] Attempts to develop cultural exports indicate a desire to have a legitimate national presence in the world of nations. That presence is conceived of as a kind of "brand name" recognition (see below). Yet in order to make sure of the culture products' viability, the state must ensure the survival of the forms it wants to promote. Hence a campaign of cultural preservation has emerged, not in the service of building self-esteem but in the service of protecting an investment. Thus state elites, the middle classes, and the media in Trinidad continually stress the importance of education vis-à-vis Carnival and the "knowing of one's history" (Ministry of Education Report 1972: 24). These things are stressed in the name of the nation, but they can really only have import if the nation is being compared to other nations. The solidification of a discrete body of cultural knowledge not only creates a patriotic and "moral" populace, it ensures a nation with a culture. A crucial element here is that the existing state must be seen to be *in control of* the regulation, distribution, promotion, and sale of culture as a marker of its legitimacy. The acts of the state toward this end are by no means received uncritically, especially by certain members of the intelligentsia in Trinidad. For example, at a symposium on Carnival and religion in 1994, a key point of concern was that culture was being preyed upon by the state like "corbeaux" (the term for vultures in Trinidad) and being carved up and sold off. Yet not a month later at another symposium, this time at the University of the West Indies, the topic was "Carnival: Exploring the Export Potential." There were also radio programs and television specials devoted to the export question. In these instances the potential contribution cultural export could make to Trinidad's economy took precedence over the possible deleterious effects of "commercializing" culture.

Mandate to Commodify: The Export of Culture

The main government or government-related administrative bodies responsible for cultural development are the National Carnival Commission and Tourist and Industrial Development Corporation; there are also specific Carnival organizations such as the National Carnival Bandleaders Association and Pan Trinbago, the steelband body. There are also the many entrepreneurs and culture brokers such as Dr. Vijay Ramlal of Carnival Judges Association and a whole host of minor marketing and advertising organizations. The Trinidad Industrial Development Corporation (TIDCO), as the state organization responsible for cultural marketing, has recently made great strides toward this end with a massive marketing campaign. In their own words, they describe this mission as "pursuing . . . a new awareness of [Trinidad] in the international marketplace" (*Trinidad Express*, Feb. 19, 1996). It is no accident that the newly reorganized bureaucratic department responsible for the expansion of tourism resides in the same physical and intellectual space as that responsible for the development of other industries. In the rhetoric mobilized by this agency there is a clear tendency toward the language of commodification. By pushing Trinidadian objects of culture such as Carnival, TIDCO hopes not only to sell products from Trinidad but also to address a more pressing problem, which is "to make Trinidad [as a country] known internationally." The success of such a project would result in Trinidad taking its place alongside other legitimated and recognized Caribbean nations, like Jamaica, that have, one might say, "brand name" cultural forms such as reggae. For example, TIDCO claims that "Jamaica clearly understands this type of marketing and is out front in selling all that it has to offer" (*Trinidad Express* 1996: 12). One can see here, then, the implicit recipe for international sovereignty and legitimacy. These "ingredients" comprise the economic success of a nation's cultural products, the one-to-one relationship such products have to a nation and the ultimate recognition of legitimacy that such a relationship bestows upon the nation. The nation, finally, becomes a corporation that successfully sells its identity, the consumption of which resolves the nation's existential crisis. Although this is ultimately supposed to strengthen the nation and "stamp [it] indelibly on the world map," the case of Jamaica shows the possible negative results of aggressive tourist and cultural marketing.

Carnival Development Committee, the governing body of the festival, underwent a transformation (and name change) in 1987 with the arrival of the National Alliance for Reconstruction to power, the first change of government since independence in 1962. In 1991, under Act 9 of Parliament, the NCC was given a new charter, which provided for new responsibilities and a greater degree of autonomy. The character of the new staff was largely of a marketing and advertising nature. Many of the new administrators had backgrounds in these fields and had been in the world of advertising and marketing in the private sector. The clear articulation of this mission is stated under the heading "Objects of the Commission," paragraph 4, subheading *a*: "To make Carnival a viable national, cultural and commercial enterprise" (Charter of the National Carnival Commission 1991: 2). As phrased, the objective of the charter articulates national, cultural, and commercial priorities and binds them together in a way so as to create an insoluble whole, the implementation of which is a national, cultural commodity. This charter has been taken quite seriously, if not always successfully, by subsequent members of the NCC; and the recent activities of TIDCO have demonstrated a renewed vigor in all matters relating to the marketing of Carnival as a tourist attraction and as an important industry alongside other serious industrial endeavors within the country, such as the production and sale of petroleum and related products or the expansion of aquaculture, citrus, and other agricultural products.

Commodification: Strategies for Building National Culture Internationally

One major aspect of the construction and promotion of Trinidadian culture is its externality. It is directed at the rest of the world. Describing Carnival as the "greatest show on earth," a boast utilized quite frequently and often without any knowledge of its association with the Barnum & Bailey Circus, is indicative of the comparative nature of national culture-building. The point is to connect with the globe and, ultimately, to safeguard national sovereignty through the attraction of tourists and the exploitation of an existing transnational community. There are differences in the ways in which nationalist sentiments are fostered or urged on the one hand and actively lived on the other.

In the case of Trinidad's Carnival, whatever nationalist substantiation it provides it does in large part through its emigrants. The plea to preserve Trinidadian culture is often heeded most strongly by those who have an understanding of what is meant by Trinidadian culture, who tend to have a nostalgia for it, and who are not involved with it on a day-to-day basis. Thus the transmigrant community is instrumental as an audience for nationalist rhetoric. They are the ones who are more likely to subscribe to the kind of nostalgic sentiment served up by the state and tourist agencies, and in fact they do participate in the spirit of nostalgia. They do consume state-generated narratives. In that sense they are involved in nationalist substantiation and legitimation, yet they are not nationals strictly speaking. Their participation is limited and serves quite a different agenda. And their willingness to consume Trinidadian culture is limited by the parameters of the transnational reproductive imagination.

Movement and flow—of goods, of people, of money, of ideas—mark the Trinidadian community in Brooklyn, and it is a community that is capable of committing to different kinds of identities in different situations. On certain occasions Trinidadians will forgo their national allegiances in favor of regional ones (i.e., Caribbean) or forgo their regional allegiances in order to be in solidarity with African Americans as black people. The most visible cultural form that Trinidadians have is Carnival, and it, too—given different occasions—can be mobilized for different purposes. But overall Carnival and the community found themselves on the requirements of the reproductive imagination with regard to "identity."

Carnival, on one level, is about remembering Trinidad, but the event itself bears little relation to the Trinidadian Carnival. As we have seen, in its Brooklyn incarnation, Carnival has been forced into parade form and has had to negotiate the very different world of American racial and ethnic politics. Yet Carnival is thought of as a true Trinidadian event, and the Trinidad to which it refers is an actual place with an authentic culture. I have noted earlier that as more and more works of social science condemn the assumed isomorphism of locale and culture, they often ignore the role that such conflations play in the minds of those very displaced peoples who are said to call such categories into question. It is one thing to talk about the reality of communities as imagined but quite another to assume that by determining this it will cease to have import to those doing the imagining. As Gupta has remarked, "The irony of these times . . . is that as actual places and localities become ever more blurred and indeterminate, *ideas* of culturally and ethnically distinct places become perhaps even more salient" (1992: 10). In fact, what is often overlooked in the effort to identify the breakdown of the space/place conjunction is that this may be a very good way to examine the praxis of nationalist imagination. If we take the position that the reproductive imagination of cultural identity "happens," at least in part, in situations of transnationalism, we might also begin to see the variables involved in the formation of very different kinds of identities. Too, we may be able to gain some perspective on the role of the state, which appears, in this light, not as a monolithic entity but rather a highly variegated amalgam of interests and goals. In the Carnival King and Queen Competition the imaginative needs of the transnation were not served. Even the somewhat different imaginations of foreign tourists were not excited by the event. Meanwhile, the various entities involved in the competition's production were in conflict. What went wrong?

Since 1987, the year the National Carnival Commission received its mandate, there has been a strong emphasis on cultural reclamation in that agency's publications and policies. The main theme that emerges is that Carnival is losing its distinctiveness. By becoming nothing more than a street party in bathing suits Carnival has lost its singular character. The state's preoccupation with having a unique culture for the nation, one that distinguishes it in the world of nations and their cultures, makes the homogenization of Carnival of deep concern. The fixation on distinctiveness on the part of those involved with the National Carnival Commission and with TIDCO reflects the members' general training as advertising executives and directors of marketing in the private sector. Thus, although Carnival as it is today is perhaps the main tourist attraction in Trinidad, there persists a spirit of improvement. In classic advertising mode, "brand name" recognition has become instrumental in the NCC's and TIDCO's attempt to capture a portion of "the market," that being, in this case, the world not just of tourism but of Carnivals and festivals in particular.[3] The goal in advertising, to use the terms of Marxist political economy, is for use value to provide incentive for consumers to enter into an act of exchange. Without name recognition the product's potential use value is diminished (Haug 1986: 14–16). In an effort to redress this balance the National Carnival Commission recently began encouraging the portrayal of old-time masquerades. In the words of one NCC official these older Carnival characters "create a differentiation of the product as Trinidad and Tobago Carnival claims a niche in the world economic market." Many of these are masquerade forms that were discouraged on the grounds of vulgarity by the middle classes of previous generations, as well as others that were abandoned after they lost relevance to the changing society. For instance, quite a few of the World War I and II–inspired characters disappeared after the conflicts ended overseas; many of the characters whose portrayal relied upon ritualized speech died in the wake of large "fancy bands" accompanied by mobile sound systems. The disappearance of these characters, however, in the official discourse of the NCC, is the lamentable by-product of public apathy, poor cultural education, and an *unwanted form of commercialization* that draws upon foreign influence for inspiration.

The NCC has, by way of attempted correction, tried to preserve elements of cultural loss. By encouraging and staging cultural shows and competitions, the NCC is hoping to keep characters such as Blue Devils, Baby Dolls, Jab Molassis, Jab Jabs and Burrokeets alive. The most significant of these attempts is the Viey

Fig. 8. Viey La Cou: Devils torment tourist.

La Cou show started in 1987. Utilizing the language of natural preservation, the state has spoken of saving endangered species and has held these competitions in a fenced car-park next to the national zoo (probably not by design, but certainly in fitting manner). This sort of policy is the state's version of the production of nostalgia, created firmly in the belief, as Hill has put it, "that the last obstacle to achieving a true . . . identity is the cultural one" (1985: 14–34). Seeing the commodification of old masquerades as purely a commercial venture would be a mistake, however. In situating itself as the guardian of culture the state justifies both a capitalist enterprise *and* its own position as the author of the commodity's aesthetic and thus its use value; a position that ensures (it is hoped) state hegemony. Thus, by slightly broadening our conception of the logic of exchange we can include the actions of governmental agencies such as the NCC, TIDCO (Tourism and Industrial Development Company of Trinidad and Tobago), and others. These bodies have recently been given a great deal more money, power, and attention in recent years. The UNC under Basdeo Panday promised to focus more attention on the possibilities of cultural export in their campaign platform and, since their ascension to power, have been true to their word. Yet we do not want to carry the political/economic analysis too far. One runs the risk of economic determinism and of losing sight of the position of the "consumer."

In order for the culturalist project to be effective, the state must construct an authoritative position for itself vis-à-vis authentic national culture. This process in Trinidad, when successful, blends the commodification of culture with nostalgia. Carnival is not, strictly speaking, a culturalist event, though it contains within it culturalisms and spawns other culturalist events alongside it. The International King and Queen of the World Competition held in Port-of-Spain in September 1994 provides a very good example of a culturalist endeavor, but one that failed. Not all culturalist programs fail, however, and both within Carnival itself as well as at other times of the year there exist public activities that are primarily culturalist and that are quite successful. In determining which events are culturalist and which ones are not anthropologists become entangled once again in questions of authenticity and invention and further run the risk of reproducing essentialized views of culture that spring from "the people" as *volkskultur*.

My goal here, however, is not to establish a categorical and qualitative difference between culturalisms and something else that might be more "genuine" in its production. I am more interested in which culturalisms do well and which do not. I do see culturalisms, however, as the products of middle-class, elite, and state involvement in the production of cultural forms that are self-consciously nation-building, didactic, and programmatic. Often the state (and here I mean not only governmental bodies but the class-habitus complex that controls and surrounds the state as a particular segment of Trinidadian society) will promote or construct an environment that is conducive to culturalisms. But their success requires more than simply adequate marketing, propaganda, or capital investment.

Middle-class involvement with Carnival has long been marked by the reform-through-competition strategy. The results of this strategy are frequently culturalisms, in that cultural forms produced under the auspices of state-controlled competitions or showcases are often either self-consciously performed in the service of displaying identity or devised for such a purpose. Culturalisms, however, are not the only possible result of sponsored competitions. In the early years of Carnival competitions, the intent was the reform of what were considered vulgar practices within Carnival. However, even in these cases issues of national identity and national culture could play a part. As independence approached Carnival competitions and Carnival itself were pitched as examples of national culture, while the character of reform activity shifted toward a concern with national identity and national reputation. Differently put, the attention on Carnival stressed the development of a purely local, yet virtuous, content. National culture-building always contains within it a sense of moral imperative. As the Trinidadian writer Willie Chen remarked in a newspaper editorial concerning the state of Carnival music, "I say bring back the golden art of yesteryear tunes. . . . They are pleasurable exercises of art and discipline in the control of mind and body movements. Only animals jump uncontrollably which leads to lewdness and vulgarity" (*Trinidad Express*, Feb. 19, 1994).

The true culture of the nation, which resides in the past and must be recovered, is not only aesthetically superior but morally superior as well. The revitalization process proposed by the state and the middle class has an imbricated set of goals that include rescue or recovery, moral improvement, international standing, and profit-making.

Why the Competition Failed

The KQC was an attempt at creating a business opportunity made by entrepreneurs who mistook the proliferation of Carnivals for the success of a marketed and engineered entertainment event. In reality the rise of almost every Trinidad and Tobago–style Carnival in the United States and the UK is the result of the presence of a significant number of Trinidadians as well as other West Indians, who arrived in these places because of major shifts in the organization of global capital and who were attracted by the possibility of making some kind of living on foreign soil. These transmigrants never left their own homes completely, nor did they cease their contact with those they left behind. Their Carnivals arose for many different reasons and were organized by different kinds of people with different motives. In general, however, it is possible to say that Carnivals became successful because of the nature of the transmigrant situation. Their success had less to do with marketing concepts, or the "professional product" as some would have it, than with a desire to preserve a cultural identity in environments that were perhaps initially hostile to but later demanded such displays (see chapter 3). The competition backers fatally misunderstood that the enthusiasm for Carnival is not generated only partly by the lure of parties nor solely by the grandeur of the kings and queens and by the musical attractions.

When the KQC finally got under way it sank dramatically. At one of the concerts only thirty-eight people attended. For the final competition, rather grandly called "The Glory—The Final Challenge," nearly all the seats in the stadium were empty. The press, sometimes merciful, was also spiteful at times. Many members of the press, Carnival craftsmen, and average Trinidadians concurred that the event was a "bacchanal," in this case in the negative sense of that term. Much was made of the fact that it was geared toward foreign audiences, with much of the advertising budget going to overseas media. Some Trinidadians felt slighted by the fact that the prize money was more than the organizers were prepared to pay the local steelband members, who, in the long run, were asked to play for free. In order to escape the fact that the prize money, at the time of the show, was nowhere to be found, the winners had to be drawn from the Trinidadian participants (Joseph interview 1994). Many, including the foreign contestants themselves, frowned on this development as a show of bad faith. Ultimately, it played into the hands of the organizers as they tried to use it as further proof that Trinidad is the "Mecca" of Carnival.

On the final day of the week-long contest a "Street Parade" was scheduled. It was, as it turned out, the most enthusiastically received part of the whole affair. It was free and so the promoters, the National Carnival Bands Association, and the National Carnival Commission did not make any money from it.

People came out in makeshift costumes, daubed themselves with oil or paint, danced behind disc jockeys on trucks, and generally enjoyed themselves.

Commodification without Context: Losing the Audience

State agencies responsible for the creation of national cultural commodities are also charged, then, with the creation of national culture. The success of this kind of culture is largely measured by the returns realized from its sale, both internally as well as globally. Using the terminology of Marxist political economy we might categorize it in the following way: Culture is, first of all, conceived by the TIDCO, the NCC, and other sponsored or related institutions as a means to two related ends: the legitimation of the state's sovereignty and the ability to mediate relationships between ethnic groups within its boundaries. Both ends can be reached through the process of commodification.

I define commodity here, following Appadurai (1986a: 13), as that point in the life of a thing when its exchangeability is foregrounded. The state conceives of culture as a collection of things, with attributes that can be exchanged either for money or some form of symbolic capital (Bourdieu 1984: 291). Yet by dealing with unstable public forms the state's attempt to commodify (and therefore, by necessity, objectify) culture runs into the problem of resistance, not to objectification per se, but to a fixed understanding of the object and therefore to exchangeability. This is especially true in the relation between the state and the transnation. The social uses to which objectified and commodified cultural forms can be put by others, transnationals for example, are not necessarily the same uses designed for them. Thus it is not in resistance to objectification that agency emerges, but in the implementation of those objectified and commodified cultural forms. There must be an audience. In thinking about relations of commodification in this way one can avoid the romantic association often made between cultural forms that exist within and those that exist without commodification. That is, it is not some purer relation to a cultural form that has only a use value (implying it does not exist in the world of exchange) where one can find "real culture."

Agency is not to be found in resisting commodification itself, but rather in the recontextualization of commodified cultural forms that have, perhaps, been produced elsewhere or by other actors. The implication here is that there is only culture where there is exchange (considered here broadly to include many forms of capital), which is a corollary to my earlier contention that there is only culture where there is a need for recognition. In the case of New York

City, in the case of the Trinidadian state, and even in the case of individuals operating in the world of the transnation, culture is mobilized in an exchange relationship that requires its objectification/commodification. That exchange relationship comprises the exchange of cultural forms for recognition, for money, for other goods and services.

The entrepreneurs and Carnival organizations that put on the International Carnival King and Queen of the World Contest in 1994 were hoping to extend Carnival season, to promote national culture, and to make a healthy profit by doing so. The enterprise ultimately failed because the commodified entity served no one. There was no context in which to consume the object offered. When contrasted to the successful cultural productions of Carnival time— Panorama, Dimanche Gras, the calypso tents—one notices a glaring lack of "buyers." There is nothing served by having a Carnival show in Trinidad in September and therefore no level of exchange.

In the next chapter I examine a competition, also mounted by the state, that was a success. Nostalgia figured into the advertisement of the competition much more heavily and ultimately in ways that resonated with Trinidadian returnees. The King and Queen Competition misread the allure of Carnival as spectacle, as an attraction in and of itself that could transcend the particular associations that Trinidadians have with it. Crudely put, it misunderstood its own product's use value. To paraphrase Terry Joseph, a Trinidadian journalist, you can't just use Carnival when you want to, you have to respect what it is to *people* (Joseph interview 1994).

6

Playing Sailor Mas', or When "Natives" Become Tourists of Themselves

Transnational Returnees

> Wherever Trinidadians have settled in sufficient numbers—Toronto, Harlem, Brooklyn, London, the outskirts of Caracas—they have taken Carnival with them. Yet great numbers troop back home annually from these and other places for the master celebration. For them, carnival stands as a time of renewal, of self-affirmation, which can occur in no other way. To miss carnival is to be diminished.
>
> John Stewart, "Patronage and Control in the Trinidad Carnival"

Steelbands with their sailors made their way through the massive Port-of-Spain crowds, sound systems, and vendors on Carnival Tuesday in 1996 in a spirit of "longtime Carnival" or Carnival of long ago. All Stars, Exodus, Phase II Pan Groove, Laventille Sounds Specialists, Invaders, Tokyo, Starlift—all vied for a TT$100,000 prize. The steelband contest was a new feature and was instituted to bring the sounds of the steelband back into Carnival. The contest was a success. When comparing this contest to the King and Queen competition, I noticed the attraction that the steelband and sailor contest held for returning migrants, who participated heavily in the event itself. In investigating the two competitions I saw that there were at least two commonalties: (1) the role of the National Carnival Commission in the institutionalization of certain Carnival forms, which were identified as in danger of disappearance and required preservation in the name both of cultural heritage and commerce (outlined in the previous chapter), and (2) the impact of such strategies of preservation on the community of costume makers and musicians, who remain dedicated to portraying and continuing such forms. Yet there is a third factor here, one that was generally absent from the King and Queen competition, namely, the impact of preservation strategies on the emigrant population of Carnival returnees who have a nostalgic and emotional investment in seeing the masquerades of their youth maintained. In both cases the state and organizations working with the state supported tourist attractions that would attract both foreign visitors and transnationals. Foreigners played very little part in both contests, yet transnationals figured overwhelmingly in the success of the steelband and sailor event.

Frequently, in dealing with the issues raised by the phenomenon of ethnic tourism, scholars point to the level of exploitation reached by such ventures (MacCannell 1992). The reconstruction of ethnicity for consumption by tourists is destructive and coercive, they maintain. It objectifies cultural forms and insinuates a "way of life" into a market-driven economy. When groups turn themselves into tourist attractions, it becomes a marker of the way in which dominant notions of cultural authenticity and their relation to a marketable identity have been internalized by traditionally subordinated groups (MacCannell 1992: 178–79).

But what other kinds of meanings might be generated when states create tourist destinations and attractions out of their landscapes and cultural forms for former nationals living abroad? Certainly tourism of oneself is nothing new. Places like Disney's Main Street, usa, are created for nostalgic consumption by Americans who have never experienced the items preserved there but that have been purportedly lost. Other examples might include tourists from Tokyo "rediscovering" pilgrimage spots in Japan (Ivy 1996). In all of these cases the desire is to capture a culture as if it were being recaptured, as if it should have somehow belonged in the experiences of the tourists themselves but never did. It was the culture and lifeway of "ancestors" or "forefathers" and therefore rightfully belongs to the alienated and drained latter-day "ethnics" or nationals who bear little of those ways themselves.

Yet this is not the case with many Trinidadians and Carnival. For first-generation Trinidadian Americans, Carnival was a factor in their lives *even if they never played.* Carnival is an unavoidable feature of Trinidadian life. One has to make a conscious and concerted effort to avoid it. "For almost one-third of the year carnival accounts for a significant share of all public events in Trinidad" (Stewart 1986: 290). For many second-generation Trinidadian Americans, trips back "home" are regular events, and exposure to Carnival begins at an early age. In addition, the presence of the Brooklyn Carnival means that Trinidadian Americans can keep up with Carnival events, bands, calypsos, and Panorama champions, all of which may become a part of the events in Brooklyn. Calypso monarchs from the previous year, bandleaders (or at least their portrayals), and steelband arrangers and performers from Trinidad are routinely invited to participate in the Brooklyn version of Carnival. For many such performers the Carnival circuit (including the festivals in London, Toronto, Miami, Boston, and elsewhere) is a good way to earn extra money throughout the year. It is even the intent of Carnival organizers abroad and their umbrella organization, the International Caribbean Carnivals Association (ICCA), to stagger the events in order to maximize participation by both spectators, players, and Carnival artists. With all of this Carnival activity, most Trinidadians that I spoke with were no strangers to the event.

Even so, there is still an element of what Fredric Jameson has called "the desperate attempt to appropriate a missing past" (1991: 19). Carnival in Trinidad is frequently referred to as the "real" Carnival. Before many interviews that I conducted (or at some point during them), in nearly every conversation, and even in polite chatter on the streets as the costumed performers skipped past, I was told that I must experience true Carnival in Trinidad. Many of the organizers and band leaders I spoke with maintained that the quality in Brooklyn had reached that of Trinidad, and one organizer even stubbornly refused to acknowledge that there was any difference at all. Yet for the vast majority of Trinidadians who had no stake in "selling" me on Brooklyn Carnival, Trinidad was where I had to go.

Trinidad remains, in the words of one Carnival-goer, "the mother of all Carnivals." The festival in Trinidad, however, has another, special resonance for the Trinidadian abroad. It holds a particular place in the transnational imagination. Carnival of the present, however, is not the one that is so powerfully meaningful to returnees. It is a different Carnival that many, especially older Trinidadians remember from their youth. That was the era of the famous and elaborate fancy masquerades of George Bailey and Harold Saldenah, those were the glory years of the steelband, the calypso, before the advent of the massive sound systems, before the "wine" and "jam" Carnivals.[1] Those were also the years of the massive military and sailor bands. For Trinidadians returning home there is a quest, not simply for Trinidad, but for a place of memory, a place lodged in a particular time. To invert Lowenthal's well-known title, "the foreign country is the past."[2] At the same time the past is where the state locates its authentic national culture. The state draws its examples of a

viable, unique national culture—a culture that is marketable—from the celebrated costumes and portrayals of bygone eras. There is, then, a confluence
of two factors: on the one hand, a desire stemming from a reproductive imagination that requires authenticity, memory, legitimation; on the other, the
generation of commercially viable cultural forms, national culture, cultural
authority.

For Carnival of 1996 the National Carnival Commission inaugurated a
steelband-on-the-road contest. The prize was announced at TT$100,000. The
NCC had been concerned over the loss of the steelband presence on the road.
Steelbands over the years have slowly but surely been left behind on Carnival
Monday and Tuesday as sound systems took over. In addition the NCC and Pan
Trinbago, the steelband organization, were worried about the possible "theft"
of steelband craftsmanship and innovation by other nations. The history of the
pan (commonly referred to as the "steel drum" outside of Trinidad), many
were afraid, would be forgotten, along with the memory of its origins in
Trinidad. If other nations were allowed to appropriate the instrument without
having to give credit or pay homage to its roots in Trinidad, yet another piece
of Trinidadian history, culture, identity would be lost to the great anonymity of
"Caribbean" identity, or worse, might be lumped into some kind of Jamaican
identity, or merely forgotten as regional in any way. It might go the way of the
guitar, which hardly anyone associates with Spain any more.[3] A related concern
was that by forgetting the roots of Trinidadian culture, the performance of
celebrated Carnival traditions would be lost: no performance, no culture, no
identity at home or abroad. By way of example, in 1996 TIDCO engaged in a
massive self-promotion that included huge, multipage advertisements in the
national newspapers. In one such advertisement in *The Express,* the headline
read: "Reclaiming the Steelpan's Birthright—Born and Bred in T & T." The
article went on to describe all that TIDCO was doing to let the world know that
pan was a Trinidadian art form. Kathleen Pinder, manager of corporate communications, described a recent undertaking in which steelbands were brought
to New York to distribute flyers, give concerts, and generally "boast of their
Trinidad and Tobago roots." The group also sold pans and ended up returning
with TT$38,000. But, as Pinder stressed, "more important than the money"
was the "re-affirming of Trinidad and Tobago as the creator and home of
Steelpan in the eyes of the international community" (*Sunday Express,* Feb.
18, 1996: 26).

Thus, the NCC decided that one way to ensure the survival of the steelbands at home was to encourage them to make a showing on Carnival Tuesday as they had in the days before the mobile sound systems. The competition that was proposed rewarded the steelband with the best presentation, including the followers of the band. That is, in addition to the musicians there would have to be at least fifty costumed supporters who walked with the band. On Carnival Tuesday most of the large steelbands came out with their followers, many of who dressed in the sailor costume traditionally associated with steelband portrayals. A significant number of these sailors were from New York, Canada, and England. Their return and participation in a state-sponsored nostalgia competition highlights an important feature of the formation and continuation of the transnation.

The interaction of transnationals with their home countries nourishes both nationalist sentiment at home and ethnic identity abroad. The relationship is neither neat nor symmetrical. Returnees and locals, state representatives, culture brokers from Trinidad and from abroad, the tourist industry, all have different agendas that are in part served by and in part undermined by the promotion of and participation in contests such as this one. The steelband on the road contest is another example of a culturalism like the King and Queen competition. It differs from the King and Queen, however, in that it was quite successful both from the point of view of spectator response and participation. Yet its presence supplies the reproductive imagination of the transnation in ways that go beyond its purpose. For the returnees do not merely consume nostalgia and commodified culture passively or in the service of a state-nationalist agenda. They appropriate the raw materials of nostalgia for use in the ethnic political struggles of the metropole. What this implies, then, is that the success of the contest is only partly attributable to the efforts of the state.

Nostalgia and the Craftsman: Jason Griffith

The sailor is one of the most celebrated and oldest of masquerades, with roots extending back into the nineteenth century. As a working-class masquerade it was perhaps the most commonly played mas' by male Trinidadians who emigrated to the United States. It is also the mas' most widely remembered, at least among my informants in Brooklyn, as the mas' of their youth. Sailor bands, until their general demise in the 1960s, were routinely the largest bands on the

Fig. 9. Fancy sailors on the road.

road on Carnival Tuesday. One Trinidadian man, who has been involved with mas' since the early 1950s, described sailor bands over 3,000 strong. On one occasion, he recalled, the Silver Stars Steelband had so many sailor masquerad- ers in its ranks that the front of the band was crossing the judging venue in downtown Port-of-Spain while the rear of the band was coming up French Street in Woodbrook, a middle-class neighborhood about half a mile away.[4] One of the last sailor-band specialists still working in Carnival is Jason Griffith. I interviewed Griffith in his home in the Belmont section of Port-of-Spain. Belmont lies at the foot of the Laventille hills and is primarily a working-class neighborhood. Unlike other parts of the city, its streets are not arranged in a grid pattern but wind gently up from the eastern side of the Queen's Park Savannah. Most of the land had belonged to the Warner family, whose mem- bers included Charles Warner, the powerful attorney-general of the island from 1844 to 1870. The land was sold, incorporated into the city limits of Port- of-Spain, and brought under the jurisdiction of the government, which pro- vided for its development with the Belmont Improvement Ordinance of 1905. With the introduction of arc and incandescent lamps many hundreds of new homes were built, so that by 1907 Belmont was a thriving suburb.

Fig. 10. Fancy sailors with birds.

The area has a long history of involvement with Carnival. Like the storied neighborhoods of Woodbrook and Laventille and like the suburb of Barataria, Belmont has produced its share of notable masmen, including Harold Saldenah, who brought his band out from Oxford Street. Jason Griffith, whose name is practically synonymous with fancy sailor bands, began in 1946. He brought out his own band by 1949 after an apprenticeship with Jim Harding, one of the first fancy sailor masmen (see chapter 1). Griffith worked steadily in sailor mas' until 1955, when he shifted to working in historical and fancy mas'. Throughout the 1960s he freelanced as a costume maker, but was not deeply involved in the sailor masquerades. It was only in 1969 that he stepped back into the role of masman, making sailor costumes and headpieces and bringing out his own band from his home on Pelham Street.

When Griffith returned full-time to costume production, the steelbands and their sailor masquerades were still quite popular. Michael Anthony reports that in 1967 Desperadoes played "Fancy sailors from USS *Spikenose*"; Tokyo played sailor, calling the band "In Harms Way"; and Invaders played sailors from the USS *Wasp*. With 5,000 members, "Invaders had by far the biggest band of Carnival" (1989: 329). Yet only two years later sailors were on the wane, even if steelbands were still a fixture on Carnival Tuesday. Carnival of 1969 reflected the deep impression that Black Power politics had made on many masmen. There were at least fifteen bands that year that carried African-inspired themes, such as "Afromania '69," "Psychedelic Afro," "African Power," "Tribute to Africa," "Modern Africa," and many more. Anthony notes of that year that "All these bands seemed to swamp out the usual sailor band and other military bands," with the possible exception being Winston Gordon's band "Sailor's Ashore in Africa" (1989: 339, 341). The sailor band recovered, however. As the steelbands became less and less of an option for masqueraders, it was left to other mas' bands to pick up the sailor portrayal. A steelband boycott in 1979 probably had some small role to play, but it was the advent of soca and the massive sound systems that helped diminish the presence of steelbands.

In 1982 Jason Griffith brought out a band called "Old-Fashioned Sailors Gone Fancy," and in 1983 he designed a band called "Hats Off to Old-Fashioned Sailors." These bands were enthusiastically received but were not massive bands the way the old sailor bands were. Anthony indicates that the latter band gave viewers an idea of what "old-time Carnivals looked like." The big bands that had taken the sailor theme, Anthony points out, had had to transform the basic costume to fit the expectations of the masqueraders who demanded contemporary styles and fabrics (1989: 429). They were no longer playing sailor the way it had been played before and of all the sailor productions only Griffith remained faithful to the styles and concepts of the past masters. Griffith himself does not entirely agree with this assessment. He points to the many innovations he and his associates have made over the years, including the inclusion of historical and fantasy themes within the parameters of the sailor's basic structure. Yet this is not what he is primarily known for. By the late 1980s Griffith's bands were an expected feature of Carnival Tuesday, but some felt that they should not be judged along with the other large fancy bands (Anthony 1989: 467). They were certainly not of the same size or magnitude, even though they were some of most spectacular and finely crafted costumes present.

As the sailor mas' waned and as Jason Griffith's portrayals became more and more relegated to the realm of "living history," his bands began to attract more and more Trinidadians from abroad. In my conversations with him he mentioned that "at least two or three sections a year are made up of people from Brooklyn" (Griffith interview 1993). This is not to say that the majority of people from Brooklyn who come to Carnival play sailor. But the sailor bands are largely supported by Brooklynites and older Trinidadians within Trinidad. The gradual supercession of the sailor by other types of portrayals reflects broader changes in Carnival. Griffith pointed out to me that his is one of the last types of masquerade in which men and women both play in relatively equal numbers. What is most remarkable about that fact is that the sailor is perhaps the last masquerade that men play in at all. The sailor bands carry more male participants proportionately than any other kind of mas' band. They are the last bands that look and feel like old-time masquerade, and that is due in large measure to the supporters from home and abroad who like to keep it that way.

Carnival Nostalgia and the Transnation in New York City

Transnationalism, in many ways, takes place "on the ground." In exploring the ways in which individuals returning from abroad, especially from the older generations, choose to play mas', I was able to see a source from which they were able to draw images of ethnicity, a sort of ethno-capital. Appadurai's notion of the ethnoscape is useful here, as he notes that "even as the legitimacy of nation-states in their own territorial contexts is increasingly under threat, the idea of the nation flourishes transnationally. Safe from the depredations of their home states, diasporic communities become doubly loyal to their nations of origin. . . . As populations become deterritorialized and incompletely nationalized, as nations splinter and recombine, as states face intractable difficulties in the task of producing "the people," transnations are the most important social sites in which the crises of patriotism are played out" (1993: 424, 428). I would argue that transnations are only one of many important sites in which to view the crises of patriotism. What the example of Trinidad shows us is that the crisis of the nation's identity is not always the same as the crisis of national identity. In the serendipitous confluence of official, state-sponsored nostalgia and the nostalgia of the returning migrant we can see such disparities at work in the formation of a global ethnoscape.

It has been said that nostalgia is a particularly powerful mode of cultural expression that emerges with a great intensity in relation to the postmodern fragmentation of social life (K. Stewart 1988: 229). Stewart maintains that nostalgia "rises to importance as a cultural practice as culture becomes more and more diffuse." Nostalgia is manifested as a kind of narrative of wholeness, which seeks to redress the disruptive nature of exile and dislocation. Nostalgia, the sickness for home, is a way of re-membering not only the past but the cultural forms that presumably existed coterminously with the space and place of their occurrence. I am speaking here not only of personal nostalgia, rooted in the experiences of the individual, but of the production of a nostalgic collective memory intended to capture the common ground of individuals with specific reference to public/national cultural forms.

Important in the formulation of the contemporary ethnoscape, especially in the Trinidad case, is the overlay, the imbrication, of the forces of cultural production and consumption. By looking at official, unofficial, and semi-official discourse it is possible to map a relation between the active construction of nostalgic identities and the growth of commodity aesthetics and fetishism in the service of national culture. In addition, these currents run toward a larger stream: the formation of digestible identities, which themselves become consumed in a marketplace of identity both at home and abroad. In the previous chapter we looked at the official discourse of nostalgia as it relates to other issues such as national culture, sovereignty, and economics. This chapter has been much more concerned with the ways in which nostalgia figures into the transnational imagination. Jason Griffith is both a "national treasure" from the state's perspective and a "transnational treasure" from the point of view of returning migrants, yet he is a private individual who works in an independent capacity. The competition in 1996 was an attempt to further capitalize on the sailor nostalgia and to create a version that the state could organize and benefit from.

The Current State of the Sailor: Sailor as Nostalgia

The disappearance of the steelband from the road and the subsequent passing of the elaborate sailor and military bands that accompanied them was due largely to the middle and upper classes and their state-mandated carnival organizations, the precursors to the NCC. Steps were taken to limit steelband violence through the formation of a steelband association in 1960. The national Panorama competition was instituted a few years later, in 1963, to channel steelband rivalry into less violent outlets. Corporate sponsorship of bands, combined with new developments in mobile music technologies, ultimately rendered obsolete the steelband on the road on Carnival Tuesday. Steelbands no longer required large portrayals to help them with revenue due to corporate involvement, and mobile sound trucks became the musical choice of most other kinds of masquerade bands.

Ironically, the very class that helped to bring it about later lamented the passing of the steelband from the road. Once the steelband had been appropriately tamed through competition and sponsorship, it was reintroduced to society as an example of bona fide cultural heritage. In 1996 many of the older, more established steelbands emerged to vie for the TT$100,000, quite a few of them playing sailor. The masqueraders were no longer the rowdy youths of the 1940s and '50s, but an older set, playing nostalgia mas'. In a sense, they were playing a masquerade of the masquerade of another era. The presence of the steelbands brought with it the possibility of experiencing something like the old-time Carnival. Something that Jason Griffith could not provide was the steelband presence. Furthermore, these were not the elaborate fancy sailors of Griffith's band but the old sailors on shore leave whose era had passed nearly twenty years before.

Sailor Mas' 1996: The "Utopia of Use Value"

The steelband competition exoticized Carnival to returnees. In doing so the state established a crucial separation between the past and the here and now and privileged the former over the latter. Yet the state, in general, sees this process as a form of recovery different from that of the returnees. For the state, recovery carries with it the promise of product differentiation; in the objectification of the past the state trades on the power of "use value" as a form of marketing. The object's cachet as artifact becomes its attraction in exchange such that its use value (imagined, in this case, as the sailor masquerade's existence outside of commercial and degraded Carnival and, ironically, its capacity to restore and supply authenticity to the returning consumer) *is* its exchange value. Susan Stewart treats this connection between use value and nostalgia and concludes that what she calls the "souvenir's" power is not only its separation from the present but also its ability to figure into a narrative of restoration: "The souvenir must be removed from its context in order to serve as a trace of it, but it must also be restored through narrative and or reverie. What it is restored to is not an 'authentic', that is, a native context of origin but an imaginary context of origin" (1993: 150). Stewart points out the importance of context for the nostalgic object, a crucial difference that, in this case, determines the success or failure of state-sponsored cultural forms. Stewart claims that such narratives relate to an "imaginary" context of origin, which to me implies the "invention" of a context, a fabrication. If we take her meaning to be that the context is imaginary in that it is no longer the immediate context and must be supplied by the imagination, then I would certainly agree that its presence is vital in reinforcing ideas of identity in the realm of the reproductive imagination.[5]

Conclusion

The growth of a thriving Carnival industry between Trinidad and the United States relies not only on the presence of Trinidadians in the foreign metropole but also on the persistent desire on the part of dislocated nationals to want to cultivate and perpetuate a cultural heritage. This requires two interconnected yet distinct circumstances: lack of—or, more accurately, resistance to—assimilation on the one hand, and adaptation to local identity politics on the other. Lack of assimilation is marked not so much by a maintenance of radical difference but by a conformity to the general shape of difference required by American-style multiculturalism. By looking at the sailor mas' as it developed in Trinidad, we have seen the unstable and fluid relationship that masqueraders have to the state and state-sponsored institutions there, as well as the ways in which players in masquerade bands have been partially successful in negotiating political-identity terrain that has expanded to include more than just the neighborhoods, city, and national boundaries. Traces of Brooklyn and the United States in general hang over the actions of Trinidadians in Trinidad, sometimes in ways that are clearly perceived and sometimes in ways that are only partially understood or understood not at all.

In creating a Trinidadian identity, Trinidadian transmigrants abroad must negotiate the fragmented and dislocated nature of the transmigrant experience. To that end Trinidadians in New York frequently draw upon essentialized cultural forms from which to imagine a concrete social identity. Such forms are frequently found in the nationalist cultural mythologies of the "homeland" from which the transmigrants have come. These mythologies take the form of cultural and historical narratives that serve to legitimize Trinidadian sovereignty and autonomy within the global family of nations. But such narratives must be relevant and must resonate with the other versions maintained in the minds and practices of the transnationals themselves. And this often carries the production of meaning away from the one envisioned by the state. Thus even as the state counts its projects successful by seeing them played out on the streets of Port-of-Spain, it may be watching those projects slipping from its grasp.

Conclusion

Implications of the Transnation, Querying Culturalism

What is the point of emphasizing the exchange quality of cultural goods? This book has taken as its task the various uses of cultural forms in the production of identity, part of which lies in showing how individuals mobilize cultural forms in relations of exchange. Such relations can be broadly construed but share a commonality in the presentation of objects in return for money, recognition, sovereignty, and other forms of capital. I have extrapolated from a definition of culture that emphasizes difference, de-emphasizes essence, and focuses on interaction. This definition of culture was arrived at primarily because the definition of culture that is in circulation in official circles tends to stress difference, but in an essentialized manner.

The politics of recognition that arose in opposition to monocultural views has given way in many instances to repressive forms of multiculturalism. Demonstrating the shared strategies of multiculturalist, emancipatory politics, and, for instance, advertising, tourism, bureaucratic administrations, and other potentially repressive or exploitative organizations suggests that pursuing strictly multiculturalist politics does not necessarily make for a progressive agenda.

But, by way of contrast, the existence of transnations, such as the Trinidadian example, shows us that people make use of cultural forms even after they have been commodified or objectified. The results can be quite different than those expected or desired by the originators. Thus, it is not the commodification of cultural forms but their negotiation that is of interest. In many ways the act of commodification facilitates the formation of the transnation. That is, in the context of the economy of identity, tangible cultural forms make for easier negotiation and exchange. This, in part, helps the transnational imagination. I say in part because what I have tried to show is that such processes are always at risk of being undermined. We have seen how the actions of limers, or the particular needs of the groups doing the "imagining," will play a part in the general formation of a transnation. Thus being Trinidadian will always be modified by *also* being a woman, being from a different generation, being a masman, or a culture broker. The processes of imagination are also never purely "resistant" to official discourse. Many of the attitudes consciously or unconsciously held by Trinidadians show that there is a great deal of agreement between the two. Finally, such agreements may exist for very different reasons. As we saw with "Fuzzy" Davis, his feelings about mas' are similar to the sentiments expressed by state agencies in Trinidad, but they are not clear evidence of those agencies' hegemony.

This study has attempted to show the numerous variables that go into the process of imagining a transnational community. Hemmed in from many sides, with agency and structure in a continuous dialectical engagement, the transnation emerges as a collective sense during certain moments but does not necessarily last or even make itself present for much of the time. The transnation is about presentation, but it is also outside of conscious strategy. To return to the image given in the introduction of the winnowing tray, I would stress that the transnation idea is present on many occasions, but sometimes only as a tacit frame. That is, as long as events exist in New York at which West Indians gather to seek each other out *as West Indians* the transnation will be there.

The negotiation of identity that results in the transnation takes place within the larger ideological framework of recognition politics. Working from micro- to macro-perspectives, anthropologists can begin to see the myriad relations that local actions have to large "vistas" of ideology.[1] That is, we can look more closely at the dialectical nature of identity formation as it engages with ideological parameters that may (but need not) exist outside of the conscious actions of people.

I see the larger "vista" as comprising a very specific conception of culture that has a unique and Western pedigree. I do not believe that it is the only concept of culture to have emerged from the West, nor do I believe that its circulation has left it unaltered. I do see, however, that its currency is increased by the spread of global media, capitalism, and other contemporary transformations. I also see that a kind of universalized notion of culture is prominent in the rhetorical strategies of nation-states as well as in the language of marketing and advertising. I cannot help but see them as related. However I would caution anthropologists not to overemphasize the efficacy of "culturalist" discourse. The transnation, to my mind, is a unique kind of imagined identity in that it must incorporate the kinds of narratives that lend it coherence and thus may draw upon "official discourse," yet at the same time transnationals find themselves amongst many such discourses *and* living in situations that no official, administrative, or governmental body quite controls.

This situation, almost a kind of international liminality, produces a new kind of international *communitas* (to borrow, loosely, from Turner 1969). Carnival provides an ideal cultural form for the reproductive imagination essential in the formation of the transnation. It is tangible, marketable—an object. It has a relationship to a nation (Trinidad) that provides imaginants with plenty of official rhetoric. Its form can be suited to New York City's ethnic politics, and within the cultural form itself individuals are encouraged to act out their personal fantasies and imaginations: "When you playing mas' your whole self free up. You could be anything, do anything. You could be warrior, or goddess or something from the imagination. You know what I am saying? But is Trinidad where you get the Carnival, is a Trinidadian thing too. So you could just be a Trinidadian" (Morris interview 1993).

Anthropology and "Culturalist" Discourse

Much of the theoretical preoccupation in this book has been with establishing the subtlety and complexity of the relationships between people's lives and actions and the institutional rhetoric they encounter in cultural contexts. Toward this end I have developed a way of thinking about these relationships as forms of exchange. These types of exchanges are symbolic in nature but have very real connections to economic and political realities as well. Certainly a good deal has been written about the role of culture in a globalizing economy (Featherstone 1990; King 1997; Tomlinson 1999; Lash and Urry 1994; Jameson and Miyoshi 1998), but little of it has been rooted in close examination of a particular community or cultural form (but see Davila 1997). By turning ethnographic method to focus on the specifics of commodification, official rhetoric, and what may be seen as institutionalization, anthropology begins to engage with the complex interplay between city-, nation-, or state-sponsored culture and its life within a given community. Here the focus should fall squarely on the issue of "culturalisms," and their contribution to what

Raymond Williams has called "structures of feeling" (Williams 1977). Why is this so crucial? Because it is the mobilization of ethnic sentiment through the medium of political rhetoric and "culture" seen as primarily "ethnic" or national that may contribute to the kinds of violence seen in Crown Heights. The discourse of culture is not neutral in its applications, which becomes clear when it is perceived in relation to the kinds of social contexts I have explored here; social contexts that to me are contexts of exchange (and not simply resource competition) and that play an enormous role in molding the structures of a given identity.

As students of ethnicity our first task is to understand that comprehending the social construction of identity or the creation of official national cultures is only part of the problem. The relationship between the two is deeply problematized by internal differences in the targeted constituency of any group. My own experience showed the deep divide and ongoing struggle to define the "national culture" let alone impose it, whole cloth, onto a homogenous pre-existing collective called Trinidadians. Age and gender are only a small part of the picture when we consider that the ethnic tensions between African and Indian Trinidadians simply do not go away in the face of the foregrounding of national or regional identities in New York.[2] Similarly, Trinidadians are "defining" themselves not solely within the context of a nation-state but also in a wide range of political contexts in places as diverse as London, New York, and Toronto. Each locale has its own set of issues and complications, but the Trinidadians existing in and between these sites are in a kind of contact with each other that both seems to necessitate a coherent cultural façade and promotes continual disjuncture. In the face of these developments future studies of Caribbean cultural forms must explore the growth of new kinds of institutions and strategies both at home and abroad to handle issues of cultural identity.

With regard to culturalisms scholars should begin to pay more attention to the increasing role that legal recourse plays in managing and controlling cultural forms linked with cultural identity. Copyright in particular is emerging as a serious strategy for institutions involved with or charged with the guardianship of national culture (Coombe 1998; Ziff and Rao 1997). This phenomenon is ostensibly concerned with curbing the depredations of something called *cultural appropriation,* which is vague in its substance. The guiding idea, though, seems to be that cultural forms, which belong to a group, are threatened by globalization, diaspora, foreign influence, and theft and must be protected by legal means. In most cases those institutions responsible for these objectified cultural forms are acknowledging the limits of their control and seeking recourse in international bodies such as the World Intellectual Property Organization or UNESCO. The future success or failure of these strategies is less important here than understanding the impulses that compel them. Because as legal strategies gain in importance, anthropologists and the legitimizing work of anthropology become more and more central as "witnesses for the defense." In the legal rhetoric, "any utilization made with both gainful intent and outside the traditional or customary context of folklore, without authorization by *a competent authority* or the community concerned" (WIPO/UNESCO Model Provisions for National Laws on Sui Generis Protection of Expressions of Folklore against Illicit Exploitation and Other Prejudicial Actions 1982).

Anthropologists are one of several of these "competent" authorities who may both decide what is legitimately cultural and subsequently grant license to "use" such forms. This is an area of concern. On the one hand, anthropologists have often championed the indigenous cultural form, beleaguered folkway, or stolen expression and set themselves up as a line of defense against appropriation without paying strong enough attention to the subsequent uses of their work in political processes that may not be agreeable. Furthermore, through this kind of work anthropologists champion an idea of culture that, as I have indicated, is essentialist.

As I have mentioned, one element in the debate over cultural appropriation that seems routinely ignored or downplayed is appropriation or re-appropriation from within. Who acts to represent the "culture" in question? What do they have to gain? We cannot assume the monolithic nature of another "culture" or group, especially when discussing the political and legal protection of heritage. Interests are at work. Preservation, broadly construed, has powerful resonance in that it creates a situation of "stakes" that were not there before. We must be careful to explore all the ramifications of preservation and appropriation at the local level. Appropriation is not about one group taking from another group by "reaching into" some static, primordial corpus of cultural goods that are equally shared. The power of the politics of appropriation derives from an understanding that groups, defined by their cultural forms, preexist these disputes. Organizations that can position themselves to recapture lost cultural forms are in a position to define local culture and secure their own authority over it. But it is in the dispute that group identity is formulated and heritage defined.

Ultimately, it is not really the fact or act of appropriation or commodification that is at stake here. Appropriation, from the perspective of many artists, is a good thing in that it spreads awareness of and promotes the popularity of certain artistic or expressive forms, which can be good for business. It's the recourse or control of appropriation that matters—that credit be given or awareness of sources heightened. Origins become forgotten, and as a consequence groups disappear as their objects float without anchor. Cultural amnesia hurts the state cultural organizations that may profit financially and symbolically from control over unique and recognizable cultural forms.

Carnival has never been merely a collection of roles and characters but the actions and activities of people who play with a given framework and may reinvent perceived traditions even as they invent novel expressive practices. Carnival provides a forum for expression that, by necessity, needs to respond to shifting contexts and transformations not only within the society but also on a global scale. The popularity of the sailor bands in the 1940s and '50s, the midnight robbers, the Dames Lorraine was always due to the efficacious way in which these forms engaged with historical phenomena of immediate importance. The "wine and jam" carnival of today is actively constructed and responds to the concerns of those who play in it. It has become middle class, commodified, and hybridized. It may be unrecognizable to many Trinidadians who lived through the Carnivals of the 1940s, but it has created a new kind of identity and community. It draws on sources from outside of Trinidad, which becomes a chief cause of concern for any preservation project that has, at least in part, the maintenance of cultural sovereignty as its goal. The preservationist strategy relies upon scholarly documentation and recourse to international legal bodies to define what is properly cultural and thereby limits or excludes significant portions of society as they seek to construct meaningful forms, culturalisms, for themselves.

Anthropologists, therefore, find themselves in a difficult situation. Attempting to report on the practices of people who are not necessarily involved in the construction of culturalisms always runs the risk of institutionalizing those practices, primarily because anthropologists still betray a desire to seek out the authentic, the uncommodified, the elusively resistant form. It is that very quality that gives anthropology a reputation as the discoverer of the authentic and thus the appropriate voice for authenticating cultural forms. I do not mean to attribute to anthropology some inordinate power in this process. Frankly, there are some cultural forms we might "celebrate" that would never be incorporated in a nationalist cultural project of any sort. Even so, many do.[3] As we come to understand how fully we are implicated in these processes, it is also important to understand that we do not fully determine their outcomes. By focusing attention on the shifting terrain of cultural construction, the specific historical and political circumstances, we come to understand the full complexity of the process of transnational cultural formations.

Notes

Introduction

1. I originally devised the term transnation to describe, generally, the idea of an imagined community (in Benedict Anderson's [1983] sense) in diaspora. Arjun Appadurai has since expanded on the term in a much more profound manner. See section in this chapter.

2. Some attempt has been made to distinguish global communities, transnational communities, and diasporic communities in order to refine our understanding of how culture change might be linked differently to different processes of dispersion. Yet the distinctions that have been made, for instance, between transnational communities referring to migrant communities that span two nations (Basch et al. 1994) and diasporic communities in which community members are scattered more widely (Gonzalez 1992) seem inadequate as ways of accounting for cultural developments if they focus on scale of dispersion.

3. It took the followers of Marx—e.g., Antonio Gramsci, the members of the Frankfurt School, Georg Lukács, Jürgen Habermas, and others—to refine the relationship between commodification and culture. Yet their particular notions of culture are by no means identical to understandings of culture as they have developed in anthropology.

4. Symbolic capital is "prestige, or authority" the making of a name for oneself, with the ability to imbue other objects with this value and therefore to accumulate economic or other kinds of capital. Cultural capital is more specifically the knowledge, talent, or skill required to participate as a legitimate player. The two "capitals" are intimately linked, especially with regard to Carnival.

5. Thus I am in basic agreement with Appadurai's (1996) usage of imagination, which owes something to ideas developed by Anderson (1983). My interest here, however, is not primarily in the role that the mass media plays in the imagination (although I will be citing mass-media sources) but more in the groups that are behind the creation of historical and cultural narratives of identity.

Chapter 1. Carnival in Trinidad

1. This practice is not followed by all historians. For instance, Brereton (1979) calls African only those people born in Africa.

2. It is common in Trinidad for people of Indian descent to be called "East Indian."

3. In brief, the binary scheme Miller (1994) uses is meant to overcome traditional dichotomous explanations of Caribbean society. Miller is not opposed to seeing the Caribbean in dualistic terms (an approach that has marked a good deal of Caribbean anthropology), but he sees the roots of these oppositions in the legacy of modernity conceived of as a kind of self-consciousness, not as the result of primordial cultural differences (African versus European), gender differences, class differences, etc.

4. Miller provides an account of the "respectability" versus "reputation" dualism that has marked some Caribbean anthropologists' approach to Caribbean social organization and gender roles (Miller 1994: 260–63), as has van Koningsbruggen (1997).

5. There are a host of local terms for "bad" women in Trinidad, including Jagabat and Wabeen, the latter being derived from Guabine, a fish that thrives in dirty water.

6. Talking broad is characterized by public, competitive performance. Abrahams notes that "women are often as quick to enter such an on-the-spot contest of wits as men" (1983: 3).

7. American culture is not uniformly accepted or absorbed by Trinidadian audiences in any monolithic way. Black audiences in Trinidad tend to listen to black American music and emulate black American style. Indian teenagers, while still often fans of black music, will be much more likely to listen to white heavy metal or alternative rock than their black counterparts.

8. See Barbara E. Powrie (1988 [1956]: 101) for a fuller discussion of the varieties of middle-class identities in nineteenth-century Trinidad.

9. Thomas, in his book *Froudacity,* talks about the potential of Africans outside of Africa to raise up the race (1969 [1889]: 179).

10. See, for instance, van Koningsbruggen (1997).

11. Trinidad today has an enormous number of competitions both inside and outside of Carnival. Success is measured by performance in competitions almost exclusively. There are competitions for sport, beauty (pageants), Indian dance and singing, calypso, steelband, scholarships, fashion, cooking, and a host of competitions within the business world. The daily newspapers are filled with award winners and plaque recipients.

12. Competition judges were drawn from a wide range of sources but were generally members of the "respectable" classes. For instance, an early calypso competition in 1927 boasted the services of Captain A. A. Cipriani, a wealthy planter but also a staunch laborite politician.

13. This is not to say that there were no standards of judgment prior to middle-class

competitions. There certainly were and continue to be such standards (see Davis interview, chap. 4). However, the competition creates a new forum of exchange. The calypsonian who sang in praise of his stickfighters or in condemnation of the authorities could continue to do so in the sponsored tents, but was subject to standards of decency and decorum that were not present in the barrack yards or rumshops.

14. Calypso singing, even before official tents were established, was social and often competitive. It is part of the New World African tradition of competitive singing that encompasses a wide variety of forms including blues, jazz, rap, and dancehall reggae, to name a few.

15. Rohlehr offers a thorough account of the role of the *Argos* in its support of Carnival and its opposition to the Crown Colony administration (1990: 90–91).

16. Calypsos lamenting the passing of the Tamboo Bamboo bands appear in the late 1930s, citing a preference for them over newer forms of music from abroad such as jazz (see Rohlehr 1990: 178).

17. Rohlehr (1990) has outlined these struggles in great detail. Of chief importance is the basic division between the middle class, Savannah-St. Clair, Carnival Queen competition and the Carnival Improvement Committee, and the Carnival Bands Union that stressed the Calypso King competition and the continuance of the Carnival in something like its pre–World War I form. Although all the various committees and organizations had moralizing goals, the real test was to wrest control from the other organizations to shape the Carnival in one particular bourgeois image or another.

18. Errol Hill also makes mention of this event (Hill 1972: 101) but cites the *Trinidad Guardian* of 1938. I am not sure if this is a misprint and he meant for it to read 1838 (the date of Joseph's book), but in any case Joseph implies that the event happened sometime before the writing of the book, which would place it before 1838. It may be that the *Guardian* was merely citing Joseph (the wording of the two accounts is very similar) as an example of the glory of old-time masquerade costumes. As it is, I use the Joseph account here.

19. Recently Peter Minshall has attempted set pieces on the Savannah stage and is often criticized for it. However, in 1995 he portrayed an allegorical scene for his band "Hallelujah" that won the Band of the Year award.

20. Rohlehr (1990) has discussed the substitution of commercialism for eroticism in the post-War Carnival, with special emphasis on the evolution of the calypso. I would agree with perhaps one addition, which might be deemed the commercialization *of* eroticism. The appearance of erotic and suggestive themes were at one and the same time decried by the conservative/religious sectors of society while at the same time recognized as assets in the budding Carnival tourism industry. Foreigners liked to see beautiful bodies cavorting in the sunshine—there was really no way around it. Furthermore, a whole generation of young middle-class women suddenly entered into Carnival for the first time. Their portrayals were generally of the more "erotic" kind, and they

generally supported masquerades of this type. These kinds of contradictions repeatedly split the middle classes in Trinidad, and it is unwise to view the bourgeoisie as a unified whole in its dealings with Carnival matters. It is also unwise to view the steady march of middle-class encroachment and rapid commercialization as inevitable and in no way resisted.

21. I am reminded of my first trip to a calypso tent during the Carnival in 1994. I arrived late and was searching for a seat in the darkened hall when the national anthem, ubiquitous in Trinidad, was begun. Used to conditions at, say, sporting events in the United States, I did not let the playing of the anthem deter me from continuing to search for a seat. My activity caused some consternation and finally one man tapped me on the shoulder and gruffly reminded me that the national anthem was playing and that I should stop, face the stage, and be quiet. I was attentive to that practice from then after.

22. My discussion of the sailor in this context is limited to its form and development in Trinidad specifically. Nautical masquerade themes are widespread throughout the Caribbean and can be found in masking traditions across the globe. In Barbados the Land Ship was an important festival portrayal, as were the ship headpieces in Jonkonnu in both Jamaica and the Bahamas.

23. There are many calypsos that deal with this particular feature of the American presence in Trinidad. There were also many stories told of husbands and boyfriends being cuckolded. One such story has a man questioning his partner about the lightness of their newborn baby's skin. The woman replies that she has been drinking milk of magnesia to lighten the complexion of the baby (a common conception at the time), to which the man replies that she must have eaten the bottle as well, as the baby had blue eyes. The story underlies the position that American servicemen held in the eyes of many Trinidadian women, whose goal was not necessarily marriage but the advancement of the prospects of their children in a system based heavily on skin color. The triumphant calypso by the Mighty Sparrow, "Jean and Dinah," effectively signaled the end of such foreign humiliation of Trinidadian masculinity, as Sparrow sings of the Yankee departure and his restoration to a rightful position of dominance.

Chapter 2. The Brooklyn Carnival

1. I was often struck by how many people in Trinidad wear articles of clothing that refer to Trinidad. Afraid of looking too much like a tourist, I assiduously avoided wearing "Trinidad" t-shirts until I began to realize that (a) my fears were the product of an absurd pretension and (b) *many* people wore such shirts.

2. There is a voluminous literature on West Indian migration to the United States, the United Kingdom, and Canada, as well as intra-Caribbean migration. For a thorough treatment of West Indian movement to the United States see Palmer (1995). This is a very good treatment of the migration literature in general, although see also Chaney and Bryce-Laporte, respectively, in Sutton and Chaney (1987).

3. Jean Grugel (1995: 180), for instance, notes that even with the oil boom, foreign investment slowed down in Jamaica and Trinidad, with divestment occurring. Prices for other main exports fell at the same time as agriculture and food production declined.

4. A recent radio program in Trinidad cited this trade as a possible area for expansion for the Trinidadian economy. Local scholars from the University of the West Indies pointed out that as Trinidadians have established a presence in New York and other foreign locales they have carried with them their culture and exposed foreigners to cultural products such as Carnival, soca music (Trinidadian Carnival music), and West Indian foods. It only remained for the government to seize upon these opportunities to both make profit and promote national culture abroad (Breakfast Club Radio Program, Trinidad, December 1993).

5. *New York Age,* September 7, 1957.

6. Advertisements and notices concerning the parade could be found in African American newspapers up and down the East Coast. For example, a notice from 1955 in the *Afro-American*, a Baltimore journal, announced plans for the ninth annual parade.

7. Perhaps the most significant event to affect the Carnival occurred in 1991 when West Indians, African Americans, and Jews in Crown Heights became embroiled in conflict after a car driven by a Hasidic Jew struck and killed a young West Indian boy. Hours later a Hasidic student was stabbed to death nearby in retaliation. This series of events and their relationship to the Carnival will be discussed in greater detail in chap. 4.

8. Much of the data on this portion of the Carnival comes from Kasinitz's excellent study, *Caribbean New York* (1992).

Chapter 3. Mas' Camps and Masqueraders

1. In Trinidad the Carnival season begins in September or early October when bands are "launched" with fetes. The newest crop of soca songs, however, does not generally emerge until after Christmas, especially on New Year's Eve. After that they are heard almost to the exclusion of all else on popular radio until after Carnival, when their play is greatly reduced, and they all but disappear by the summer. At this point radio stations will resume their normal fare of soul hits from the United States and Jamaican dub and dancehall reggae. This has continued to cause some controversy amongst soca artists and calypsonians, who tend to be frustrated by what this seasonality does to their ability to sell records and pursue their careers year round. The grand continuum of Carnivals that now exists is vital to the livelihood of most soca artists (with a few exceptions).

2. This does not imply that people are refused because they are "too dark," although a tacit color barrier is maintained in other areas of Trinidadian life. One young woman, for instance, who was a bit darker than one of her group of friends was bitter about the kinds of clubs they went to. Although she was admitted to the same places as they were it was clear that it was because she was exceptional in her looks and an exception was being made. Some of her other friends and relatives, however, might have been barred

from entrance. The color line in Carnival is more flexible and seems rather self-selective. This does not mean that color discrimination is absent from Carnival bands, however.

3. I am using pseudonyms in this section.

4. For a penetrating fictional treatment of barrack yard life, see C.L.R. James's *Minty Alley.*

5. For a full treatment of the Fancy Indian see Daniel J. Crowley, "The Traditional Masques of Carnival," *Caribbean Quarterly* (1956).

Chapter 4. Bureaucratic Multiculturalism and West Indian American Day

1. Basch (1987) gives some idea here of the entrenched philosophy of ethnicity-based political policy in New York. N.B. The Mayor's Ethnic Advisory Council was dissolved after the Dinkins administration. In Brooklyn the Bureau of Ethnic Affairs, a branch of the borough president's office, continues to handle such disputes, as it has for nine years.

2. The following account was pieced together from a number of newspaper accounts, editorials, and academic articles that purported to describe the event. Their accuracy cannot, of course, be fully guaranteed. For a partial list of sources please see the bibliography section at the end of the book.

3. It is not clear what percentage of protesters, throughout the disturbance, were West Indian, of West Indian descent, or native African Americans.

4. It is not within the scope of this chapter to detail the growth and changes in the political character of the Caribbean community in New York. See Kasinitz's excellent study (1992) for a detailed overview of these issues. It is worth noting, however, that Caribbean Americans have often acted like "traditional" immigrant groups *and* members of a "racial" minority during the course of their history in the United States.

5. This is one significant problem, for instance, with the pluralism model advanced by M. G. Smith in the Caribbean. Smith's model was meant to explain multiethnic societies in colonial or postcolonial settings where culturally unrelated groups interact under the administrative framework of a colonial power. These societies cannot integrate successfully because they lack a common "social will" (M. G. Smith 1965). Smith assumes throughout, however, that the separate cultures he is describing are unproblematically "given."

6. Here I am referring to public statements expressed by local leaders and editorialists in some of the leading Caribbean publications in New York. See, for example Sleeper (1988) for an overview.

7. It is not only the "people on the street" who manipulate the forms or practices of elements within the Carnival. Officials responsible for the presentation of the festival, despite some protests to the contrary, have actively changed the Carnival for their own purposes over the years. See Kasinitz 1992 and, for example, Cohen 1993 for examples from London's Notting Hill Carnival.

8. At one such symposium at Medgar Evers College a featured guest speaker was one Rabbi Yisrael Francis, described as an "African-Caribbean-American-Hasidic Jew."

9. The case of the Koreans is problematic because it has resulted in the inclusion of another ethnic group *within* the Carnival, which, if even only minutely, begins to dilute the festival as an ethnic display event.

10. Dean MacCannell has called ethnic tourism, for instance, the mirror image of racism. He draws a distinction between constructed ethnicity and reconstructed ethnicity, the difference being that constructed ethnicity is generally undertaken by the ethnic group as a way of developing a political voice while reconstructed ethnicity is undertaken by the tourist market. I fundamentally agree with MacCannell that these two processes are related. I am particularly interested in the blurring of these definitions, however. The internally generated ethnic construction often serves the reconstruction process quite well (see MacCannell 1992: 158–59, 172–80).

11. See the special issue of *Cultural Anthropology* 11, no. 4 (November 1996) edited by Daniel Segal.

12. I am referring here to the enormously influential volumes *Imagined Communities,* by Benedict Anderson, and *The Invention of Tradition,* by Eric Hobsbawm and Terrence Ranger.

Chapter 5. Bringing It All Back Home

1. These issues were discussed at a symposium entitled "Carnival: Exploring the Export Potential" and comprised a conference and workshop held at the University of the West Indies, February 18, 1994.

2. In chapter 6 I explore the "culture panic" phenomenon more specifically, drawing upon the case of the steelband and the pan or steel drum. The fear of culture loss or theft manifests itself differently for people outside of strictly governmental or entrepreneurial capacities. These divisions tend to coincide with the divisions in the narratives of Carnival's meaning discussed in the first chapter.

3. The Carnival in Rio de Janeiro, Brazil, is one major "competitor," as is Mardi Gras in New Orleans.

Chapter 6. Playing Sailor Mas', or When "Natives" Become Tourists of Themselves

1. Wining and jamming are descriptive terms for dancing. They are especially erotic and symbolize to many the downfall of the Carnival, its loss of craftsmanship, and its defeat by the forces of debauchery and commercialism.

2. This is a reference to Lowenthal's *The Past Is a Foreign Country* (1985).

3. The fervor over pan reached a peak during my stay in Trinidad. Articles appeared routinely in the newspapers that seemed to contribute to the "pan-ic" or "steal-

band," as I began to think of it. Innovations in pan design by Canadians or the Swiss, which were being patented, Americans teaching pan in Japan instead of Trinidadians, and steel orchestras being founded in Europe without Trinidadian input or expertise were all sources of anxiety. The final controversy surrounded the debate over the teaching of the pan versus the harmonium in schools. Many Trinidadians, especially those of African descent, considered the pan the logical choice of instrument for musical instruction in the schools because it is the only instrument to have been invented in Trinidad and is routinely cited as the only new acoustic instrument to have been invented in the twentieth century, anywhere. The harmonium, championed especially by Indo-Trinidadians as an example of their cultural heritage, is rejected as a colonial instrument, introduced by the English into India and therefore not even "authentically" Indian, let alone Trinidadian. The positioning of Indians within Trinidad as ethnic minorities, no matter what their numbers in the population, has been a feature of Trinidadian cultural negotiation. Indo-Trinidadians have often emphasized their separateness from Trinidadian culture and their connection to India, leaving, by exnomination, African Trinidadians as the bearers of the national culture in their capacity as "Creole." This has emerged historically both by conscious withdrawal from national culture and by exclusion from it. This trend has changed dramatically since the majority Indian party, the UNC, has come to power. There now seems to be a greater interest in demonstrating the Indian contribution to Trinidadian culture and society.

4. This story was related to me by Winston Carr, the son of well-known Trinidadian folklorist Andrew Carr.

5. Susan Stewart (1993).

Conclusion

1. By "vista" of ideology I mean a widespread body of ideas, concepts, and assumptions that exists in the popular consciousness and may be traceable through a kind of genealogical intellectual exercise. Appadurai has termed these vistas "ideoscapes" (1996), and Taylor has traced the ideological roots of "recognition" to similar effect (1992). Both authors set current intellectual concerns against these backdrops to show the pervasive, often naturalized forms they can take.

2. For a similar discussion related to Carnival in Canada, see F. Manning 1983.

3. Some years ago I had the good fortune to meet Daniel Crowley, an American scholar who is a well-known and much beloved figure in the older intellectual circles of Trinidad. He was one of the first of a group of scholars to make Carnival the object of serious intellectual inquiry. In that regard he contributed valuable essays to a 1956 issue of the *Caribbean Quarterly* dedicated to Carnival. In one essay he wrote about the "Traditional Masques of Carnival" (Crowley 1956b), in which he cataloged the

most important Carnival characters. We were discussing this essay at lunch with several other Carnival and Caribbean scholars, and he confessed he did not recall ever hearing the term Dimanche Gras before he wrote about it and suspected he might have invented it. It is now thoroughly canonized in the official Carnival as the Sunday night before Carnival starts.

Glossary of Trinidadian Terms

Baby Doll: A costume somewhat similar to the Dame Lorraine, accompanied by a drama in which passersby are accosted by the masquerader who accuses them of fathering an illegitimate child (a doll). The baby doll threatens to call a policeman if the accused does not give some money for "child support."

Bacchanal: A key term in Trinidad and Tobago. Although most usage carries with it the general sense of confusion, uproar, and disorder, it can be both good and bad. Thus it can be used to describe a noisy and joyous occasion as well as extremely disreputable and scandalous conduct.

Bad John: An outlaw, a man of violent behavior and criminal reputation.

Band: A group of masqueraders, organized around a theme and divided into sections that participate in Carnival. The band is organized by a bandleader and competes against other bands for the band of the year title. Historically the term was used to designate groups of stickfighters, or the associated female singing and dancing societies.

Bandleader: The organizer and (sometimes) designer of a Carnival band.

Barataria: An eastern suburb of Port-of-Spain, Barataria has a rich Carnival tradition including two of the best known wirebenders: Cito Velasquez and Geraldo Vieira.

Barrack Yard: The yards created by the formation of barracks around central space. Such barracks provided housing for laborers in and around Port-of-Spain and consisted of a long, low building with small rooms divided from one another but under the same roof. The barrack yards were communal and often held the one, shared water source. Barrack yards became associated with rough language and behavior and have also been cited as the source and performance center for many masquerade types, especially the Dame Lorraine.

Belmont: A working-class neighborhood in Port-of-Spain, Belmont is home to one of the last Fancy sailor bands, that of Jason Griffith.

Blue Devil: A masquerade figure dressed in shorts and painted blue. The blue devils travel in bands and make an eerie, high pitched whooping noise. They often have one of their number in chains who must be forcibly restrained. They gather money from spectators in return for keeping the dangerous devil away.

Borokeete (also **Burroquite, Borokeet, Boroquite,** etc.): A masquerade costume in which a man or woman appears to be riding on a donkey. The donkey costume is worn around the waist, and the masquerader's torso rises up from the middle of the donkey's back. This masquerade is very popular with Indian masqueraders.

Brass Band: Term used to describe musical band at Carnival and to distinguish it from a Carnival band. There need not be any brass instruments in the band, but there are frequently horns.

Buljol and Bake: Traditional Carnival breakfast food often served with coffee. Buljol is made from salt fish that has been soaked and shredded and made into a salad with hot peppers, tomatoes, cucumbers, and other ingredients. The word comes from the French *brûle-gueule*, or burn-mouth. Bake is a deep fried bread.

Calypso (also **Kaiso, Cariso**): A popular song marked, traditionally, by clever rhyming and social commentary. Calypsos may be either written or extemporaneous and are generally topical.

Calypso Monarch: Awarded at a competition held at the Savannah, the calypso monarch (formerly calypso king) is the performer judged to have the best new calypsos of the year.

Carnival King: The largest and fanciest male costume of any band. The winner of a competition of such costumes held during Dimanche Gras is crowned carnival king for that year.

Carnival Queen: The largest and fanciest female costume of any band (*see* **Carnival King**). Not to be confused with the Queen of Carnival, who was the winner of the prestigious beauty pageant (now defunct) of the same name.

Chipping, Chip: A light, easy, shuffling dance used as both rhythmic locomotion and a way to rest while marching in a band or following a steelband.

Dame Lorraine: A Carnival figure of a man dressed as a woman with exaggerated buttocks and oversized breasts. The buttocks sway in a comical fashion when the masquerader walks.

Dimanche Gras: From the French meaning fat Sunday, or meat Sunday, this is the Sunday before Ash Wednesday and the beginning of Lent. In Trinidad, Dimanche Gras is marked by Carnival competitions including the calypso monarch competition and the king and queen of Carnival costume contest.

Fancy Sailor: A version of the sailor costume characterized by elaborate decoration and intricate, often humorous headpieces. (*See also* **Sailor; King Sailor.**)

Fatigue: To bother or pester verbally, to tease.

Grand Stand: Area of seating on the south side of the Savannah stage where the judges and the quieter audiences sit. One can generally hear better in the grand stand and this is where pan aficionados sit during Panorama.

Headpiece: That part of Carnival costume worn on the head.

Jab Jab: From the French *diable* (devil), a Carnival costume in which the masquerader dresses as a devil. Now associated primarily with J'ouvert.

Jab Molassi: Molasses devil. This character covers himself with molasses or some sticky substance such as oil or pitch and dresses in shorts, horns, and a tail. Traditionally the jab molassi would threaten to rub the offending substance on onlookers unless they gave him money.

Jagabat: A loose woman, a woman of questionable morals. Also used for a woman chasing a wealthy man (origin unknown, probably Hindi). (*See* **Wabeen.**)

Jamette: A bad woman, possibly derived from the French *diamètre* for the imaginary line dividing the social circle into upper and lower halves. The word may also come from the French slang for a whore, *jeannette*. The jamettes constituted the "obscene" element in Carnival in the nineteenth century and were the focus of middle-class reform.

John John: A poor neighborhood on Port-of-Spain, also known as "behind the bridge." It shares a Carnival tradition and deep rivalry with other neighborhoods both in the immediate area and across town. (*See* **Belmont, Woodbrook, Laventille.**)

J'ouvert (jouvay, jouvert, etc.): From the French *jour ouvert* (open day, or daybreak), J'ouvert is the beginning of Carnival at which time King Carnival is given the keys to the city and the revelry begins. In Trinidad J'ouvert begins around two o'clock in the morning when people come out into the street to celebrate. There is a wide variety of costumes associated almost exclusively with J'ouvert, many of which include covering oneself with paint or mud or oil.

Kaiso: *See* **Calypso.**

Land Ship: A Friendly Society developed in Barbados and modeled on the British navy. Land Ship groups were identified by a ship's name and had a hierarchy of officers from Lord High Admiral on down. At selected times the Land Ship societies parade, perform drills, and perform coordinated dances.

Las Lap: The final period in Carnival taking place in the hours before midnight on Shrove Tuesday after the parade of the bands.

Laventille: The neighborhood just a little further east of John John and further up into the hills overlooking the city. Laventille is home to one of most famous steelbands, Desperadoes.

Lime: As a verb the term means to hang around with friends, pass the time, and talk. The word seems to have reappeared in Trinidad during World War II with the arrival of American sailors in Trinidad. Liming derives from the word for English sailors—limeys—so-called because of their habit of carrying citrus on long ocean voyages to avoid scurvy. In Trinidad limey came to be used to describe any low-class white. The socializing and loafing about of sailors in Port-of-Spain and their often rude and disorderly behavior inspired the new usage. The term survived the departure of the Americans and has lost its derogatory connotation. As a noun the word is used to describe loosely organized social gathering. The gathering may be around an event or some kind of purpose (a beach lime, a movie lime). In this sense, too, a lime may be the group of friends that hang around with each other, even if they are not together at that moment. Thus, a cohort, a group of companions.

Mamaguy: Deception by flattery but also used to mean lighthearted banter and teasing. Derived from a Spanish (probably Venezuelan) cockfighting term referring to a cock that only pretends to fight.

Mas': Short for masquerade, the term usually refers to the costume of an individual or to the whole costume theme of a band. The term also, however, is used to mean a confusion, a trouble. In this latter sense it is often expressed as Ole Mas' (*see* **Ole Mas'**).

Mas' Camp: The headquarters of a masquerade band, where the costumes are assembled. Often, this is also where registration for the band takes place, but it need not be. The site may be temporary or permanent. In Brooklyn many of the Mas' camps are temporary while in Trinidad some camps run all year from the same location, constructing costumes for carnivals around the world.

Masman (Masmen): This term is primarily used to designate someone who constructs masquerade costumes. It is most commonly associated with either the person in charge of the band (*see* **Bandleader**), someone who is an expert at one of the higher skilled crafts such as wirebending, papier-mâché, etc., or someone who designs the band itself. These roles may be embodied in one person, or they may be separate.

Midnight Robber: Masquerader whose costume consists of a broad-brimmed hat fringed with tassels, an elaborate cape, baggy trousers, and tunic generally bearing a skull and crossbones, who carries a dagger and pistol. The midnight robber gives elaborate and terrifying speeches in which he boasts of his destructive power and evil reputation. He demands money to spare the onlooker's life.

Moko Jumbie: A masquerader who stalks about on very high stilts. The moko jumbie used to collect money from people in second-story balconies. The name is a compound derived from distinct Africa sources, *moko* most likely being derived from Hausa for "ugly" and *jumbie* from Kongo sources for "spirit."

Monday Mas': Period of Carnival on Monday night before Shrove Tuesday. This mas' is generally more mellow and is played with steelbands and with only parts of costumes or t-shirts.

North Stands: The temporary bleacher-style seating erected across from the Grand Stand in the Savannah at Carnival time. The North Stands are where the more riotous audiences sit, especially during Panorama.

Ole Mas': Refers to the type of masquerade portrayed during J'ouvert and typified by characters such as Jab Molassis, Jab jabs, Blue Devils, Baby Dolls, and Dame Lorraines (among many others). Masquerade costumes lampooning public officials and current events are also popular. The term is also used, much in the same way bacchanal is used in its negative sense, to mean a confusion or a disorganized and unpredictable situation.

Pan: The Trinidadian term for steel drum and, by extension, steelband music.

Panorama: Panorama is the national steelband competition and the largest steelband competition in the country. It takes place on the Saturday before Carnival in the Queen's Park Savannah.

Pan Yard: Open lot or space where pans are stored and where steelband rehearsals are carried out. They are a chief liming spot during Carnival.

Picong: Competitive, spontaneous verbal battle between calypsonians or others. Also used to mean teasing in general (*see* **Fatigue; Mamaguy**).

Pissenlit: An old masquerade, made illegal, in which men dressed in rags stained with fake menstrual blood.

Play(ing) Mas': To participate in Carnival. To join a band, or masquerade in some way.

Road March: The song played by Carnival bands on carnival Tuesday. It is also a competition, the winner being the song played most frequently by bands as they march during the Parade of the Bands. Each masquerade band is accompanied by a sound system and often by a live band as well (*see* **Brass Band**). As the masqueraders move through the streets various popular soca hits are played. The one played by the most bands the most often is judged the winning road march.

Roti: Specifically the round, unleavened bread made from yellow split-pea flour, salt, and water, into which is wrapped a serving of curry. Roti is used generically to describe the whole meal together. Roti may be a serving of curried potatoes (Hindi: *aloo* or *alu*) along with goat, chicken, beef, shrimp, or other meats, and various vegetables such as pumpkin, green beans (*bodi*), and spinach. Roti was brought to Trinidad by East Indians.

Savannah/Big Yard: The vast park in Port-of-Spain where Carnival competitions are held. (*See* **Grand Stand; North Stands**).

Standard: A long pole, on top of which is fixed an emblematic representation of a band's section. Standards may take the form of an addition to the costume, such as a spear for a warrior, or it may be a more abstract, symbolic form such as a banner, geometric design, etc.

Tent: Location where calypsos are sung and calypso competitions held. Admission is generally charged.

Track, the: The pathway leading up to the Savannah stage. This is the area where steelbands (also known as pan sides) wait and rehearse before performing during Panorama. The track is also used during the King and Queen of Carnival competitions.

Viey La Cou: Competition begun in 1987 to promote the preservation and continued performance of old-time Carnival characters.

Wabeen: A loose woman, named for the *guabine,* a fish reputed to live in dirty or muddy water.

Wine/Wining: A dance performed at fetes, at Carnival time, at discos, etc. Wining is marked by the erotic gyration of hips, slightly bent knees, and rotation of the buttocks.

Wirebender: Carnival craftsman responsible for shaping the wire structures upon which costumes are created.

Woodbrook: A working- to middle-class residential area just west of downtown Port-of-Spain. Woodbrook has produced a number of famous masmen, including George Bailey and Stephen Derek, as well as a number of steelbands.

Bibliography

Abrahams, Roger D. 1983. *The Man-of-Words in the West Indies: Performance and the Emergence of Creole Culture.* Baltimore: Johns Hopkins University Press.

———. 1987. "An American Vocabulary of Celebrations." In *Time Out of Time: Essays on the Festival,* edited by Alessandro Falassi. Albuquerque: University of New Mexico Press.

Abrahams, Roger, and John Szwed. 1983. *After Africa.* New Haven: Yale University Press.

Adorno, Theodore W. 1981. *Prisms.* Cambridge: MIT Press.

Alexander, M. Jacqui. 1994. "Not Just (Any) Body Can Be a Citizen: The Politics of Law, Sexuality and Postcoloniality in Trinidad and Tobago and the Bahamas." *Feminist Review* 48: 5–23.

Alleyne-Dettmers, Patricia. 1995. "Political Dramas in the Jour Ouvert Parade in Trinidad Carnival." *Caribbean Studies* 28 (2): 326–38.

Allsopp, Richard. 1996. *Dictionary of Caribbean English Usage.* Oxford: Oxford University Press.

Alonso, Ana Maria. 1990. "Men in 'Rags' and the Devil on the Throne: A Study of Protest and Inversion in the Carnival of Post-Emancipation Trinidad." *Plantation Society in the Americas* 3 (1): 73–120.

———. 1994. "The Politics of Space, Time and Substance: State Formation, Nationalism and Ethnicity." *Annual Review of Anthropology* 23: 379–405.

Althusser, Louis. 1971. *Lenin and Philosophy.* New York: Monthly Review Press.

Anderson, Benedict. 1983. *Imagined Communities: Reflections on the Origin and Spread of Nationalism.* London: Verso.

Andrain, Charles F. 1984. "Capitalism and Democracy Reappraised." *Western Political Quarterly* 37 (4): 652–65.

Anthony, Michael. 1978. *The Making of Port-of-Spain.* Port-of-Spain: Key Caribbean Publications.

———. 1983 [?]. *Port-of-Spain in a World at War, 1939–1945.* Port-of-Spain: Ministry of Sports, Culture and Youth Affairs.

———. 1989. *Parade of Carnivals of Trinidad, 1839–1989.* St. James, Trinidad: Circle Press.

Anthony, Michael, and Andrew Carr. 1975. *David Frost Introduces Trinidad and Tobago.* London: André Deutsch.

Appadurai, Arjun. 1986a. *The Social Life of Things: Commodities in Cultural Perspective*. Cambridge: Cambridge University Press.

————. 1986b. "Theory in Anthropology: Center and Periphery." *Comparative Studies in Society and History* 28 (1): 356–61.

————. 1993. "Patriotism and Its Futures." *Public Culture* 5: 411–29.

————. 1996. *Modernity at Large: Cultural Dimensions of Globalization*. Minneapolis: University of Minnesota Press.

Appadurai, Arjun, and Carol Breckenridge. 1988. "Why Public Culture?" *Public Culture* 1 (1): 5–10.

Asad, Talal. 1973. *Anthropology and the Colonial Encounter*. Atlantic Highlands, N.J.: Humanities Press.

Austin, Diane. 1983. "Culture and Ideology in the English Speaking Caribbean: A View from Jamaica." *American Ethnologist* 10: 223–39.

Babcock, Barbara A. 1978. *The Reversible World: Symbolic Inversion in Art and Society*. Ithaca: Cornell University Press.

Bakhtin, Mikhail. 1968. *Rabelais and His World*. Cambridge: MIT Press.

Balibar, Etienne, and Immanuel Wallerstein. 1991. *Race, Nation, Class: Ambiguous Identities*. Translated by Chris Turner. London: Verso.

Baptiste, Owen. 1988. *Women in Mas'*. Port-of-Spain: Inprint Caribbean.

Barth, Frederik. 1969. *Ethnic Groups and Boundaries: The Social Organization of Cultural Difference*. Boston: Little, Brown.

————. 1989. "The Analysis of Culture in Complex Societies." *Ethnos* 54 (3–4): 120–42.

Barthes, Roland. 1972. *Mythologies*. New York: Hill and Wang.

————. 1977. *Image, Music, Text*. Translated by Stephen Heath. New York: Hill and Wang.

Basch, Linda. 1987. "The Vincentians and Grenadians: The Role of Voluntary Associations in Immigrant Adaptation to New York City." In *New Immigrants in New York, New York*, edited by Nancy Foner. New York: Columbia University Press.

Basch, Linda, Nina Glick Schiller, and Cristina Szanton Blanc. 1994. *Nations Unbound: Transnational Projects, Postcolonial Predicaments and Deterritorialized Nation-States*. Langhorne, Pa.: Gordon & Breach.

Bateson, Gregory. 1958. *Naven*. Stanford: Stanford University Press.

Baudrillard, Jean. 1983. *Simulations*. New York: Semiotext(e).

Beck, Melinda, Bruce Shenitz, and Marcus Mabry. 1991. "Bonfire in Crown Heights." *Newsweek*, September 9, 1991, 48.

Beckles, Hilary, and Verne Shepherd. 1991. *Caribbean Slave Society and Economy*. New York: The New Press.

Benitez-Rojo, Antonio. 1992. *The Repeating Island: The Caribbean and the Postmodern Perspective*. Durham: Duke University Press.

Best, Lloyd, and Allan Harris. 1991. *A Party Politics for Trinidad and Tobago*. Port-of-Spain: Tapia House.

Bethel, Clement. 1990. "Junkanoo in the Bahamas." *Caribbean Quarterly* 36 (3–4): 1–29.

Bettelheim, Judith. 1990. "Carnival in Cuba: Another Chapter in the Nationalization of Culture." *Caribbean Quarterly* 36 (3–4): 29–42.

Birth, Kevin K. 1994. "Bakrnal: Coup, Carnival and Calypso in Trinidad." *Ethnology* 33 (2): 165–77.

Blauner, Peter. 1986. "Islands in the City." *New York Magazine*, April 21, 1986, 66–73.

Bonnett, Aubrey. 1981. *Institutional Adaptation of West Indian Immigrants to America: An Analysis of Rotating Credit Associations.* Washington, D.C.: University Press of America.

Bottomore, Tom. 1996. *The Dictionary of Marxist Thought.* Oxford: Basil Blackwell.

Bourdieu, Pierre. 1984. *Distinction: A Social Critique of the Judgment of Taste.* Translated by Richard Nice. Cambridge: Harvard University Press.

———. 1993. *The Field of Cultural Production.* New York: Columbia University Press.

Boyke, Roy. 1984, 1985, 1986, 1987. *Trinidad Carnival Magazine.* Port-of-Spain: Key Caribbean Publications.

Braithwaite, Lloyd. 1975. *Social Stratification in Trinidad.* Kingston: University of the West Indies.

Brathwaite, Kamau. 1990. "Ala(r)ms of God—Konnu and Carnival in the Caribbean." *Caribbean Quarterly* 36 (3–4): 77–109.

Brenkman, John. 1987. *Culture and Domination.* Ithaca: Cornell University Press.

Brereton, Bridget. 1975. "The Trinidad Carnival, 1870–1900." *Savacou* 11.

———. 1979. *Race Relations in Colonial Trinidad, 1870–1900.* Cambridge: Cambridge University Press.

———. 1983. *A History of Modern Trinidad, 1783–1962.* Port-of-Spain: Heinemann.

Briggs, Charles. 1996. "The Politics of Discursive Authority in Research on the Invention of Tradition." *Cultural Anthropology* 11 (4): 435–69.

Bryce-Laporte, Roy S. 1972. "Black Immigrants: The Experience of Invisibility and Inequality." *Journal of Black Studies* 3: 29–56.

Bryce-Laporte, Roy S., and Delores M. Mortimer. 1981. *Caribbean Immigration to the United States.* RIIES Occasional Papers 1, vol. 1. Washington: Smithsonian Institution Press.

Buff, Rachel. 1997. "Mas' in Brooklyn: Immigration, Race and the Cultural Politics of Carnival." In *Language, Rhythm, and Sound: Black Popular Cultures into the Twenty-first Century,* edited by J. K. Adjaye and A. R. Andrews. Pittsburgh: University of Pittsburgh Press.

Burton, Richard. 1997. *Afro-Creole: Opposition and Play in the Caribbean.* Ithaca: Cornell University Press.

Busby-Montenegro, Lisa. 1994. "Canadians Patent a New Pan Design." *The Sunday Guardian,* January 23.

Caillois, Roger. 1961. *Man, Play and Games.* New York: Free Press of Glencoe.

Campbell, Carl C. 1994. *Cedulants and Capitulants: The Politics of Coloured Opposition in the Slave Society of Trinidad, 1783–1838.* Port-of-Spain: Paria Publishing.

Carnegie, Charles V. 1996. "Dundus and the Nation." *Cultural Anthropology* 11 (4): 470–509.

———. 1999. "Garvey and the Black Transnation." *Small Axe* 5.

Chambers, Iain. 1994. *Migrancy, Culture, Identity.* London: Routledge.

Chaney, Elsa M. 1987. "The Context of Caribbean Migration." In *Caribbean Life in New York City,* edited by Constance Sutton and Elsa M. Chaney. New York: Center for Migration Studies.

Charter of the National Carnival Commission. 1991. "Act No. 9 of 1991: Republic of Trinidad and Tobago: An Act to Establish a National Carnival Commission of Trinidad and Tobago." Vol. 30. *Trinidad and Tobago Gazette.* Port-of-Spain: Trinidad.

Chatterjee, Partha. 1986. *Nationalist Thought and the Colonial World*. Minneapolis: University of Minnesota Press.

Chen, Willie. 1988. *King of Carnival*. London: Hansib Publishing.

———. 1994. "Bring Back That Ole Time Carnival." *The Trinidad Express*, February 19.

Clifford, James. 1988. *The Predicament of Culture*. Cambridge: Harvard University Press.

Cohen, Abner. 1974. *Two-Dimensional Man*. London: Tavistock.

———. 1981. *The Politics of Elite Culture*. Berkeley: University of California Press.

———. 1982. "A Polyethnic London Carnival as a Contested Cultural Performance." *Ethnic and Racial Studies* 5: 23–42.

———. 1993. *Masquerade Politics*. Berkeley: University of California Press.

Cowley, John. 1996. *Carnival, Canboulay and Calypso: Traditions in the Making*. Cambridge: Cambridge University Press.

Craig, Susan. 1981. *Contemporary Caribbean: A Sociological Reader*. Port-of-Spain: Susan Craig.

Crick, Malcolm. 1989. "Representations of International Tourism: Sun, Sex, Sights, Savings and Servility." *Annual Review of Anthropology* 18: 307–44.

Crowley, Daniel J. 1956a. "The Midnight Robbers." *Caribbean Quarterly* 4 (3–4): 263–74.

———. 1956b. "The Traditional Masques of Carnival." *Caribbean Quarterly* 4 (3–4): 194–223.

Cudjoe, Selwyn R. 1993. *Eric E. Williams Speaks: Essays on Colonialism and Independence*. Wellesley, Mass.: Calaloux Publications.

Cuffy, David. 1993. "Caribbean Carnival Summit." *Trinidad Guardian*, March 30.

Cummins, Allissandra. 1997. "The Role of Museums and Heritage Institutions in the Promotion and Preservation of the Cultural Patrimony." Document prepared for the Office of Cultural Affairs, Performance Contract no. CPR 15841. Bridgetown, Barbados.

Cupid, John. 1994. "Trinidad Carnival Traditional Characters." *First Carnival King and Queen of the World Magazine* 1: 16–17.

Cvetkovich, Ann, and Douglas Kellner. 1997. *Articulating the Global and the Local: Globalization and Cultural Studies*. Politics and Culture series, vol. 5A. Boulder: Westview.

Daily Express. 1991 [?]. "The Greatest Show on Earth: Trinidad Carnival" and "Minshall: The Man and His Mas'." Port-of-Spain.

Da Matta, Roberto. 1984. "Carnival in Multiple Planes." In *Rite, Drama, Festival, Spectacle: Rehearsals toward a Theory of Cultural Performance*, edited by J. J. MacAloon. Philadelphia: Institute for the Study of Human Issues.

———. 1991. *Carnivals, Rogues and Heroes*. Notre Dame: University of Notre Dame Press.

Davis, Rey. 1996. "All Stars Wins $1M." *The Trinidad Guardian*, February 24.

Davis, Susan G. 1986. *Parades and Power: Street Theatre in Nineteenth-Century Philadelphia*. Berkeley: University of California Press.

de Certeau, Michel. 1984. *The Practice of Everyday Life*. Translated by Steven Rendall. Berkeley: University of California Press.

Deere, Carmen Diana. 1990. *In the Shadows of the Sun*. Boulder: Westview.

De Leon, Sherrie Ann. 1996. "West Indians Make Mas' in Brooklyn." *The Independent*, September 13.

de Verteuil, Anthony. 1973. *Sir Louis de Verteuil, His Life and Times: Trinidad, 1800–1900*. Port-of-Spain: Columbus Press.

————. 1984. *The Years of Revolt, Trinidad, 1881–1888*. Port-of-Spain: Paria Press.

————. 1995. *The Urich Diary, Trinidad, 1830–1832*. Translated by Irene Urich. Port-of-Spain: The Litho Press.

Diawara, Manthia. 1990. "Black British Cinema: Spectatorship and Identity Formation in *Territories*." *Public Culture* 3 (1): 33–47.

Dominguez, Jorge I., Robert A. Pastor, and R. Delisle Worrell. 1993. *Democracy in the Caribbean*. Baltimore: Johns Hopkins University Press.

Doyle-Marshall, William. 1983. "Bitter Taste in Brooklyn." *Trinidad Guardian*, October 18.

————. 1985. "New Challenge for Brooklyn Carnival." *Trinidad Guardian*, July 24.

————. 1986. "Now It's an International Carnival Association." *Trinidad Guardian*, December 10.

Duvignaud, Jean. 1976. "Festivals: A Sociological Approach." In *Festivals and Carnivals: The Major Traditions*, edited by Jean Duvignaud. Paris: The UNESCO Press and la Baconnière.

Dyck, Noel. 1992. *Indigenous Peoples and the Nation-State*. St. John's: Institute of Social and Economic Research, Memorial University of Newfoundland.

Eagleton, Terry. 1991. *Ideology*. London: Verso.

Eco, Umberto. 1986. *Travels in Hyperreality*. New York: Harcourt, Brace, Jovanovich.

Elder, Jacob D. 1972. *From Congo Drum to Steelband*. St. Augustine: University of the West Indies Press.

————. 1988. *African Survivals in Trinidad and Tobago*. London: Karia Press.

Eriksen, Thomas Hylland. 1990. "Liming in Trinidad: The Art of Doing Nothing." *Folk* 32: 23–43.

————. 1991. "The Cultural Contexts of Ethnic Differences." *Man* 26: 127–44.

————. 1993. *Ethnicity and Nationalism: Anthropological Perspectives*. Sterling, Va.: Pluto Press.

Escobar, Arturo. 1995. *Encountering Development*. Princeton: Princeton University Press.

Evanier, David. 1991. "The Lynching of Yankel Rosenbaum." *The New Republic*, 21–31.

Falassi, Alessandro. 1987. *Time Out of Time: Essays on the Festival*. Albuquerque: University of New Mexico Press.

Featherstone, Mike. 1990. *Global Culture: Nationalism, Globalization and Modernity*. London: Sage.

Ferguson, James. 1992. "Jamaica: Stories of Poverty." *Race and Class* 34 (1): 61–73.

Foner, Nancy. 1987a. "The Jamaicans: Race and Ethnicity among Migrants in New York City." In *New Immigrants in New York City*, edited by Nancy Foner. New York: Columbia University Press.

————. 1987b. *New Immigrants in New York City: Race and Ethnicity among Migrants in New York City*. New York: Columbia University Press.

————. 1987c. "West Indians in New York City and London: A Comparative Analysis." In *Caribbean Life in New York City*, edited by Constance Sutton and Elsa Chaney. New York: Center for Migration Studies.

————. 2001. *Islands in the City: West Indian Migration to New York*. Berkeley: University of California Press.

Foster, Robert J. 1991. "Making National Cultures in the Global Ecumene." *Annual Review of Anthropology* 20: 235–60.

Foucault, Michel. 1980. *Power/Knowledge*. New York: Pantheon.

Fox, Richard G. 1990. *Nationalist Ideologies and the Production of National Cultures.* Washington, D.C.: American Anthropological Association.

———. 1991. *Recapturing Anthropology.* School of American Research Advanced Seminar Series. Santa Fe: SAR Press.

Francois, David, and Carlisle Hall. 1992. "Carnival as Politics." *So Yuh Going to Carnival* 6: 19–21.

Fraser, Nancy. 1989. *Unruly Practices: Power, Discourse and Gender in Contemporary Social Theory.* Minneapolis: University of Minnesota Press.

———. 1997. *Justice Interruptus: Critical Reflections on the "Postsocialist" Condition.* London: Routledge.

Froude, James Anthony. 1888. *The English in the West Indies.* London: Longmans, Green and Co.

Frow, John. 1991. "Tourism and the Semiotics of Nostalgia." *October* 57: 123–51.

Gallaugher, Annemarie. 1995. "Constructing Caribbean Culture in Toronto: The Representation of Caribana." In *The Reordering of Culture in the Hood: Latin America, the Caribbean and Canada,* edited by A. Ruprecht and C. Taiana. Ottawa: Carleton University Press.

Gellner, Ernest. 1983. *Nations and Nationalism.* Ithaca: Cornell University Press.

Georges, Eugenia. 1990. *The Making of a Transnational Community: Migration, Development and Culture Change in the Dominican Republic.* New York: Columbia University Press.

Gilroy, Paul. 1993a. *The Black Atlantic: Modernity and Double Consciousness.* Cambridge: Harvard University Press.

———. 1993b. *Small Acts: Thoughts on the Politics of Black Cultures.* London: Serpent's Tail.

Glick Schiller, Nina, and Georges Fouron. 1990. "'Everywhere we go we are in danger': Ti Manno and the Emergence of a Haitian Transnational Identity." *American Ethnologist* 17 (2): 329–47.

Glick Schiller, Nina, Linda Basch, and Cristina Blanc-Szanton. 1992. *Towards a Transnational Perspective on Migration: Race, Class, Ethnicity, and Nationalism Reconsidered.* New York: Annals of the New York Academy of Sciences, vol. 645.

Gmelch, George. 1992. *Double Passage: The Lives of Caribbean Migrants Abroad and Back Home.* Ann Arbor: University of Michigan Press.

Gold, Gerald. 1987. *Minorities and Mother Country Imagery.* St. John's: Institute of Social and Economic Research, Memorial University of Newfoundland.

Goldberg, David Theo. 1994. *Multiculturalism: A Critical Reader.* Oxford: Basil Blackwell.

Gonzalez, David. 1991. "Hasidim Say They'll Join Parade Line: Good-Will Gesture in Crown Heights." *New York Times,* September 2.

Gonzalez, Nancie L. 1992. *Dollar, Dove and Eagle: One Hundred Years of Palestinian Migration to Honduras.* Ann Arbor: University of Michigan Press.

Gourevitch, Philip. 1993. "The Crown Heights Riot and Its Aftermath." *Commentary,* 29–34.

Grimes, John. 1975a. "Carnival Festivities Must Be Better Organized." *New York Amsterdam News,* September 24.

———. 1975b. "West Indian Carnival Exciting, Exotic." *New York Amsterdam News,* September 10.

Grugel, Jean. 1995. *Politics and Development in the Caribbean Basin.* Bloomington: Indiana University Press.

Guillermoprieto, Alma. 1991. *Samba.* New York: Vintage Books.

Gupta, Akhil. 1992. "The Song of the Nonaligned World: Transnational Identities and the Reinscription of Space in Late Capitalism." *Cultural Anthropology* 7 (1): 63–79.

Gupta, Akhil, and James Ferguson. 1992. "Beyond 'Culture': Space, Identity and the Politics of Difference." *Cultural Anthropology* 7 (1): 6–23.

Gutmann, Amy. 1992. *Multiculturalism and "The Politics of Recognition."* Princeton: Princeton University Press.

———. 1994. *Multiculturalism.* Princeton: Princeton University Press.

Gutzmore, Cecil. 1993. "Carnival, the State and the Black Masses in the United Kingdom." In *Inside Babylon: The Caribbean Diaspora in Britain,* edited by W. James and C. Harris. London: Verso.

Hall, Herman. 1982. "Inside Brooklyn's Carnival." *Everybody's Magazine* 6: 12–22.

Hall, Stuart. 1991a. "The Local and the Global: Globalization and Ethnicity." In *Culture, Globalization and the World System: Contemporary Conditions for the Representation of Identity,* edited by A. D. King. Binghamton: State University of New York Press.

———. 1991b. *Myths of Caribbean Identity.* Coventry, U.K.: University of Warwick Centre for Caribbean Studies.

Hamelink, C. J. 1983. *Cultural Autonomy in Global Communications.* New York: Longmans.

Handler, Richard. 1988. *Nationalism and the Politics of Culture in Quebec.* Madison: University of Wisconsin Press.

Hannerz, Ulf. 1989. "Notes on the Global Ecumene." *Public Culture* 1 (2): 66–75.

———. 1992. *Cultural Complexity.* New York: Columbia University Press.

Harewood, Jack, and Ralph Henry. 1985. *Inequality in a Post-Colonial Society: Trinidad and Tobago, 1956–1981.* St. Augustine: Institute of Social and Economic Research, University of the West Indies.

Harney, Stefano. 1996. *Nationalism and Identity: Culture and the Imagination in a Caribbean Diaspora.* London: Zed Books.

Harvey, David. 1989. *The Condition of Postmodernity: An Inquiry into the Origins of Culture Change.* Cambridge: Blackwell.

Haug, W. F. 1986. *Critique of Commodity Aesthetics: Appearance, Sexuality and Advertising in Capitalist Society.* Translated by Robert Bock. Minneapolis: University of Minnesota Press.

Held, David. 1995. *Democracy and the Global Order.* Stanford: Stanford University Press.

Henry, Paget, and Paul Buhle. 1992. *C.L.R. James's Caribbean.* Durham: Duke University Press.

Herskovits, Melville J., and Frances S. Herskovits. 1964. *Trinidad Village.* New York: Octagon Books. Originally published in 1947.

Hill, Donald R. 1981. "New York's Caribbean Carnival." *Everybody's Magazine* 5: 33–37.

———. 1993. *Calypso Calaloo: Early Carnival Music in Trinidad.* Gainesville: University Press of Florida.

———. 1994. "A History of West Indian Carnival in New York City to 1978." *New York Folklore* 20 (1–2): 47–66.

———. 1995. "Trinidad Pan." *Natural History* (February): 34–41.

Hill, Donald R., and Robert Abramson. 1979. "West Indian Carnival in Brooklyn." *Natural History* (August–September): 73–85.

Hill, Errol. 1972. *The Trinidad Carnival: Mandate for a National Theatre*. Austin: University of Texas Press.

———. 1976. "The Trinidad Carnival: Cultural Change and Synthesis." In *Festivals and Carnivals: The Major Traditions*, edited by Jean Duvignaud. Paris: UNESCO Press and la Baconnière.

———. 1985. "Traditional Figures in Carnival: Their Preservation, Development and Interpretation." *Caribbean Quarterly* 31 (2): 14–35.

Hobsbawm, Eric, and Terence Ranger. 1983. *The Invention of Tradition*. Cambridge: Cambridge University Press.

Horkheimer, Max. 1972. *Critical Theory*. New York: Herder and Herder.

Huizinga, Johan. 1967. *Homo Ludens*. Boston: Beacon Press.

Ivy, Marilyn. 1995. *Discourses of the Vanishing: Modernity, Phantasm, Japan*. Chicago: University of Chicago Press.

Jackson, P. 1988. "Street Life: The Politics of Carnival." *Environment and Planning D: Society and Space* 6: 213–27.

James, C.L.R. 1971. *Minty Alley*. London: New Beacon Books.

———. 1977. *The Future in the Present: Selected Writings*. Westport, Conn.: Lawrence Hill and Co.

———. 1984. *Party Politics in the West Indies*. San Juan, Trinidad: Inprint Caribbean.

———. 1993. *Beyond a Boundary*. Durham: Duke University Press.

Jameson, Fredric. 1994. *Postmodernism, or The Cultural Logic of Late Capitalism*. Durham: Duke University Press.

Joseph, E. L. 1838. *History of Trinidad*. Port-of-Spain: Columbus Publishers.

Juneja, Renu. 1988. "The Trinidad Carnival: Ritual, Performance, Spectacle and Symbol." *Journal of Popular Culture* 21 (4): 87–101.

Kadetsky, Elizabeth. 1992. "Racial Politics in New York." *The Nation*, 656–58.

Kasinitz, Philip. 1992. *Caribbean New York*. Ithaca: Cornell University Press.

Keane, Webb. 1997. *Signs of Recognition: Powers and Hazards of Representation in an Indonesian Society*. Berkeley: University of California Press.

Kearney, M. 1995. "The Local and the Global: The Anthropology of Globalization and Transnationalism." *Annual Review of Anthropology* 24: 547–65.

Keith, Michael, and Steve Pile. 1993. *Place and the Politics of Identity*. London: Routledge.

Khan, Aisha. 1991. "Ethnicity, Culture and Context." *Man* 26: 873–77.

———. 1995. "Homeland, Motherland: Authenticity, Legitimacy and Ideologies of Place among Muslims in Trinidad." In *Nation and Migration: The Politics of Space in the South Asian Diaspora*, edited by Peter van der Veer. Philadelphia: University of Pennsylvania Press.

Kifner, John. 1991a. "Blacks March by Hasidim Through a Corridor of Blue." *New York Times*, August 25.

———. 1991b. "In Brooklyn, Steel Drums and a Truce." *New York Times*, September 3.

King, A. D. 1991. *Culture, Globalization and the World System: Contemporary Conditions for the Representation of Identity*. Binghamton: SUNY Press.

Kingsley, Charles. 1871. *At Last: A Christmas in the West Indies*. 2 vols. London: Macmillan.

Klass, Morton. 1961. *East Indians in Trinidad*. New York: Columbia University Press.

————. 1991. *Singing with Sai Baba: The Politics of Revitalization in Trinidad*. Boulder: Westview.

Klein, Joe. 1991. "Deadly Metaphors." *New York Magazine*, 26–29.

Kopytoff, Igor. 1986. "The Cultural Biography of Things: Commodification as Process." In *The Social Life of Things*, edited by Arjun Appadurai. Cambridge: Cambridge University Press.

————. 1988. "Public Culture: A Durkheimian Genealogy." *Public Culture* 1 (1): 11–16.

Laclau, Ernesto. 1990. *New Reflections on the Revolution of Our Time*. London: Verso.

————. 1994. *The Making of Political Identities*. London: Verso.

Laclau, Ernesto, and Mouffe Chantal. 1985. *Hegemony and Socialist Strategy: Towards a Radical Democratic Politics*. London: Verso.

Lamming, George. 1954. *The Emigrants*. Ann Arbor: University of Michigan Press.

Lash, Scott. 1990. *Sociology of Postmodernism*. London: Routledge.

Lash, Scott, and Jonathan Friedman. 1992. *Modernity and Identity*. Oxford: Basil Blackwell.

Lash, Scott, and John Urry. 1987. *The End of Organized Capitalism*. Madison: University of Wisconsin Press.

————. 1994. *Economies of Signs and Space*. London: Sage Publications.

Lefebvre, Henri. 1991. *The Production of Space*. Translated by Donald Nicholson-Smith. Oxford: Basil Blackwell.

Lewis, Gordon K. 1968. *The Growth of the Modern West Indies*. New York: Modern Reader Paperbacks.

————. 1983. *Main Currents in Caribbean Thought*. Baltimore: Johns Hopkins University Press.

Lewis, Samella, and Mary Jane Hewitt. 1995. *Caribbean Visions*. Alexandria, Va.: Art Services International.

Lieber, Michael. 1981. *Street Life: Afro-American Culture in Urban Trinidad*. Boston: G. K. Hall.

Linke, Uli. 1990. "Folklore, Anthropology and the Government of Social Life." *Comparative Studies in Society and History* 32 (1): 117–48.

Liverpool, Hollis. 1990. *Culture and Education: Carnival in Trinidad and Tobago, Implications for Education in Secondary Schools*. London: Karia Press.

————. 1993. "Rituals of Power and Rebellion: Carnival Tradition in Trinidad and Tobago." Ph.D. diss., University of Michigan.

Logan, Andy. 1991. "Syzygy." *The New Yorker*, September 23, 102–8.

Lovelace, Earl. 1979. *The Dragon Can't Dance*. London: Longmans.

Lowenthal, David. 1985. *The Past Is a Foreign Country*. Cambridge: Cambridge University Press.

Lyotard, Jean-François. 1989. *The Postmodern Condition: A Report on Knowledge*. Translated by Geoff Bennington and Brian Massumi. Minneapolis: University of Minnesota Press.

MacAloon, John J. 1984. *Rite, Drama, Festival, Spectacle: Rehearsals Toward a Theory of Cultural Performance*. Philadelphia: Institute for the Study of Human Issues.

MacCannell, Dean. 1989. *The Tourist: A New Theory of the Leisure Class*. New York: Schocken.

————. 1992. *Empty Meeting Grounds: The Tourist Papers*. London: Routledge.

Macdonald, J. S. 1986. *Trinidad and Tobago.* New York: Praeger.

Magid, Alvin. 1989. *Urban Nationalism: A Study of Political Development in Trinidad.* Gainesville: University of Florida Press.

Mahabir, Cynthia. 1985. *Crime and Nation-Building in the Caribbean.* Cambridge: Schenkman.

Manning, Frank E. 1977. "Cup Match and Carnival." In *Secular Ritual,* edited by S. F. Moore and B. G. Meyerhoff. Amsterdam: Van Gorcum.

———. 1978. "Carnival in Antigua." *Anthropos* 73: 191–204.

———. 1983. *The Celebration of Society: Perspectives on Contemporary Cultural Performance.* Bowling Green, Ohio: Bowling Green University Popular Press.

———. 1984. "Carnival in Canada: The Politics of Celebration." In *The Masks of Play,* edited by B. Sutton-Smith and D. Kelly-Byrne. New York: Leisure Press.

———. 1990. "Overseas Caribbean Carnivals: The Art and Politics of a Transnational Celebration." In *Caribbean Popular Culture,* edited by John Lent. Bowling Green, Ohio: Bowling Green State University Press.

Marcus, George. 1995. "Ethnography in/of the World System: The Emergence of Multi-Sited Ethnography." *Annual Review of Anthropology* 24: 95–117.

Marcus, George E., and Michael M. J. Fischer. 1986. *Anthropology as Cultural Critique.* Chicago: University of Chicago Press.

Marin, Louis. 1987. "Notes on a Semiotic Approach to Parade, Cortege and Procession." In *Time Out of Time,* edited by Alessandro Falassi. Albuquerque: University of New Mexico Press.

Massey, Doreen. 1995. "Space/Place." In *Place and the Politics of Identity,* edited by Michael Keith and Steve Pile. London: Routledge.

Matthews, Les. 1960. "What Happened to the West Indies Day Parade?" *New York Amsterdam News,* September 10.

Mavrogordato, Olga. 1979. *Voices in the Street.* Port-of-Spain: Inprint Caribbean.

Miller, Daniel. 1991. "Absolute Freedom in Trinidad." *Man: The Journal of the Royal Anthropological Institute* 26 (2): 323–42.

———. 1992. "The Young and the Restless in Trinidad: A Case of the Local and the Global in Mass Consumption." In *Consuming Technologies: Media and Information in Domestic Spaces,* edited by R. Silverstone and E. Hirsch. New York: Routledge. 163–82.

———. 1993. "Spot the Trini." *Ethnos* 58 (3–4): 317–34.

———. 1994a. *Modernity an Ethnographic Approach: Dualism and Mass Consumption in Trinidad.* Providence, R.I.: Berg.

———. 1994b. "The Uses and Abuses of 'Ethnicity': A Review Article." *Ethnos* 59 (1–2): 91–99.

Millette, James. 1970. *Society and Politics in Colonial Trinidad.* London: Zed Books.

Ministry of Education. 1972. *Report of the Working Party—Chaguaramas Secondary School Conference.* Port-of-Spain: Trinidad and Tobago Government Printery.

Mintz, Sidney. 1974. *Caribbean Transformations.* Baltimore: Johns Hopkins University Press.

———. 1995. "Enduring Substances, Trying Theories: The Caribbean Region as Oikoumene." *Journal of the Royal Anthropological Institute* 2: 289–311.

Mintz, Sidney, and Richard Price. 1976. *An Anthropological Approach to the Afro-American*

Past: A Caribbean Perspective. Philadelphia: Institute for Study of Human Issues.

Mintz, Sidney W., and Sally Price. 1985. *Caribbean Contours.* Baltimore: Johns Hopkins University Press.

Mittelholzer, Edgar. 1950. *A Morning at the Office.* London: Heineman.

Moore, Dennison. 1995. *Racial Ideology in Trinidad: The Black View of the East Indian.* Tunapuna, Trinidad: Chakra Publishing House.

Moore, Sally Falk. 1989. "The Production of Cultural Pluralism as a Process." *Public Culture* 1 (2): 26–48.

Morley, David, and Kevin Robins. 1995. *Spaces of Identity: Global Media, Electronic Landscapes and Cultural Boundaries.* London: Routledge.

Moses, Knolly. 1985. "Brooklyn Mas' Still Marked by Petty Feuding, Disorganization." *Trinidad Guardian*, August 25.

Naficy, Hamid. 1991. "The Poetics and Practice of Iranian Nostalgia in Exile." *Diaspora* 1 (3): 285–302.

Naipaul, V. S. 1959. *Miguel Street.* New York: Vintage.

———. 1967. *The Mimic Men.* London: Penguin.

———. 1969a. *The Loss of El Dorado.* London: André Deutsch.

———. 1969b. *The Middle Passage.* Middlesex: Penguin.

———. 1972. *The Overcrowded Barracoon.* London: Penguin.

———. 1974. *The Return of Eva Peron with The Killings in Trinidad.* London: Penguin.

Nash, June. 1981. "Ethnographic Aspects of the World Capitalist System." *Annual Review of Anthropology* 10: 393–423.

Nettleford, Rex M. 1978. *Caribbean Cultural Identity: The Case of Jamaica.* Kingston: Institute of Jamaica.

Nunley, John. 1989. "Caribbean Festival Arts: Each and Every Bit of Difference." *African Arts* 22 (3): 68–89.

Nunley, John W., and Judith Bettelheim. 1988. *Caribbean Festival Arts: Each and Every Bit of Difference.* Seattle: University of Washington Press.

Nurse, Keith. 1996. "Trinidad and Tobago's Carnival: Toward an Export Strategy." *Caribbean Labour Journal* (March).

———. 1999. "Globalization and Trinidad Carnival: Diaspora, Hybridity and Identity in Global Culture." *Cultural Studies* 13 (4): 661–90.

———. 2000. "The Caribbean Music Industry: The Case for Industrial Policy and Export Promotion." Paper prepared for the Office of Cultural Affairs, Inter-American Cultural Program Organization of American States, Washington, D.C.

Olwig, Karen Fog. 1993a. "Defining the National in the Transnational: Cultural Identity in the Afro-Caribbean Diaspora." *Ethnos* 58 (3–4): 361–76.

———. 1993b. *Global Culture, Island Identity.* Australia: Harwood Academic Publishers.

Ottley, Carlton R. 1961. *The Story of Port of Spain.* St. James, Trinidad: Harran Educational Publishers.

———. 1974. *Slavery Days in Trinidad.* Port-of-Spain: Carlton Ottley.

———. 1978. *The Trinidad Callaloo: Life in Trinidad from 1851–1900.* Diego Martin, Trinidad: Crusoe Publishing House.

Oxaal, Ivar. 1982. *Black Intellectuals and the Dilemmas of Race and Class in Trinidad.* Cambridge: Harvard University Press.

Oxford English Dictionary (Compact Edition). 1989. New York: Oxford University Press.

Palmer, Ransford W. 1995. *Pilgrims from the Sun: West Indian Migration to America.* New York: Twayne.

Patterson, Orlando. 1969. *The Sociology of Slavery.* Cambridge: Associated University Press.

———. 1977. *Ethnic Chauvinism: The Reactionary Impulse.* New York: Stein and Day.

Payer, Cheryl. 1991. *Lent and Lost: Foreign Credit and Third-World Development.* London: Zed.

Payne, Nellie. 1990. "Grenada Mas', 1928–1988." *Caribbean Quarterly* 36 (3–4): 54–65.

Pearse, Andrew. 1956. "Mitto Sampson on Calypso Legends of the Nineteenth Century." *Caribbean Quarterly* 4 (3–4): 140–63.

Philippe, J. B. 1987 [1824]. *An Address to the Right Hon. Earl Bathurst by a Free Mulatto.* Port-of-Spain: Paria Press.

Powrie, Barbara E. 1956. "The Changing Ability of the Coloured Middle Class Toward Carnival." *Caribbean Quarterly* 4 (3–4): 91–107.

Pryce, Everton A. 1985 "The Notting Hill Gate Carnival—Black Politics, Resistance and Leadership, 1976–1978." *Caribbean Quarterly* 31 (2): 35–52.

Purdy, Matthew. 1994. "Parade Shows Off West Indian Political Clout." *New York Times,* September 7.

Reyes, Elma. 1985. "Carnival in Brooklyn: A Chip Off TT Mas'." *Trinidad Express Newspaper,* September 13.

Richardson, Bonham. 1983. *Caribbean Migrants: Environment and Human Survival on St. Kitts and Nevis.* Knoxville: University of Tennessee Press.

Robertson, George, et al. 1994. *Traveler's Tales: Narratives of Home and Displacement.* London: Routledge.

Robotham, Don. 1996. "Transnationalism in the Caribbean: Formal and Informal." *American Ethnologist* 25 (2): 307–21.

Rohlehr, Gordon. 1985. "'Man Talking to Man': Calypso and Social Confrontation in Trinidad from 1970 to 1984." *Caribbean Quarterly* 31 (2): 1–14.

———. 1990. *Calypso and Society in Pre-Independence Trinidad.* Port-of-Spain: Gordon Rohlehr.

Rouse, Roger. 1991. "Mexican Migration and the Social Space of Postmodernism." *Diaspora* 1 (1): 8–23.

———. 1995. "Questions of Identity: Personhood and Collectivity in Transnational Migration to the United States." *Critique of Anthropology* 14 (4): 351–80.

Rubinstein, Hymie. 1987. *Coping with Poverty: Adaptation Strategies in a Caribbean Village.* Boulder: Westview.

Rueschemeyer, Dietrich, Evelyn Huber Stephens, and John D. Stephens. 1992. *Capitalist Development and Democracy.* Cambridge: Polity Press.

Ryan, Selwyn D. 1972. *Race and Nationalism in Trinidad and Tobago.* St. Augustine: ISER, University of the West Indies.

———. 1988. *Trinidad and Tobago: The Independence Experience, 1962–1987.* St. Augustine: ISER, University of the West Indies.

———. 1991. *Social and Occupational Stratification in Contemporary Trinidad and Tobago.* St. Augustine: ISER, University of the West Indies.

Sander, Reinhard W. 1978. *From Trinidad: An Anthology of Early West Indian Writing.* London: Hodder and Stoughton.

Scott, David. 1991. "That Event, This Memory: Notes on the Anthropology of African Diasporas in the New World." *Diaspora* 1 (3): 261–84.

Segal, Daniel. 1989. "Nationalism in a Colonial State." Ph.D. diss., University of Chicago.

———. 1993. "Living Ancestors: Nationalism and the Past in Postcolonial Trinidad and Tobago." In *Remapping Memory*, edited by J. Boyarin. Minneapolis: University of Minnesota Press.

———, ed. 1996. "Resisting Identities: Theme Issue." *Cultural Anthropology* 11 (4).

Selvon, Sam. 1956. *The Lonely Londoners.* Essex: Longman Group UK.

Singh, Kelvin. 1994. *Race and Class Struggles in a Colonial State, Trinidad, 1917–1945.* Kingston: The Press, University of the West Indies.

Sleeper, Jim. 1988. "Playing the Ethnic Card in New York City." *American Visions* 3: 6–10.

Slymovics, Susan. 1995. "New York City's Muslim World Day Parade." In *Nation and Migration*, edited by Peter van der Veer. Philadelphia: University of Pennsylvania Press.

Smith, Anna Deavere. 1993. *Fires in the Mirror.* New York: Anchor, Doubleday.

Smith, Anthony D. 1986. *The Ethnic Origins of Nations.* Oxford: Basil Blackwell.

Smith, M. G. 1965. *The Plural Society in the British West Indies.* Berkeley: University of California Press.

———. 1991. *Pluralism, Politics and Ideology in the Creole Caribbean.* New York: Research Institute for the Study of Man.

Smith, Michael Peter. 1992. "Postmodernism, Urban Ethnography and the New Social Space of Ethnic Identity." *Theory and Society* 21: 493–531.

Smith, R. T. 1988. *Kinship and Class in the West Indies.* Cambridge: Cambridge University Press.

Soja, Edward W. 1989. *Postmodern Geographies.* London: Verso.

Stafford, Susan Buchanan. 1987. "The Haitians: The Cultural Meaning of Race and Ethnicity." In *New Immigrants in New York*, edited by Nancy Foner. New York: Columbia University Press.

Stallybrass, Peter, and Allon White. 1986. *The Politics and Poetics of Transgression.* Ithaca: Cornell University Press.

Stewart, John. 1986. "Patronage and Control in the Trinidad Carnival." In *The Anthropology of Experience*, edited by V. W. Turner and E. M. Bruner. Urbana: University of Illinois Press.

———. 1989. *Drinkers, Drummers and Decent Folk: Ethnographic Narratives of Village Trinidad.* Albany: SUNY Press.

Stewart, Kathleen. 1988. "Nostalgia—A Polemic." *Cultural Anthropology* 3 (3): 227–42.

Stewart, Susan. 1993. *On Longing: Narratives of the Miniature, the Gigantic, the Souvenir, the Collection.* Durham: Duke University Press.

Stinner, William F., Klaus de Albuquerque, and Roy S. Bryce-Laporte. 1982. *Return Migration and Remittances: Developing a Caribbean Perspective.* Washington: Smithsonian Institution Press.

Stuempfle, Stephen. 1995. *The Steelband Movement: The Forging of a National Art in Trinidad and Tobago.* Philadelphia: University of Pennsylvania Press.

Sutton, Constance, and Elsa Chaney. 1992. *Caribbean Immigrants in New York.* New York: Center for Migration Studies.

———. 1994. *Caribbean Life in New York City: Sociocultural Dimensions.* New York: Center for Migration Studies.

Sutton, Constance R., and Susan Makiesky-Barrow. 1987. "Migration and West Indian Racial and Ethnic Consciousness." In *Caribbean Life in New York City*, edited by Constance R. Sutton and Elsa Chaney. New York: Center for Migration Studies.

Taussig, Michael. 1993. *Mimesis and Alterity.* New York: Routledge.

Taylor, Charles. 1991. *The Ethics of Authenticity.* Cambridge: Harvard University Press.

Taylor, John. 1992. "The Politics of Grievance." *New York Magazine*, 18–19.

Thomas, J. J. 1969. *Froudacity: West Indian Fables by James Anthony Froude.* Port-of-Spain: New Beacon Books.

Thomas, Roy. 1987. *The Trinidad Labour Riots of 1937: Perspectives Fifty Years Later.* St. Augustine: Extra-Mural Studies Unit, University of the West Indies.

Thomas-Hope, Elizabeth. 1992. *Explanation in Caribbean Migration.* London: Macmillan.

Tomlinson, John. 1991. *Cultural Imperialism.* Baltimore: Johns Hopkins University Press.

Toney, Joyce Roberta. 1986. "The Development of a Culture of Migration among a Caribbean People: St. Vincent and New York." Ph.D. diss., Columbia University.

Trotman, David Vincent. 1986. *Crime in Trinidad: Conflict and Control in a Plantation Society, 1838–1900.* Knoxville: University of Tennessee Press.

Trouillot, Michel-Rolph. 1990. *Haiti: State against Nation.* New York: Monthly Review Press.

———. 1992. "The Caribbean Region: An Open Frontier in Anthropological Theory." *Annual Review of Anthropology* 21: 19–42.

Turner, Terence. 1993. "Anthropology and Multiculturalism: What Is Anthropology that Multiculturalists Should Be Mindful of It?" *Cultural Anthropology* 8 (4): 411–29.

Turner, Victor. 1969. *The Ritual Process.* Chicago: Aldine.

———. 1982. *Celebration: Studies in Festivity and Ritual.* Washington, D.C.: Smithsonian Institution Press.

———. 1983. "Carnival in Rio: Dionysian Drama in an Industrializing Society." In *The Celebration of Society*, edited by Frank Manning. Bowling Green, Ohio: Bowling Green University Popular Press.

Turner, Victor W., and Edward M. Bruner. 1986. *The Anthropology of Experience.* Urbana: University of Illinois Press.

van Capelleveen, Remco. 1988. "'Peripheral' Culture in the Metropolis: West Indians in New York City." In *Alternative Cultures in the Caribbean*, edited by T. Bremer and U. Fleischmann. Berlin: Bibliotheca Ibero-Americana, Vervuert Verlag.

van der Veer, Peter. 1995. *Nation and Migration: The Politics of Space in the South Asian Diaspora.* Philadelphia: University of Pennsylvania Press.

van Gennep, Arnold. 1960. *The Rites of Passage.* Chicago: University of Chicago Press.

Verdery, Katherine. 1994. "Beyond the Nation in Eastern Europe." *Social Text* 38: 1–20.

Vertovec, Steven. 1995. "Hindus in Trinidad and Britain: Ethnic Religion, Reification and the Politics of Public Space." In *Nation and Migration*, edited by Peter van der Veer. Philadelphia: University of Pennsylvania Press.

Waite, Chris. 1993. "Trinidad Masquerades: Performance, Play and Community in a Post-Colonial Carnival." Ph.D. diss., University of Western Australia.

Walcott, Derek. 1993. *The Antilles: Fragments of Epic Memory.* New York: Farrar, Straus and Giroux.

Wallerstein, Immanuel. 1974. *The Modern World System.* 2 vols. New York and London: Academic Press.

Warner-Lewis, Maureen. 1991. *Guinea's Other Suns: The African Dynamic in Trinidad Culture.* Dover, Mass.: The Majority Press.

Waters, Mary C. 1999. *Black Identities: West Indian Immigrant Dreams and American Realities.* Cambridge: Harvard University Press.

Watkins-Owens, Irma. 1996. *Blood Relations.* Bloomington: Indiana University Press.

Watson, Hilbourne A. 1989. *The Caribbean in the Global Political Economy.* Boulder: Lynne Rienner Publishers.

Watts, David. 1987. *The West Indies: Patterns of Development, Culture and Environmental Change Since 1492.* Cambridge: Cambridge University Press.

Williams, Brackette. 1989. "A Class Act: Anthropology and the Race to Nation Across Ethnic Terrain." *Annual Review of Anthropology* 18: 401–44.

———. 1991. *Stains on My Name, War in My Veins: Guyana and the Politics of Cultural Struggle.* Durham: Duke University Press.

Williams, Eric. 1962. *History of the People of Trinidad and Tobago.* Port-of-Spain: PNM Publishing Company.

———. 1964. *British Historians and the West Indies.* Port-of-Spain: PNM Publishing.

———. 1981. *Forged From the Love of Liberty: Selected Speeches of Dr. Eric Williams.* London: Longmans.

———. 1982. *Celebration: Studies in Festivity and Ritual.* Washington, D.C.: Smithsonian Institution Press.

Williams, Patrick, and Laura Chrisman. 1994. *Colonial Discourse and Post-Colonial Theory.* New York: Columbia University Press.

Williams, Raymond. 1958. *Culture and Society, 1780–1950.* New York: Columbia University Press.

———. 1977. *Marxism and Literature.* Oxford: Oxford University Press.

———. 1983. *Keywords.* Oxford: Oxford University Press.

Wilson, Peter J. 1973. *Crab Antics: The Social Anthropology of English-Speaking Negro Societies of the Caribbean.* New Haven: Yale University Press.

Wood, Donald. 1968. *Trinidad in Transition.* London: Oxford University Press.

———. 1988. "The Trinidad Carnival: A Medium of Social Change." In *Alternative Cultures in the Caribbean: First International Conference of the Society of Caribbean Research.* Berlin: Bibliotheca Ibero-Americana.

———. 1990. "The Robber in the Trinidad Carnival." *Caribbean Quarterly* 36 (3–4): 42–54.

Yarrow, Andrew L. 1991. "Brooklyn Prepares and Braces for a Parade." *New York Times,* August 30.

Yelvington, Kevin A. 1990. "Ethnicity 'Not Out': The Indian Cricket Tour of the West Indies and the 1976 Elections in Trinidad and Tobago." *Arena Review* 14 (1): 1–12.

———. 1993. *Trinidad Ethnicity.* Warwick University Caribbean Studies. London: The Macmillan Press.

———. 1995. *Producing Power: Ethnicity, Gender and Class in a Caribbean Workplace.* Philadelphia: Temple University Press.

Young, Robert. 1990. *White Mythologies: Writing History and the West.* London: Routledge.

Young, Virginia Heyer. 1993. *Becoming West Indian: Culture, Self and Nation in St. Vincent.* Washington, D.C.: Smithsonian Institution Press.

Newspapers and Magazines

Everybody's Caribbean Magazine. 1994. "Problems Between Hasidim and Community Over the 1994 Caribbean Carnival." 18: 27–31.

Everybody's Magazine. 1990. "New York's Caribbean Carnival 1990." 14: 4–14.

New York Age. 1957. "West Indies Day Fete Features Big Parade." September 7.

New York Amsterdam News. 1950. "West Indians Parade in New York City." September 9.

———. 1961. "West Indian Parade Becomes a Brawl." September 9.

———. 1974. "One Million Participate in West Indian Parade." September 7.

———. 1975. "Parks Department Asks for $10,000 to Clean Up After Carnival." August 27.

New York Daily Challenge. 1977. August 8, 4.

New York Times. 1991. "In Crown Heights, Simmering Tensions and a Fragile Peace." August 23.

Trinidad Express Newspaper. 1992. "Labour Day Also a Time for Politics." September 20.

———. 1996. "Towards a New Awareness of T & T in World Market." February 18.

Personal Interviews

Afong, Richard. December 16, 1993, January 5, 1994.

Davis, Kevin "Fuzzy." October 13, 1995.

Derek, Stephen. January 14, 1994.

Griffith, Jason. November 27, 1993, December 3, 1994.

Hinds, Neville. December 18, 1993, January 23, 1994

Joseph, Terry. September 19, 1994.

Knox, Arden. January 15, April 11, 1994.

Lee Heung, Elsie. January 6, 1994.

Lezama, Carlos. July 17, 1995.

Morris, Ray. August 28, 1993, September 10, 1995.

Poison Lime. December 28, 1993.

Velasquez, Cito. February 25, 1994.

Vieira, Geraldo. November 15, 1993.

Index

Philip W. Scher is assistant professor of anthropology at the University of Oregon and coeditor of *Perspectives on the Caribbean: A Reader in Culture and History* (forthcoming) and *Critical Mas': Nationalism and Transnationalism in the Trinidad Carnival* (forthcoming).

DATE DUE

103866	
~~220274~~	
220272	

Printed in the United States
54063LVS00003B/67

9 780813 027999